English Made *Easy*

Fourth Edition

Mary Margaret Hosler, Ph.D.
Professor
Department of Business Education and Office Systems
University of Wisconsin at Whitewater

The Late Bernadine P. Branchaw, ED.D.

 **Glencoe McGraw-Hill**

New York, New York   Columbus, Ohio   Woodland Hills, California   Peoria, Illinois

REVIEWERS

Library of Congress Cataloging-in-Publication Data

Hosler, Mary Margaret.
    English made easy / Mary Margaret Hosler, Bernadine Branchaw. –
4th ed.
      p.   cm.
    Previous ed. Published under: English made easy / Bernadine P.
Branchaw, 2nd ed. C1986.
    Includes index.
    ISBN 0-02-801961-X
1. English language—Business English.   2. English language--
Grammar.   I. Branchaw, Bernadine P.   II. Branchaw, Bernadine P.
English made easy.   III. Title.
PE1115.H64 1997
428.2'02465—dc21   97-24066
                                                    CIP

English Made Easy, Fourth Edition

Imprint 2002

Send all inquiries to:
Glencoe/McGraw-Hill
21600 Oxnard St., Suite 500
Woodland Hills, CA 91367-4906

ISBN 0-02-801961-X

  5 6 7 8 9   066   05 04 03 02

TABLE OF CONTENTS

TABLE OF CONTENTS

THE GOALS OF ENGLISH MADE EASY

No matter what career you choose—accounting, banking, end user consulting, financial planning, law, medicine, engineering, marketing, teaching—you will need to know how to communicate effectively. In the world of business, you will communicate with a variety of people:

- Sales representatives and suppliers may call you for information.
- Supervisors and managers may ask you to prepare reports.
- Administrators and directors may discuss problems with you.
- Customers and visitors may ask you for directions or explanations.
- End users may ask for help in learning a new software package.

In these and other business situations, you will take part in an exchange of information. Because the smooth flow of information is essential for every business, a company values an employee who can communicate effectively. By communicating effectively, you avoid misunderstandings, save the company time and money, and keep customers happy.

In every communication situation, your main tool for success is your command of the English language. To succeed in business, therefore, you need to improve your communication skills and to master standard English. *English Made Easy* will help you achieve these goals.

HOW ENGLISH MADE EASY REACHES ITS GOALS

The fourth edition of *English Made Easy* will help you master communication skills with a simple step-by-step approach to the correct use of the English language. This text-workbook describes and explains the basic principles of English and provides numerous illustrations of each principle.

English Made Easy consists of 51 lessons. Each four-page lesson presents two pages of instruction followed by two pages of exercises. This consistent, user-friendly format makes this communication book both practical and enjoyable.

Within each lesson are several Checkup sections—usually one for each principle taught in that lesson. The Checkup exercises test your understanding of the concept. They allow you to apply a principle immediately after you study it in the text.

Because the answer to the first item in each Checkup is given, you have an opportunity to check yourself. Cover the text answer with a card and, following the directions for that Checkup, do the first item. Then check your answer against the text answer. If your answer is correct, continue doing the Checkup. If your answer is incorrect, review the text until you understand why you made an error. Only when you are sure that you will not repeat an error should you continue doing the Checkup.

The answers to all the Checkups are in the back of this text; these answers should be used to give you immediate reinforcement of your answers. When you do check your work, make sure you understand why each answer is correct. If you do not understand, review the text material, or ask your instructor for help. Completing the Checkups conscientiously will help you to do better on the two-page exercises in each lesson. The two pages of exercises at the end of the lesson give you an opportunity to apply the principles learned in that lesson.

To further help you build skill in using the English language, each lesson contains a writing section in which you can create your own sentences, focusing on the principles learned in that lesson. Also, a short story activity will give you still another way to review the principles in that lesson.

Thus through several different activities in each lesson, you are given lots of practice in becoming proficient with using words in our language. *English Made Easy* can help you develop the communication skills you will need for success in the business world. The time you invest now will pay big dividends in the future.

ACKNOWLEDGMENTS

Special thanks must go to the reviewers of the manuscript, who are listed on the copyright page. A special thank you goes to Louella Zahn for her dedicated help in the preparation of this manuscript. If you have comments on this fourth edition of *English Made Easy*, I would like to hear from you.

Mary Margaret Hosler
Department of Business Education and Office Systems
University of Wisconsin—Whitewater
Whitewater, WI 53190
hoslerm@uwwvax.uww.edu

PRETEST

How well can you recognize all eight parts of speech? Do you remember how to punctuate sentences correctly? Do you know when to capitalize a letter or word? The following 50 exercises will give you an opportunity to review your skills with the English language. Complete all the exercises and score yourself at the end.

PART I: PARTS OF SPEECH

Is the italicized word a noun, a pronoun, and adjective, an adverb, a verb, a preposition, a conjunction, or an interjection? Write your answers in the spaces at the right.

1. Yes, *Clark*, the report is finished.
2. Susan received a *perfect* score for her performance.
3. *Complete* all the exercises on the first page.
4. Faye received a *bonus* for her efforts.
5. Although they *shipped* the order weeks ago, I have not received it.
6. A *two-thirds* majority agreed with the proposed resolution.
7. Eileen *and* Oliver both had promising careers.
8. We hoped to be finished by 2 p.m., *but* it was closer to 4 p.m.
9. *Whew!* That was a close call.
10. The dissertation will be *revised* to include faculty recommendations.
11. *We* initiated the idea, but the officers carried it out.
12. *Outspoken* critics were not in agreement with the other reviewers
13. The twins worked *energetically* for the first few hours.
14. Marion's *supervisor* approved the design for the building.
15. Give *them* the merchandise they requested.
16. Please walk *toward* the door quickly.
17. The *glaring* error appeared on the front page.
18. Rebecca will *not* sing in the school's choir.
19. The new *system* is working out nicely in our office.
20. The inspectors *wandered* through the plant.
21. The *exclusive* report was prepared by Victor Adams.
22. Standing *behind* the door, he could see the whole auditorium.
23. The *extremely* fragile vase was sitting very close to the edge of the president's desk.
24. *Glenda* was the number one choice for the position.
25. Construction on the new building *began* last week.
26. Members *of* the committee voted in favor of a bonus.
27. Theresa *and* Brian went to the theater.
28. *Oh!* I forgot to make that change.
29. The directions were *very* difficult to follow.
30. We will address *their* concerns at the meeting.

1. _noun_
2. _adjective_
3. _verb_
4. _noun_
5. _verb_
6. _adjective_
7. _conjunction_
8. _____
9. _interjection_
10. _____
11. _pronoun_
12. _adjective_
13. _adverb_
14. _noun_
15. ~~preposition~~ _pronoun_
16. ~~adverb~~ _preposition_
17. _adjective_
18. _____
19. _noun_
20. _verb_
21. _adjective_
22. _adverb_
23. _____
24. _noun_
25. _____
26. _____
27. _____
28. _interjection_
29. _____
30. ~~preposition~~ _pronoun_

PART II: PUNCTUATION

Insert commas, semicolons, colons, periods, questions marks, hyphens, quotation marks, and apostrophes as needed in the following sentences. Circle your answers.

31. If we finish our work by 3 oclock may we leave
32. No you are not allowed to go
33. First she typed the long report for her manager then she typed several letters
34. His objective is clear He wants to help the poor the sick and the homeless
35. This mornings meeting was at 830 this afternoons meeting will be at 330
36. The professor assigned Chapter 3 Making Oral Presentations for reading
37. As we left the office Mellanie said Lets go out for dinner tonight
38. Will you please give this package to Ms. Albright
39. One sixth of the estate went to his nieces and nephews
40. We can leave here in the morning or we can leave after lunch

PART III: CAPITALS

Underline any letters that should be capitalized in the following sentences.

41. students were asked to read the autobiography of benjamin franklin.
42. while shopping for victorian furniture in austin, we stopped and had a danish roll and coffee.
43. she and her family were vacationing at lake powell, utah, in august.
44. after taking english, latin, and spanish courses, I was happy to be enrolled in an economics class.
45. mother and dad will be attending the graduation at milton high school.

PART IV: NUMBERS

Rewrite correctly each incorrect item listed below. If an item is correct, write OK.

46. 2/3 majority	46. _____
47. January 15th	47. _____
48. five thirty-two cent stamps	48. _____
49. two $10 bills	49. _____
50. 24 and a half miles	50. _____

UNIT 1

WHY STUDY ENGLISH AGAIN?

✓ Lesson 1. Origin of the English
Language

UNIT 1 OVERVIEW

The study of the English language is a study of languages from all over the world. Many words that we use have come to us from other countries and have evolved from centuries of use. Other words have been coined as society has changed due to technology and the quantity of information available.

The English language is an evolving language that reflects the way people live and work. English is a dynamic, fluid language that adapts to the changes in society.

The lexicographers (dictionary makers) have had a challenge for centuries, whether writing on clay tablets or placing words on a CD-ROM, to reflect the current language of society. In Unit 1 we will look at the origin of words in the English language.

UNIT OBJECTIVES

When you complete Unit 1, you will be able to:

- identify words derived from various countries.

- identify root words from other languages.

- describe how new words have been added to the English language.

- form blended words.

- identify abbreviated words.

- form compound words.

LESSON 1

ORIGIN OF THE ENGLISH LANGUAGE

HOW DID LANGUAGE BEGIN?

No one really knows how or when language began, but most theories support one of two ways. Language might have started with grunts and groans, or with movements and gestures that were interpreted as words. Written language began to evolve around 3100 B.C. Prior to that time, spoken language had been in use for thousands of years. Eventually, people wrote a symbol for each sound, thereby devising an alphabet.

CHECKUP 1

List four words or expressions you use most often. If you do not know what words you tend to repeat in a conversation, ask a friend to tell you. (Answers will vary.)

1. Okay _____
2. _____
3. _____
4. _____

HOW DID WE GET OUR WORDS?

In the early centuries, wandering tribes and conquerors of lands brought their language to the overthrown people causing language to become a blend of the languages used by the conquered and the conquerors. The English language emerged when the dialects of the Saxons, Angles, and Jutes mixed with the British to form the Anglo-Saxon language. With Christianity came the addition of Latin words such as *creed, verse, clerk, rose,* and *lily.* Later the Danish added words such as *law, call, care, fellow,* and *husband* to the English language. French influence is in words such as *age, aunt, beauty, card,* and *copy.* Thus, the English language is a blend of many languages.

GREEK AND LATIN ROOTS

The English language has retained words or word roots from the Greek and Latin languages. If you know the meaning of root words, you will be able to define many English words.

GREEK ROOTS

Root	Meaning	English Word
cycl	circle, ring	cycle, encyclopedia
ast	star	astronaut, astronomy
graph	write	telegraph, photograph
scop	see	microscope, stethoscope
gram	letter, written	monogram, diagram

CHECKUP 2

For each word, write the Greek root and its meaning.

WORD	GREEK ROOT	MEANING
1. asterisk	ast	star
2. bicycle	_____	_____
3. telegraph	_____	_____
4. biography	_____	_____

LATIN ROOTS

Root	Meaning	English Word
aud	hear	auditorium, audience
loc	place	locate, allocate
urb	city	suburb
rupta	break	bankrupt

For each word, write the root and then its meaning.

WORD	LATIN ROOT	MEANING
1. bankrupt	rupta	break
2. location	_____	_____
3. suburb	_____	_____
4. audible	_____	_____

WORDS ADDED BY AMERICANS

People who settled in America took the English language as it had evolved and added more words. The Spanish added *potato*, *cargo*, *banana*, and *burro*. The French in America added *depot*, *levee*, *bayou* and place locations such as *Butte* and *Boise*. The Indian language gave us words like *moccasin*, *toboggan*, and place locations such as *Spokane*, *Chautauqua*, and *Willamette*.

BLENDED WORDS

As people use the English language, they constantly alter it. Some words have been blended to form new words. For example:

bit = binary + digit   goodbye = God + be (with) + ye
motel = motor + hotel   of (the) clock = o'clock

CHECKUP 4 Using the two separate words, can you identify the blended word? Write the blended words in the spaces at the right.

1. breakfast + lunch
2. modulator + demodulator
3. motor + pedal
4. split + slice

1. brunch
2. _____
3. _____
4. _____

ABBREVIATED WORDS

Through everyday use, many of the words in our language have become abbreviated. Look at the following examples:

ORIGINAL FORM	ABBREVIATED FORM	ORIGINAL FORM	ABBREVIATED FORM
advertisement	ad	gasoline	gas
dormitory	dorm	limousine	limo
mathematics	math	telephone	phone

CHECKUP 5 Write the abbreviated form for each word in the spaces at the right.

1. automobile   auto
2. hamburger   _____

3. examination   _____
4. memorandum   _____

COMPOUND WORDS

Commonly used words are sometimes put together to form new, or compound words. Examples are *afternoon*, *backyard*, *bathroom*, and *blueprint*.

CHECKUP 6 In the spaces provided, write the compound word that is formed from the two separate words.

1. wind   shield   windshield
2. touch   down   _____

3. side   walk   _____
4. door   knob   _____

LESSON 1

Name _____ Date _____ Score _____

EXERCISES

EXERCISE 1 Identify the new, or blended, word formed from the two separate words. Write your answers in the spaces at the right.

1. day's + eye
2. fare + ye + well
3. gleam + shimmer
4. splash + spatter
5. twist + whirl
6. blot + botch
7. flutter + hurry
8. squirm + wiggle
9. fourteen + nights
10. twilight + night

1. _____
2. _____
3. _____
4. _____
5. _____
6. _____
7. _____
8. _____
9. _____
10. _____

EXERCISE 2 Combine the words in each line to form two compound words. Write the compound words in the spaces at the right.

1. basket   fire   ball   camp
2. apple   mate   class   sauce
3. copy   way   right   high
4. stick   watch   lip   wrist
5. birth   point   day   pin
6. nut   pea   dog   bull
7. back   port   air   bare
8. cup   dream   day   butter
9. paper   tail   news   pony
10. driver   screw   nail   toe
11. made   volley   home   ball
12. book   up   hold   note
13. fold   bird   fill   black
14. beam   table   time   sun
15. water   end   week   fall
16. rain   break   bow   fast
17. wire   wild   tap   cat
18. way   film   door   strip
19. guard   beat   life   off
20. mate   sand   play   quick
21. shirt   sweet   sweat   heart
22. china   leaf   ware   clover
23. web   slaw   cole   cob
24. dove   father   land   tail
25. rest   rack   hay   head

1. _____
2. _____
3. _____
4. _____
5. _____
6. _____
7. _____
8. _____
9. _____
10. _____
11. _____
12. _____
13. _____
14. _____
15. _____
16. _____
17. _____
18. _____
19. _____
20. _____
21. _____
22. _____
23. _____
24. _____
25. _____

Identify the complete word from its abbreviated form. Write your answers in the spaces at the right. *Note:* There may be more than one answer.

1. tux
2. vet
3. mum
4. taxi
5. teen
6. lube
7. flu
8. trig
9. cuke
10. lunch

1. _____
2. _____
3. _____
4. _____
5. _____
6. _____
7. _____
8. _____
9. _____
10. _____

WRITING ACTIVITY

Write a sentence using the abbreviated word. (Answers will vary.)

1. champ _____
2. lab _____
3. grad _____
4. prof _____
5. fridge _____

SHORT STORY

Underline the compound words and the blended words in the following paragraph. Write the words in the spaces at the right. If you have no underscored words in a line, write *NONE*.

I decided to try out my new skateboard at
sunrise when the air is crisp and clear. So
I put on my outfit just for the occasion, went
down the driveway, and on to the sidewalk.
What an outstanding activity! I passed the
drugstore, the newspaper stand, and the used
paperback bookstore. Since it was early, six
o'clock, few people were around, and I could
observe the sights of the downtown. The smog
was burning off and the skyscrapers were
silhouetted against the sky. It was very pretty.
However, it was time to stop and return home to
prepare for the day. I had brunch scheduled for
eleven with a wholesale buyer and an appointment
for a haircut at two. Another busy day would soon begin.

1. _____
2. _____
3. _____
4. _____
5. _____
6. _____
7. _____
8. _____
9. _____
10. _____
11. _____
12. _____
13. _____
14. _____
15. _____

UNIT 2

SENTENCE STRUCTURE

UNIT 2 OVERVIEW

To communicate your ideas to others, you need to express your thoughts in complete sentences. In this unit, you will learn to identify the main elements of a sentence, the subject and the verb. You will also learn to write sentences that make a statement, raise a question, give a command, or prompt an exclamation. Speaking and writing in complete sentences put you in command of communication!

UNIT OBJECTIVES

When you complete Unit 2, you will be able to:

- name the main verb in a sentence.

- select the subject(s) of a sentence.

- identify a sentence.

- write a sentence using a subject and a verb.

- complete a sentence using an appropriate subject or verb.

- recognize the four classifications of sentences—declarative, interrogative, imperative, and exclamatory.

- write examples of each one of the four classifications of sentences.

LESSON 2

THE SENTENCE

THE SENTENCE—A COMPLETE THOUGHT

A *sentence* is a group of words that express a complete thought. If a group of words does not express a complete thought, it is not a sentence. The sentence must have two parts, the *subject* and the *verb*.

The fax machine, located on the first floor. This is not a sentence. It does not express a complete thought. By themselves, the words *The fax machine, located on the first floor* make no sense. You need more information.

The fax machine, located on the first floor, will be available for public use. This is a sentence. It expresses a complete thought. Why discuss the fax machine on the first floor? The fax machine will be available to the public.

CHECKUP 1

Decide whether each of the following word groups is a sentence. If the group of words is a sentence, circle *S*. If the group of words is not a sentence, circle *NS*.

1. The tone of his voice.	1. S	(NS)
2. You should highlight the important dates in the paragraph.	2. S	NS
3. The files on the Smith manufacturing proposal are gone.	3. S	NS
4. Now that we have completed the report.	4. S	NS
5. Short-term goals, from one day to three months.	5. S	NS

THE SUBJECT

The *subject* of a sentence names the person, place, or thing that is performing or receiving the main action in the sentence. The action being performed or received can be a physical action (throw, hit, bounce) or a state-of-being action (is, feels, smells, are, seem).

Performing the action: **Juan threw Marguerite the keys.** The subject, *Juan*, performs the action of *throwing*.

Receiving the action: **The keys were thrown to Marguerite by Juan.** The subject, *keys*, received the action of *thrown*.

Performing the action: **You seem happy today.** *You* is the subject that is performing the state-of-being action expressed by the verb *seem*.

CHECKUP 2

Underline the subjects in the following sentences. Then write the subjects in the spaces at the right.

1. <u>Amy</u> insisted on going to the roller rink with us.   1. Amy
2. A close friend of mine volunteered to donate money.   2. _____
3. Her appearance was elegant.   3. _____
4. An oral presentation needs to be well organized.   4. _____
5. More businesses are providing day-care centers.   5. _____

The Understood Subject   In sentences that give a command or make a request, the subject is always understood to be *you*. But the word *you* frequently does not appear in such sentences. It does not appear because the word *you* is understood when one person is speaking directly to another.

> **Please be ready by 10 a.m.** The sentence makes a request. The subject is understood to be *you*: (You) Please be ready by 10 a.m.
>
> **Write the practice material for homework.** The sentence gives a command. The subject is understood to be *you*: (You) Write the practice material for homework.

CHECKUP 3   Write the subjects for the following sentences in the spaces at the right. If the subject is understood to be *you*, write (*you*).

1. The software program inserts the graphics automatically.   1. <u>program</u>
2. Use secondary sources of information for your report.   2. _____
3. The procedures manual contains useful information.   3. _____
4. She will interview for the consulting job.   4. _____
5. Her ability to design houses is well known.   5. _____

THE VERB—THE ACTION WORD

Part of Speech   Just as every sentence must have a subject, so every sentence must have a verb. The *verb* is a word that tells what the subject does, what the subject is, or what happens to the subject.

> Tells what the subject does: **Our neighbor walks his dog every morning.** The verb *walks* tells what the neighbor does.
>
> Tells what the subject is: **Ms. Carlyle is our department chairperson.** The verb *is* tells what Ms. Carlyle is.
>
> Tells what the subject is: **Mr. Lopez is very happy today.** The verb *is* tells about Mr. Lopez's state-of-being or condition.
>
> Tells what happens to the subject: **The city manager was given a 3 percent raise in salary.** The verb *was given* tells what happened to the city manager. Note that this verb has two words.

CHECKUP 4   Underline the verbs in the following sentences. Then write the verbs in the spaces at the right.

1. The emergency team <u>received</u> a commendation for their work.   1. <u>received</u>
2. Read the user's manual first.   2. _____
3. Each group wants a different topic.   3. _____
4. Buy your ticket before the offer expires.   4. _____
5. The visitors from France toured our plant and offices.   5. _____

Name _____ Date _____ Score _____

EXERCISES

EXERCISE 1 Decide whether each of the following word groups is a sentence. If the group of words is a sentence, circle *S*. If the group of words is not a sentence, circle *NS*.

1. The birds flocked to the feeder after the snow storm. 1. S NS
2. The driveway with the pillars. 2. S NS
3. Showing the card to him. 3. S NS
4. Although there have been many manufacturers of the car. 4. S NS
5. Our dog is at the groomer. 5. S NS
6. Place the emphasis on accuracy. 6. S NS
7. You play the piano beautifully. 7. S NS
8. Learn how to use the new database software. 8. S NS
9. The time is right for a new product line. 9. S NS
10. Working until midnight. 10. S NS
11. Because of the challenge it offers. 11. S NS
12. The store is advertising for clerks. 12. S NS
13. If you can find a vacant table. 13. S NS
14. The facts did not reveal the fundamental problem. 14. S NS
15. The red collar with bells. 15. S NS
16. We received your estimates yesterday. 16. S NS
17. A number of elements in the proposal were modified. 17. S NS
18. Another frustrating situation that may occur. 18. S NS
19. The word *uno* means one. 19. S NS
20. Standards need to be established before proceeding with the plan. 20. S NS

EXERCISE 2 Underline the subjects and the verbs in the following sentences. Then write the subjects and the verbs in the spaces provided. If the subject is understood to be you, write (*you*).

1. My black sweatshirt was stained from bleach. 1. _____
2. The car wash opens at 7 a.m. 2. _____
3. Sound strategy works. 3. _____
4. Introduce yourself first to the host. 4. _____
5. We ordered a limousine for our drive to the airport. 5. _____
6. Snow caused the road to be icy. 6. _____
7. The bakeries in our neighborhood make fantastic pastries. 7. _____
8. Engrave the name of the person on the pen. 8. _____
9. The tank holds 20 gallons of gasoline. 9. _____
10. The carpet was laid in the living room. 10. _____
11. Computers were installed in the new offices. 11. _____
12. Allen graduated from college with honors. 12. _____
13. The deck provides a place for people to socialize. 13. _____
14. She authored a book on training in corporations. 14. _____
15. Please respond via e-mail. 15. _____

16. Bob purchased three franchises in Texas last year.   16. _____
17. Everyone made a contribution to the flower fund.   17. _____
18. Proofread the letter carefully before lunch.   18. _____
19. The contract goes to the lowest bidder.   19. _____
20. The settlement appears imminent.   20. _____
21. Yes, we raised our prices on all our products.   21. _____
22. His hair is a golden brown.   22. _____
23. She is waiting for the bus.   23. _____
24. Vacation time is scheduled to begin in July.   24. _____
25. Florists sell many roses for Valentine's Day.   25. _____
26. Traffic moves slowly after 5 p.m.   26. _____
27. Listen carefully to the directions.   27. _____
28. The proceeds exceeded $12,000.   28. _____
29. This apple tastes sour.   29. _____
30. Please accept this gift as a token of our appreciation.   30. _____
31. The card measures 5 by 7 inches.   31. _____
32. The store announced its annual sale.   32. _____
33. The snowmobilers raced across the snowy fields.   33. _____
34. The car's headlights blinded the pedestrian.   34. _____
35. Large rocks were used in the landscaping.   35. _____

EXERCISE 3   The subject is missing from the following sentences. Write a subject that would complete each sentence. (Answers will vary.)

1. All (?) must register at the desk.   1. _____
2. The (?) stops at all railroad crossings.   2. _____
3. (?) bought an expensive mirror.   3. _____
4. (?) gushed from the broken main.   4. _____
5. My (?) does not write smoothly.   5. _____
6. After the storm, a (?) appeared.   6. _____
7. Several (?) were involved in the accident.   7. _____
8. (?) will be going to the conference tomorrow.   8. _____
9. Most (?) turned in their forms early.   9. _____
10. The (?) made it through the harsh winter.   10. _____

EXERCISE 4   The verb is missing from the following sentences. Write a verb that would complete each sentence. (Answers will vary.)

1. The countertop (?) from marble.   1. _____
2. The batteries in the flashlight (?) weak.   2. _____
3. The report (?) advantages and disadvantages of the process. 3. _____
4. The color of his suit (?) grey.   4. _____
5. The cat (?) the furniture.   5. _____
6. My office (?) on the fourth floor.   6. _____
7. Bob's newspaper (?) away last night.   7. _____
8. The fax machine (?) off the stand.   8. _____
9. Darlene's new briefcase (?) genuine leather.   9. _____
10. The new printer (?) yesterday.   10. _____

SUBJECTS AND VERBS

THE MAIN SUBJECT

The *main* subject performs the action of the sentence or has the action performed on it. Modifiers—adjectives and adverbs—are not part of the main subject.

The spongy red ball was used in training the dogs. The main subject is *ball.* The words *The spongy red* are modifiers; they are not part of the main subject.

CHECKUP 1 Underline the main subjects in the following sentences. Then write the main subjects in the spaces at the right.

1. <u>Promises</u> need to be kept.
2. The youth choir practices on Wednesday.
3. His shiny red car was parked near the curb.
4. The well-known author had written several books.
5. The eye glasses were tinted to prevent glare.

1. <u>promises</u>
2. _____
3. _____
4. _____
5. _____

THE MAIN VERB

The *main* verb is the most important verb that expresses the action. When the verb has more than one word in it, the main verb is always the *last*.

Carole *sent* her reply to the invitation by e-mail. There is only one verb—*sent.* It is, of course, the main verb.

The orders *had been received* earlier. The main verb is the last verb, *received.* The other verbs, *had* and *been,* are helpers.

CHECKUP 2 Underline the main verbs in the following sentences. Then write the main verbs in the spaces at the right.

1. The building was <u>demolished</u> by the crane.
2. Where have you been staying all this time?
3. Members of the brass choir played at the reception.
4. I could have worked all week on the manuscript.
5. Audrey has been reading for two hours.

1. <u>demolished</u>
2. _____
3. _____
4. _____
5. _____

THE COMPOUND SUBJECT

A subject is *compound* when it has two or more parts that are joined by a conjunction (*and, or,* or *nor*). These parts have the same verb.

When two or more nouns or pronouns are joined by *and,* the verb is always plural.

The boys and the girls hit the pinata. The nouns *boys* and *girls* form the compound subject. The two parts of this compound subject are plural; they are joined by the conjunction *and.* They require the plural verb, *hit.*

The boy and the girl hit the pinata. The nouns *boy* and *girl* form the compound subject. Both nouns in this compound subject are singular, but they require a plural verb because they are joined by the conjunction *and*. The nouns in this compound subject require the same plural verb, *hit*.

When two or more nouns or pronouns are joined by *or*, *nor*, *either . . . or*, or *neither . . . nor*, the noun or pronoun closest to the verb determines whether the verb is singular or plural.

The boys or the girls hit the pinata. The nouns *boys* and *girls* are joined by *or* to form the compound subject. Look at the noun closest to the verb. *Girls* is plural; therefore, the verb must also be plural. *Hit* is plural.

The boys or the girl hits the pinata. The nouns *boys* and *girl* are joined by *or* to form the compound subject. The noun closest to the verb is *girl*, which is singular. *Hits* is also singular.

| **CHECKUP 3** | Underline the compound subjects in the following sentences. Then write the compound subjects in the spaces at the right. |

1. A circus <u>wagon</u> or a <u>float</u> is used in the parade.   1. <u>wagon, float</u>
2. The sheriff and prisoner enter the courtroom.   2. _____
3. Papers and pencils are necessary to take the qualifying exam.   3. _____
4. Neither the brother nor the sister wants the prize.   4. _____
5. Men and women are needed as volunteers for the Red Cross.   5. _____

| **CHECKUP 4** | Underline the correct verb for each of the following sentences. Then write the word in the space at the right. |

1. Charlene or Lee (*supervises, supervise*) the installation of the computers.   1. <u>supervises</u>
2. A computer or books (*are, is*) needed for the auction.   2. _____
3. Books or a computer (*is, are*) needed for the auction.   3. _____
4. The president or vice president (*is, are*) coming to our open house.   4. _____
5. The students and the teacher (*plan, plans*) to review the syllabus.   5. _____

THE COMPOUND VERB

A *compound verb* consists of two or more verbs that are joined by a conjunction (*and*, *or*, *nor*). The verbs have the same subject.

You can sing or dance in the variety show. The words *sing* and *dance* form the compound verb. They have the same subject, *You*.

The sales associate plans and promotes special events. The words *plans* and *promotes* form the compound verb. They have the same subject, *associate*.

| **CHECKUP 5** | Underline the compound verbs in the following sentences. Then write the compound verbs in the spaces at the right. |

1. The seaside home <u>shook</u> and <u>rattled</u> from the high wind.   1. <u>shook, rattled</u>
2. The land was plowed and disked before planting the seeds.   2. _____
3. Jane opened and distributed the mail to all departments in the company.   3. _____
4. I carefully combed and styled my hair.   4. _____
5. He studied hard and graduated with honors.   5. _____

EXERCISES

EXERCISE 1 Underline the main subjects in the following sentences. Then write the main subjects in the spaces at the right.

1. Kathy will lead us in song this morning.   1. _____
2. All branches of the bank will be remodeled.   2. _____
3. Our largest department store in town is Hudson's.   3. _____
4. A red sweater was knit by Terri.   4. _____
5. Student members were recognized at the banquet for their achievements.   5. _____

EXERCISE 2 Underline the main verbs and helping verbs in the following sentences. Then write the *main* verbs in the spaces at the right.

1. The bottle contains a mixture of water and sugar.   1. _____
2. Your constitutional rights may have been violated.   2. _____
3. The chow chow dog originated in China.   3. _____
4. Does this new car require a specific grade of oil?   4. _____
5. You have decided about the job already?   5. _____

EXERCISE 3 Underline the compound subjects in the following sentences. Then write the compound subjects in the spaces provided.

1. Diet and exercise contribute to a healthy lifestyle.   1. _____
2. Several organs or a piano is for sale.   2. _____
3. Memos and letters comprise much of our written communication.   3. _____
4. The author and publisher were meeting in New York City.   4. _____
5. Management or marketing is Kaye's major.   5. _____

EXERCISE 4 Underline the compound verbs in the following sentences. Then write the compound verbs in the spaces provided.

1. Gloria spoke and wrote French fluently.   1. _____
2. The hair stylist trims and styles long hair.   2. _____
3. The assistant composes and keys his own letters.   3. _____
4. I inspected the pens and pulled the rejects.   4. _____
5. Kelly made a shopping list and placed a checkmark beside each purchased item. 5. _____

EXERCISE 5 Decide whether each of the following groups of words is a sentence. If the group of words is a sentence, write the subject and the *main* verb in the space provided. If the group of words is not a sentence, write *no sentence*.

1. The dollar a basic monetary unit.   1. _____
2. A new furniture polish was developed by the company.   2. _____
3. Dictionaries vary greatly in size, purpose, and reliability.   3. _____

4. Dwarf trees were planted on the grounds.   4. _____

5. John pretended that he had given a lecture on space travel.   5. _____

EXERCISE 6   Either a subject or a verb is missing from the following sentences. For each sentence, underline *S* if a subject is needed in place of the question mark; underline *V* if a verb is needed. Write a subject or a verb that would complete each sentence in the spaces at the right. (Answers will vary.)

1. The train engineer (?) the whistle.   S V   1. _____

2. They (?) their engagement.   S V   2. _____

3. The (?) entered the bay and headed toward the dock.   S V   3. _____

4. If employees want to keep their jobs, (?) will work hard.   S V   4. _____

5. The program automatically (?) all errors.   S V   5. _____

EXERCISE 7   In each of the following sentences, make the subject compound by adding another subject in place of the question mark. Write your answers in the spaces at the right. (Answers will vary.)

1. Cookies and (?) were served to the children.   1. _____

2. Cars and (?) filled the company parking lot.   2. _____

3. A rabbit or (?) eat lettuce.   3. _____

4. Bugs or a (?) eats lettuce.   4. _____

5. The King and (?) of Spain were in the United States for a five-day visit.   5. _____

EXERCISE 8   In each of the following sentences, make the verb compound by adding another verb in place of the question mark. Write your answers in the spaces at the right. (Answers will vary.)

1. The bear cubs rolled and (?) in the sunshine.   1. _____

2. Prices rise and (?) depending on the economy.   2. _____

3. Use spellcheck and (?) the letter before mailing it.   3. _____

4. His fingernails were trimmed and (?) by the manicurist.   4. _____

5. Bob looked at the cars and (?) the one he wanted.   5. _____

EXERCISE 9   Follow the directions for each numbered item.

Write a sentence using a verb. Circle the verb. (Answers will vary.)

1. _____

Write a sentence using a main subject. Circle the subject. (Answers will vary.)

2. _____

Write a sentence using a compound verb. Circle the compound verb. (Answers will vary.)

3. _____

Write a sentence using a compound subject joined by *and*. Circle the words that form the compound subject. (Answers will vary.)

4. _____

Write a sentence using a compound subject joined by *or*. Circle the words that form the compound subject. (Answers will vary.)

5. _____

KINDS OF SENTENCES

SENTENCE CLASSIFICATIONS

There are four classifications of sentences. Sentences are classified according to what they do. The following chart shows the four kinds of sentences.

Declarative Sentence	Presents information or states a fact . . . .
Interrogative Sentence	Asks a question ????
Imperative Sentence	Gives a command or states a request . . . .
Exclamatory Sentence	Expresses strong feeling !!!!

DECLARATIVE SENTENCE

A *declarative sentence* states, or declares, a fact, a belief, or an opinion. End the sentence with a period.

Fact: January is a cold month of the year.

Belief: Medical science will have a cure for most ills by the year 2050.

Opinion: The movie was the best I have seen.

CHECKUP 1 Write three declarative sentences using the words presented as the subjects. *Remember:* End your sentences with periods. (Answers will vary.)

1. birthday   Judi's birthday is on Saturday. _____
2. dish   _____
3. CD-ROM   _____
4. Vegetable   _____

INTERROGATIVE SENTENCES

An *interrogative sentence* asks a question. End the sentence with a question mark.

How long will you be gone?   **When will the network be installed?**

A sentence that asks an *indirect* question, such as "He asked me what my thoughts were," is *not* an interrogative sentence; it is a declarative sentence.

Direct Question   Where should I sit?   How are you?

Indirect Question   Marcia asked where she should sit.

When a sentence is phrased as a question but a response is not wanted, then the sentence is really a request or a command. End the sentence with a period, not a question mark.

Will you please give me more time. This is a request, not really a question.

CHECKUP 2 Write three interrogative sentences that start with the words listed below. End your sentences with question marks. (Answers will vary.)

1. What   What would you like to have for dessert tonight? _____
2. Who   _____
3. How   _____
4. When   _____

CHECKUP 3 Write two sentences that start with the words listed below. Phrase each as a question to which you expect no response. End your sentences with a period. (Answers will vary.)

1. Can   Can you sit still. _____
2. Will   _____
3. When   _____
4. How   _____

IMPERATIVE SENTENCES

An *imperative sentence* makes a request or gives a command. The subject of the imperative sentence is generally the pronoun *you*, even though it does not appear in the sentence.

Please feed the cat while I am gone. This sentence is a request; *you* is the subject.

See your supervisor before tomorrow. This sentence is a command; *you* is the subject.

An imperative sentence ends with a period *unless* it makes a strong command that calls for the use of the exclamation point.

Quiet!   **Hush!**   **Go!**   **Stop it!**

CHECKUP 4 Write three imperative sentences that give a command. If the sentence makes a *strong* command, end it with an exclamation point. (Answers will vary.)

1. Be here by 8 o'clock. _____
2. _____
3. _____
4. _____

CHECKUP 5 Write three imperative sentences that make a request. End your sentence with a period. (Answers will vary.)

1. Eat your vegetables. _____
2. _____
3. _____
4. _____

EXCLAMATORY SENTENCES

An *exclamatory sentence* expresses strong feeling. It is a declarative sentence stated with great emotion or excitement. An exclamatory sentence *always* ends with an exclamation point.

No!   **Good for you!**   **I can't wait to see you!**

CHECKUP 6 Write three exclamatory sentences. End your sentences with exclamation points. (Answers will vary.)

1. The building is on fire! _____
2. _____
3. _____
4. _____

CHECKUP 7 Identify the following sentences as declarative (**D**), interrogative (**I**), imperative (**IM**), or exclamatory (**E**) by circling the proper symbol.

1. When will you buy an ergonomically designed keyboard?   1. D Ⓘ IM E
2. Oh! I didn't know that before.   2. D I IM E
3. Early spring rains caused much flooding in the country.   3. D I IM E
4. Place the books on the top shelf in the cabinet.   4. D I IM E

Name   Date   Score

EXERCISES

EXERCISE 1 — Identify the following sentences as declarative (**D**), interrogative (**I**), imperative (**IM**), or exclamatory (**E**) by circling the proper symbol.

1. Please stop to see our newly remodeled store.
2. The book signing starts at 2 p.m.
3. Have you seen the new grammar software?
4. Watch where you step.
5. Are you sure it is true?
6. Quiet so I can hear the show!
7. Make sure the computer is turned off when you leave.
8. What do you intend to do about it?
9. Just a minute now!
10. Check the oil level in your car before leaving.

1. D I IM E
2. D I IM E
3. D I IM E
4. D I IM E
5. D I IM E
6. D I IM E
7. D I IM E
8. D I IM E
9. D I IM E
10. D I IM E

EXERCISE 2 — With each set, write the type of sentence requested.

Write three declarative sentences using the words listed below as the subjects of the sentences. *Remember:* End your sentences with periods. (Answers will vary.)

1. information   _____
2. dispute   _____
3. telephone   _____

Write three interrogative sentences that start with the words listed below. *Remember:* End your sentences with question marks. (Answers will vary.)

4. How   _____
5. When   _____
6. Where _____

Write three imperative sentences. *Remember:* End your sentences with periods. If a sentence makes a strong command, end it with an exclamation point. (Answers will vary.)

7. _____
8. _____
9. _____

Write three exclamatory sentences. *Remember:* End your sentences with exclamation points. (Answers will vary.)

10. _____
11. _____
12. _____

EXERCISE 3   Follow the directions given for each set of sentences.

Change the following sentences from indirect questions to direct questions. *Remember:* Use a question mark after each direct question. (Answers will vary.)

1. He asked for my e-mail number.

_____

2. The interviewer asked for my work experience.

_____

3. I asked if she planned to attend the teleconference.

_____

4. She asked if I would go with her.

_____

Change the following sentences from direct questions to indirect questions. (Answers will vary.)

5. Dina asked, "When will you complete the drawing?"

_____

6. Mike exclaimed, "Why did you cancel the order?"

_____

7. Joni asked, "Did you have any difficulty with the directions?"

_____

8. Ms. Brown said to the applicant, "How much experience do you have?"

_____

9. Jake asked, "How fast can you throw the ball?"

_____

10. The instructor yelled, "Everyone exit through that door!"

_____

EXERCISE 4   Punctuate the following sentences by placing a period (.), question mark (?), or exclamation point (!) in the spaces at the right.

1. Marketing majors can find jobs in retail management   1. _____

2. What were his motives   2. _____

3. Hurry   3. _____

4. She was careless with the computations   4. _____

5. When is the mortgage payment due   5. _____

6. Do not criticize a person in front of other people   6. _____

7. What is another word that sounds like principal   7. _____

8. The spear-fishing season will close in another week   8. _____

9. What are you thinking   9. _____

10. Cool   10. _____

UNIT 3

NOUNS

UNIT 3 OVERVIEW

The word *noun* is a label used to identify words that have certain characteristics and functions. One characteristic of nouns is that they name persons, places, things, concepts, and qualities. We label words as nouns to distinguish them from other words that have different characteristics and functions. In this unit, we will look at the different *types* of nouns (such as common or proper), *classifications* of nouns (such as concrete and abstract), and *functions* of nouns.

UNIT OBJECTIVES

When you complete Unit 3, you will be able to:

- identify nouns and their function in a sentence.

- describe common and proper nouns.

- recognize concrete and abstract nouns.

- distinguish between compound and collective nouns.

- form the plural of nouns.

- use singular and plural possessive nouns correctly.

- write sentences using the correct form of a noun.

LESSON 5

COMMON AND PROPER NOUNS

NOUNS

Part of Speech

Nouns are one of the eight parts of speech. Nouns name people, places, things, concepts, and qualities. There are basically two classifications of nouns—concrete and abstract. Within each of these classifications, there are two types of nouns—common and proper. Most nouns are common, but if they name *particular* people, places, things, concepts, and qualities, they are *proper* nouns.

A person:	boy, Maria, cowboy, accountant, doctor
A place:	Milwaukee, outdoors, India, downtown
A thing:	door, message, computer, Talmud
A concept:	entrepreneurship, independence, capitalism
A quality:	tender, happiness, joy

Our friends drove their car to Washington, D.C., to visit national monuments, parks, and cemeteries. Notice how many nouns can be used in one simple sentence. *Friends, car, Washington, D.C., monuments, parks,* and *cemeteries* are all nouns. Each word names something.

CHECKUP 1

Underline the nouns in the following sentences.

1. Please order supplies for Ms. Rinehard.
2. You receive five benefits when you join the plan.
3. Henry, please take this tray down to the cafeteria.
4. Use the large brush when you groom the dog.

CHECKUP 2

The words at the left tell what kind of noun to look for in each line. Underline the correct noun for each line. Then write that noun in the space at the right.

1. person:	floor	light	captain	1.	captain
2. place:	Alaska	tray	peanut	2.	_____
3. thing:	briefcase	Mexico	Homer	3.	_____
4. quality:	bird	grass	lush	4.	_____
5. idea:	lost	beard	democracy	5.	_____

Common Noun

boy

building

COMMON NOUNS

Common nouns refer to *general* persons, places, or things. They are not capitalized.

Name of persons:	child	student	adult	professor	prisoner
Name of places:	district	state	county	mall	theater
Name of things:	telephone	magazine	desk	check	pan

The cat and the dog live in the barn located on the farm. *Cat, dog, barn,* and *farm* are all common nouns. These nouns are not capitalized.

CHECKUP 3

Underline the common nouns in the following sentences.

1. An abbreviation is a shortened form of a word or phrase.
2. The doctor will give your wife the results of the test.
3. The carpenter went into town to get more material.
4. The auditor and director encouraged Emilia to interview for the position.

Underline the nouns used in the following paragraph. Write each noun in the space at the right.

On a clear, cold <u>night</u>, the <u>sky</u> can be lit up with the <u>brightness</u> coming from the twinkling stars. An ancient astronomer drew up the earliest list of the brightness of the stars. He listed about twenty-five of the brightest stars of the first magnitude.

1. _night, sky, brightness_
2. _____
3. _____
4. _____

Proper Noun

Juan

Empire State Building

PROPER NOUNS

Proper nouns name *particular* persons, places, or things. Proper nouns are capitalized.

Names of particular persons:	Susan	Jacob	Mr. Manogue	Ms. Fowler
Names of particular places:	Halifax	Seattle	Australia	Mexico
Names of particular things:	Lake Michigan		Empire State Building	
	Mt. Rushmore		Jefferson Memorial	

Amy and ***Shaun*** purchased a ***Harley-Davidson*** last ***August***. *Amy, Shaun, Harley-Davidson* and *August* are all proper nouns. They are all capitalized.

CHECKUP 5 Underline the proper nouns in the following sentences.

1. <u>Oliver Medford</u> donated 1,000 acres of land near <u>Boulder, Colorado</u>.
2. It took Ken Burns five years to film a documentary on the Civil War.
3. This was the year for the Green Bay Packers to win the Super Bowl.
4. The National Archives plans to release excerpts from five videotapes.

FUNCTION OF NOUNS

Nouns may function as *subjects, direct objects, indirect objects, objects of prepositions, subject complements,* and *appositives.* Because nouns perform these different functions in a sentence, it is important for you to learn to identify and use them correctly.

My ***husband*** grew a three-pound ***tomato***. *Husband* is the subject of the verb *grew*; *tomato* is the direct object.
Leggs threw the ***baseball***. *Leggs* is the subject of the verb *threw*; *baseball* is the direct object.
Leggs threw ***Star*** the ***baseball***. *Leggs* is the subject of *threw*; *baseball* is the direct object; *Star* is the indirect object.
The ***collision*** caused damage to the ***car***. *Collision* is the subject; *car* is the object of the preposition *to*.
The ***pineapple*** is a tropical ***plant***. *Pineapple* is the subject of the verb *is*; *plant* is a subject complement.
Marty Wendt, the ***treasurer***, presented the audit results. *Marty Wendt* is the subject; *treasurer* is an appositive (an appositive gives more information about Marty Wendt).

CHECKUP 6   Write a sentence illustrating each of the functions of a noun in a sentence. Circle the noun showing the function. (Answers will vary.)

1. subject of the verb   (Maria) can report suspected animal abuse.
2. object of a preposition _____
3. object of a verb   _____
4. appositive   _____

EXERCISES

EXERCISE 1 — Identify the nouns in the following sentences by underlining common nouns once and proper nouns twice. *Remember:* Identify only nouns.

1. Your doctor will tell you that many people in the hospital are admitted because of illness brought on by worry.

2. We placed an advertisement in the American Medical Journal and almost 10,000 doctors responded.

3. Jayne was driving from Chicago to Wisconsin when she passed a sign for Lambs Farm and decided to stop in.

4. Our costs have gone up so much in the year that we can no longer maintain our current prices and continue to operate at a profit.

5. Replacements were brought in from Scotland, Wales, and England.

6. Tom graduated from Central University Medical School in Chicago in June.

7. When you go on vacation, do you manage to put business completely out of your mind?

8. Catherine was vacationing at Lake Powell, Utah, in August when she learned about her promotion.

9. Just up the road, Mark and Joe had been searching the area for an unusual spiral-grain wood.

10. Present this card at our main store, and we will give you a substantial discount.

11. We are building our new store at the corner of Rutledge Avenue and Wall Street.

12. The ambassador to the Soviet Union was on the telephone.

13. Do you usually eat turkey on Thanksgiving Day?

14. From Florida to Alaska, 19 states contain about 460 million acres of federally-owned land.

15. Loopholes in laws and regulations must be corrected.

16. We are prepared to offer you a large salary.

17. The booklets, Music for Children, costs only a few cents a day to own.

18. Laughing and weeping Germans chipped away at the Berlin Wall.

19. In two weeks, the sororities and fraternities will hold pledge week.

20. Vera attended a convention in San Antonio, Texas.

21. Brokers receive a commission on every bond they sell.

22. Prompt action in returning the enclosed card may prove to be the wisest step you take.

23. James Lee has proposed your name for membership.

24. Some artists and writers left the region to find artistic freedom.

25. The Stelter Agency can offer you a package that covers your entire family.

26. Every July the Defense Department receives about 5,000 inquiries from Capitol Hill.

27. Vera, a Republican, visited the White House and the Democratic Congress, which was in session during her visit.

28. The Brentwood Conservancy has started a fund-raising drive with a goal of $500,000.

29. Julio invited us to visit him at his ranch in California.

30. Columnist William Sellars described the low point in his career as a journalist.

31. After five seasons, Jerry Rose of the San Francisco 49ers was the greatest deep-threat wide receiver in professional football.

32. Three phases of management will be explained in this course.

33. After a day of working over kilns, the potter looked forward to an evening of fine food.

34. The abacus, which was used in China, Rome, and Greece, was an early computing device.

35. The best time to buy a new car is at the end of the month because salespeople want their monthly reports to look good.

EXERCISE 2   The nouns listed below are commonly used in discussing technology. Use each noun correctly in a sentence. Use a dictionary to check the meaning of any noun you do not know. (Answers will vary.)

1. bulletin board   _____
2. CPU (central processing unit)   _____
3. graphics   _____
4. documentation   _____
5. commands   _____
6. input   _____
7. icon   _____
8. screen saver   _____
9. output   _____
10. mouse   _____
11. keystrokes   _____
12. applications   _____
13. menu   _____
14. computer   _____
15. disk drive   _____
16. password   _____
17. monitor   _____
18. screen   _____
19. spell check   _____
20. merge   _____

SHORT STORY   Underline once the common nouns and twice the proper nouns in the following paragraph. Write all the nouns in the spaces at the right.

The troop traveled to the coast and to see the mountains that they had heard so much about. Mr. Smith wanted the boys to see the peak that was named after his father. Smith's Peak isn't the highest but it means more to Troop 104 than any of the other peaks.

1. _____
2. _____
3. _____
4. _____
5. _____

LESSON 6

CONCRETE, ABSTRACT, COMPOUND, AND COLLECTIVE NOUNS

CLASSIFICATION OF NOUNS

Nouns are classified as concrete or abstract. Concrete nouns, which are more specific than abstract nouns, are preferred for use in business writing.

CONCRETE NOUNS

Concrete nouns refer to persons, places, and objects that you can see, hear, smell, touch, or taste. The following nouns are concrete; you can use your senses to identify them.

umbrella	see, touch
hotdog	see, touch, taste, and smell
noise	hear

CHECKUP 1

One concrete noun is in each group of three words below. Identify the concrete nouns by writing them in the spaces at the right.

1. raw	cartoon	action	1. <u>cartoon</u>
2. tuba	care	emboss	2. _____
3. cooperation	cost	curtain	3. _____
4. primary	imagery	tomato	4. _____

CHECKUP 2

 List four concrete nouns and tell why each is concrete. *Remember:* A concrete noun identifies or names something that can be seen, heard, smelled, touched, or tasted. (Answers will vary.)

1. <u>hammer</u>   <u>It is a concrete noun because it can be seen and touched.</u>
2. _____   _____
3. _____   _____
4. _____   _____

ABSTRACT NOUNS

Abstract nouns identify or name ideas or qualities. Abstract nouns refer to something that cannot be seen, heard, smelled, touched, or tasted. The following nouns are abstract because they cannot be identified by using the five senses.

oversight   joy   peace   emotion   wisdom   beauty

CHECKUP 3

One abstract noun is in each group of three words. Identify the abstract nouns by writing them in the spaces at the right.

1. spirit	house	leaves	1. <u>spirit</u>
2. liability	boat	lumber	2. _____
3. owl	jar	jealousy	3. _____
4. system	money	paper	4. _____

CHECKUP 4

 List four abstract nouns. Use each in a sentence. (Answers will vary.)

1. <u>democracy</u>   <u>Democracy means different things to different people.</u>
2. _____   _____
3. _____   _____
4. _____   _____

KINDS OF NOUNS

Nouns can further be described as compound and collective.

COMPOUND NOUNS

Compound nouns are formed from two or more words that act like one unit. A compound noun may be written as one word, as two separate words, or as a hyphenated word.

ONE WORD	TWO OR MORE WORDS	HYPHENATED WORD
chopsticks	chop suey	attorney-at-law
childproof	point of view	ball-and-socket joint
airlines	ice age	pay-TV

Some proper nouns contain a compound noun.

Marshall *Middle School*   Tourist *Airlines*   Harper *Community College*

My *mother-in-law* used a *money order* to pay for a ticket on Midwest Express *Airlines*.

CHECKUP 5

Identify the compound nouns in the following sentences. Underline the compound nouns, and write them in the spaces at the right.

1. I have a <u>sweatshirt</u> that shows the <u>lighthouses</u> on the <u>Great Lakes</u>.

2. I had never seen so many oil wells in my life.

3. The stopwatches were unpacked and put in the storeroom.

1. <u>sweatshirt, lighthouses,</u> <u>Great Lakes</u>

2. _____

3. _____

CHECKUP 6

Make the following nouns compound by combining each with other words of your choice. Write the compound nouns in the spaces at the right. (Answers will vary.)

1. candle   1. <u>candlelight</u>   3. father   3. _____

2. free   2. _____   4. post   4. _____

COLLECTIVE NOUNS

A collective noun names a group or collection of persons, places, or things. The collective noun considers the group of persons, places, or things as *one* person, *one* place, or *one* thing unless the members of that group act individually.

Group of persons:	crew	team	people	committee	denomination
Group of places:	union	nation	federation	republic	
Group of things:	herd	flock	swarm	litter	gaggle	cluster

Collective nouns may be either singular or plural. They take a singular verb when the group is acting as one unit; they take a plural verb when the members are acting as individuals.

The audience is applauding.   **The audience are going home.**

CHECKUP 7

Write a collective noun for each of the words listed below. (Answers will vary.)

1. soldiers   1. <u>military</u>   3. trees   3. _____

2. cattle   2. _____   4. wolves   4. _____

Name _____   Date _____   Score _____

EXERCISES

EXERCISE 1   Read the following sentences. Then write the *concrete nouns* in the spaces at the right.

1. Members pay a fee for each selection.   1. _____
2. Learn how to eloquently express the words you use.   2. _____
3. Paychecks were distributed on Tuesday.   3. _____
4. Last year was the best year ever for our business.   4. _____
5. The boxes held about 20 books.   5. _____

EXERCISE 2   Read the following sentences. Then write the *abstract nouns* in the spaces at the right.

1. The love of reading is a habit started in childhood.   1. _____
2. Learn how to express your ideas forcefully.   2. _____
3. Jake has an excellent memory.   3. _____
4. Problems often offer you opportunities.   4. _____
5. Because of his fairness in dealing with others, he was well liked.   5. _____

EXERCISE 3   Read the following sentences. Then write the *compound nouns* in the spaces at the right.

1. Matt started on a goodwill tour to four states.   1. _____
2. The spotlight will be on those who meet their quota.   2. _____
3. The headlines did not tell the entire story.   3. _____
4. The finer sportswear will go on sale Friday.   4. _____
5. How can I overcome stage fright?   5. _____

EXERCISE 4   Read the following sentences. Then write the *collective nouns* in the spaces at the right.

1. Medicine has made many advances for the good of humanity.   1. _____
2. A bevy of quail landed in the field.   2. _____
3. The faculty was meeting to discuss class schedules.   3. _____
4. Only a minority of voters will come out on election day.   4. _____
5. Myron sat on several important boards within the community.   5. _____

EXERCISE 5   List five concrete nouns. Tell why each noun is concrete. (Answers will vary.)

1. _____
2. _____
3. _____
4. _____
5. _____

Name ten abstract nouns. (Answers will vary.)

1. _____   6. _____
2. _____   7. _____
3. _____   8. _____
4. _____   9. _____
5. _____   10. _____

EXERCISE 7 Make the following nouns compound by combining each word with other words of your choice. Write the compound nouns in the spaces provided. (Answers will vary.)

1. jack   1. _____   5. news   5. _____
2. key   2. _____   6. sun   6. _____
3. latch   3. _____   7. wheel   7. _____
4. land   4. _____   8. black   8. _____

EXERCISE 8 One concrete noun is in each group of three words below. Identify the concrete nouns by writing them in the spaces at the right.

1. corn   controversy   emotion   1. _____
2. power   fair   eye   2. _____
3. factor   tire   spite   3. _____
4. gaiety   stapler   devotion   4. _____
5. water   warmth   quiet   5. _____

EXERCISE 9 Write a sentence that contains the following. (Answers will vary.)

1. Compound noun:

_____

2. Collective noun:

_____

SHORT STORY Underline the compound nouns in the following paragraph. Write the compound nouns in the spaces at the right.

Plan now to attend our open house and see our   1. _____
new method for painting classrooms. Our powerful airbrush   2. _____
shoots paint through a specially designed spray gun.   3. _____
Paint flows smoothly through the bristles of the paintbrush.   4. _____
Everyone who uses our method can achieve   5. _____
professional-looking results.

LESSON 7

PLURAL NOUNS

A noun may be singular or plural. A noun that refers to *one* person, place, or thing is *singular* in number. A noun that refers to *more than one* person, place, or thing is *plural* in number.

FORMING REGULAR PLURAL NOUNS

RULE 1

Most nouns form the plural by adding *s* to the singular.	
Singular	**Plural**
hand	hands
dog	dogs
driver	drivers

RULE 2

Nouns ending in *s, x, z, ch,* or *sh* form the plural by adding *es* to the singular.	
Singular	**Plural**
virus	viruses
sketch	sketches
wish	wishes
fax	faxes
quartz	quartzes
But: quiz	quizzes

CHECKUP 1 Identify the following nouns as singular or plural by writing *S* or *P* in the spaces at the right.

1. birds   electors   paper _P, P, S_   3. editor   grills   caps _____

2. oven   rivers   record _____   4. cities   replies   box _____

CHECKUP 2 Write the plural for each singular noun.

1. pass _passes_   3. tax _____

2. push _____   4. march _____

RULE 3

When a singular noun that ends in *y* is preceded by a *consonant,* form the plural by changing the *y* to *i* and adding *es.*	
Singular	**Plural**
copy	copies
study	studies
industry	industries

RULE 4

When a singular noun that ends in *y* is preceded by a vowel (*a, e, i, o, u*), form the plural just by adding *s.*	
Singular	**Plural**
guernsey	guernseys
delay	delays

CHECKUP 3 Write the plural for each singular noun.

I'm dizzy from all these rules.

1. fifty   1. _fifties_   5. holiday   5. _____

2. policy   2. _____   6. attorney   6. _____

3. finery   3. _____   7. boy   7. _____

4. corollary   4. _____   8. bay   8. _____

When a noun ends in an *o* and the *o* is preceded by a vowel, form the plural by adding *s* to the singular.

Singular	Plural
radio	radios
portfolio	portfolios

Singular nouns ending in an *o* that is preceded by a *consonant* form their plurals by adding *s* or *es*.

	Singular	Plural
add *s*	logo	logos
add *es*	potato	potatoes

Singular musical terms ending in *o* form their plurals by adding *s*.

Singular	Plural
piano	pianos
banjo	banjos

Most nouns ending in *f*, *fe*, or *ff* form the plural by adding *s*, but some change the *f* or *fe* to *ve* first before adding the *s*.

	Singular	Plural
add *s*	belief	beliefs
	safe	safes
	sheriff	sheriffs
Change *f* or *fe* to *ve*, then add *s*.	half	halves
	wife	wives

CHECKUP 4 Write the plural of the following nouns.

1. two   twos
2. cello
3. echo
4. cameo

5. tariff
6. proof
7. belief
8. thief

FORMING IRREGULAR PLURAL NOUNS

Some nouns form their plurals in irregular ways. Just memorize these nouns.

Singular	Plural
foot	feet
mouse	mice

Some nouns have one form for both the singular and the plural.

Singular	Plural
trout	trout
fish	fish

Some nouns are *always* singular. Some nouns are *always* plural.

Always Singular	Always Plural
measles	scissors
honesty	oats

Compound nouns generally form the plural by adding *s* to the most important word.

Singular	Plural
father-in-law	fathers-in-law
couch potato	couch potatoes

Remember: When you are in doubt about forming the plural of a noun, check the dictionary. You'll always find the correct spelling there.

CHECKUP 5 Review the plurals you have studied in this lesson by correcting the following sentences. Underline any incorrect plurals, and write the correct plurals in the spaces at the right. If a plural is correct, write *OK*.

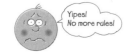

Yipes! No more rules!

1. The four <u>rule of thumb</u> are listed on the next page.
2. Several loafs of bread were on the table.
3. My two pony are named Sadie and Honey.
4. Anna sent her faxs from her home computer.

1. rules of thumb
2.
3.
4.

Name   Date   Score

EXERCISES

EXERCISE 1   Write the plurals for the following nouns in the spaces at the right. If the plural is the same as the singular form, write *same*.

1. elf	1. _____	41. concrete	41. _____
2. automobile	2. _____	42. institute	42. _____
3. vote	3. _____	43. morale	43. _____
4. daisy	4. _____	44. alto	44. _____
5. deer	5. _____	45. genius	45. _____
6. crash	6. _____	46. ferry	46. _____
7. staff	7. _____	47. wrench	47. _____
8. dollar	8. _____	48. mouse	48. _____
9. trout	9. _____	49. club	49. _____
10. child	10. _____	50. scissors	50. _____
11. cassette	11. _____	51. tweezers	51. _____
12. cookie	12. _____	52. watch	52. _____
13. berry	13. _____	53. vitamin	53. _____
14. country	14. _____	54. gasoline	54. _____
15. thing	15. _____	55. emergency	55. _____
16. economy	16. _____	56. fiasco	56. _____
17. studio	17. _____	57. eighty	57. _____
18. program	18. _____	58. dalmatian	58. _____
19. portfolio	19. _____	59. gravy	59. _____
20. bear	20. _____	60. bylaw	60. _____
21. prize	21. _____	61. patch	61. _____
22. sheep	22. _____	62. butterfly	62. _____
23. luggage	23. _____	63. wagon	63. _____
24. style	24. _____	64. supervisor	64. _____
25. computer	25. _____	65. cemetery	65. _____
26. business	26. _____	66. economics	66. _____
27. dish	27. _____	67. fire	67. _____
28. security	28. _____	68. injury	68. _____
29. glass	29. _____	69. fly	69. _____
30. wolf	30. _____	70. disability	70. _____
31. goose	31. _____	71. series	71. _____
32. world	32. _____	72. goods	72. _____
33. hobby	33. _____	73. fairy tale	73. _____
34. sister-in-law	34. _____	74. feather	74. _____
35. electrode	35. _____	75. miss	75. _____
36. notch	36. _____	76. story	76. _____
37. statistics	37. _____	77. waffle	77. _____
38. crash	38. _____	78. journey	78. _____
39. finch	39. _____	79. impurity	79. _____
40. peony	40. _____	80. parka	80. _____

Write singular nouns that end in *s, x, z, ch,* and *sh* in the first column. Then write the plurals of these nouns in the second column. (Answers will vary.)

SINGULAR   PLURAL

1. _____   _____
2. _____   _____
3. _____   _____
4. _____   _____
5. _____   _____
6. _____   _____
7. _____   _____
8. _____   _____
9. _____   _____
10. _____   _____

EXERCISE 3 Write singular nouns that end in *y* and are preceded by a consonant in the first column. Then write the plurals of these nouns in the second column. (Answers will vary.)

SINGULAR   PLURAL

1. _____   _____
2. _____   _____
3. _____   _____
4. _____   _____
5. _____   _____
6. _____   _____
7. _____   _____
8. _____   _____
9. _____   _____
10. _____   _____

WRITING ACTIVITY Write a singular noun on each line following the number. Write a sentence using the plural form for that noun on the line next to the noun. (Answers will vary.)

1. _____   _____
2. _____   _____
3. _____   _____
4. _____   _____

SHORT STORY Read the following paragraph. Underline plural nouns. If a plural noun has been misspelled, write the correct spelling in the space at the right. If the line has no misspelled plural nouns, write *OK* in the blank.

Sometimes I wish I had proxys to take my quizes in math.   1. _____
My scores are average; however, there is room for improvement.   2. _____
My studys in three other courseses—accounting, music, and   3. _____
international business—are very good. For music I have access   4. _____
to two pianoes—one at home and one at school—so I can practice   5. _____
many houres a day. I know wishs cannot come true, so   6. _____
maybe I need to practice math at home and at school also.   7. _____

POSSESSIVE NOUNS

Tom's bike

FORMING POSSESSIVE NOUNS

Possessive nouns show ownership or possession. The apostrophe (') is used to show the possessive form of nouns. Note that the word following the possessive word is always a noun.

the editor's viewpoint   **Mike's truck**   **a book's title**

POSSESSIVES OF SINGULAR NOUNS

Singular Nouns Not Ending in an *s* or *z* Sound   To form the possessive of a singular noun not ending in an *s* or *z* sound, add an apostrophe and *s* ('s) to the noun.

editor	editor's
corps	corps's (ends in the *letter s* but not the *sound* of *s*)
Illinois	Illinois's (ends in the *letter s* but not the *sound* of *s*)

Singular Nouns Ending in an *s* or *z* Sound   Forming the possessive of a singular noun that ends in an *s* or *z* sound depends on how the noun is pronounced as a possessive.

If pronouncing the noun as a possessive adds a syllable, then write the noun with an apostrophe and *s* ('s).

boss *Boss* is a one-syllable word that ends in the *s* sound. When pronounced as a possessive, it has *two* syllables. Therefore, write the possessive as *'s*. **His boss's car is in the garage.**

Lucas *Lucas* is a two-syllable word that ends in the *s* sound. When pronounced as a possessive, it has *three* syllables. Therefore, write the possessive as *'s*. **Mr. Lucas's barbershop is closing.**

Cortez *Cortez* is a two-syllable word that ends in the *z* sound. When *pronounced* as a possessive, it has *three* syllables. Therefore, write the possessive as *'s*. **Cortez's book is being published this year.**

If pronouncing the noun as a possessive does not add a syllable because doing so would make it too awkward to pronounce, then write the noun with only an apostrophe (no *s*).

New Orleans *Orleans* is a two-syllable word that ends in the *s* sound. Adding a syllable when pronouncing it as a possessive is awkward. Therefore, write the possessive by adding only an apostrophe (no *s*). **This is New Orleans' busiest restaurant.**

POSSESSIVES OF PLURAL NOUNS

Be sure to change the singular noun to its correct plural form before forming the possessive of a plural noun.

To form the possessive of a plural noun that ends in *s*, add only an apostrophe (').

Singular	**Plural**	**Plural Possessive**
baby	babies	babies' blankets
Jones	Joneses	Joneses' yard

To form the possessive of a plural noun that does *not* end in *s*, add an apostrophe and *s* ('s).

Singular	**Plural**	**Plural Possessive**
child	children	children's games
woman	women	women's fashions
man	men	men's shoes

Avoid using the possessive form for inanimate objects. Use the *of* phrase instead.

the blade *of* the saw (**NOT**: the saw's blade)

It is correct to use the possessive form for time, distance, quantity, and celestial bodies.

Singular	Plural	Plural Possessive
year	years	years' experience
dollar	dollars	dollars' worth
sun's warmth (only one sun)		
today's schedule (only one today)		

CHECKUP 1 Write the singular possessive, the plural, and the plural possessive for each of the nouns listed below.

	Singular Possessive	Plural	Plural Possessive
1. hero	hero's	heroes	heroes'
2. witness	_____	_____	_____
3. ox	_____	_____	_____
4. lady	_____	_____	_____

POSSESSIVES OF COMPOUND NOUNS

For compound nouns, form the *singular possessive* by adding an apostrophe and *s* (*'s*) to the end of the word. To form the *plural possessive*, first form the plural. If the plural form ends in *s*, add only an apostrophe (*s'*). If the plural form does not end in *s*, add an *apostrophe* and *s* (*'s*).

Compound Noun	Singular Possessive	Plural Possessive
eyewitness	eyewitness's	eyewitnesses'
stockholder	stockholder's	stockholders'
sister-in-law	sister-in-law's	sisters-in-law's

SEPARATE POSSESSION

When two or more nouns are used to show *separate ownership*, write *each* noun in the possessive form. If we wish to write about the bike that Tom owns and the bike that Judd owns, we would say *Tom's and Judd's bikes*.

When two or more nouns are used to show *joint* ownership, that is, ownership of the same item, then only the last noun is possessive. If we wish to write about the bike that Tom and Judd own together, we would say *Tom and Judd's bike*.

Tom's bike

Tom's and Judd's bikes

Tom and Judd's bike

CHECKUP 2 Correct any errors in the use of possessives in the following sentences. Underline each error. Then write your corrections in the spaces at the right.

1. <u>Tanya's</u> and Homer's wedding date has been changed.
2. Dick's and Pat's business was near the airport on South Street.
3. Brown and Hickman's novels are on the reserved shelves.
4. Her son's-in-law apartment had a lovely view of the lake.

1. Tanya
2. _____
3. _____
4. _____

EXERCISES

EXERCISE 1   In the spaces provided, write the singular possessive, the plural, and the plural possessive for each of the nouns listed below.

	Singular Possessive	Plural	Plural Possessive
1. brother-in-law			
2. informant			
3. maid			
4. saleswoman			
5. gypsy			
6. county			
7. senator			
8. sister			
9. cameraman			
10. jungle			

EXERCISE 2   Write the correct possessive form for each of the italicized expressions below. (*Hint:* Rewrite only the *italicized* words.)

1. The *car of the vice-president* was decorated with flags.   1. _____
2. The *experiment of Dr. Boggs* was reported in literature.   2. _____
3. The *toy of the dog* went rolling down the hill.   3. _____
4. The *letter of the president* was received with delight.   4. _____
5. The *votes of the citizens* were counted and verified.   5. _____
6. The *rattle of the baby* was found under the crib.   6. _____
7. Our *office of the accountant* overlooked the Hudson River Valley.   7. _____
8. The *headline of the newspaper* was shocking.   8. _____
9. The *testimony of Judd* helped to send the man to jail.   9. _____
10. The *return of the Sandhill Cranes* marked the start of spring.   10. _____
11. The *business of Mack and Jeff* earned over $10,000 the first year.   11. _____
12. The *address of the sender* appeared on the envelope.   12. _____

EXERCISE 3   Underline the nouns that should be written in the possessive form. Then write the correct possessive forms in the spaces at the right. If a sentence is correct, write *OK*.

1. The teams coach was praised for the great season.   1. _____
2. Gus's Department Store sells at discount prices.   2. _____
3. Krista office needs a painting.   3. _____
4. This years' events were summarized in the paper.   4. _____
5. A politician's speech usually contains much jargon.   5. _____
6. The girls competitor is her best friend.   6. _____
7. All employees e-mail messages are subject to monitoring.   7. _____
8. The Meyerses car was left unlocked overnight.   8. _____

9. John's and Spring's performance in the debate was excellent.   9. _____
10. Eleanor and Larry took several months vacation last year.   10. _____
11. Rita's room was a mess.   11. _____
12. Mondays ceremony gave viewers an opportunity to see new faces.   12. _____
13. Andrew Lloyd Webber's masterpiece was performed by the drama club.   13. _____
14. Allen agreed to do the work for a week salary.   14. _____
15. Winning the board game was just beginner luck.   15. _____
16. Now is the best time to buy the company stock.   16. _____
17. Timothy's and Mark's computers were being delivered Tuesday.   17. _____
18. His family's love of maps led to his interest in geography.   18. _____
19. Did you know that Hal took Joeys lunch?   19. _____
20. Did you get your money worth?   20. _____

WRITING ACTIVITY   Write a sentence for each one of the following words. (Answers will vary.)

1. Jill's   _____

_____

2. brother-in-law's   _____

_____

3. eyewitnesses'   _____

_____

4. student's   _____

_____

5. families'   _____

_____

SHORT STORY   Correct any errors in the use of possessives in the following paragraph. Underline each error. Then write your corrections in the spaces at the right. If the line is correct, write OK.

The councils decision last night will no doubt get the   1. _____

publics attention because the council okayed an admissions'   2. _____

charge of $1 for this springs opening of the Rotary Gardens.   3. _____

The senior citizens club had opposed the charge; however,   4. _____

the citys supervisor of parks spoke in favor of the charge.   5. _____

He said the public would easily get their moneys worth   6. _____

because the Gardens offer beauty as well as education to   7. _____

those who stroll the paths. The surrounding communities   8. _____

fees will be $2.   9. _____

UNIT 4

PRONOUNS

UNIT 4 OVERVIEW

Pronouns are called "noun substitutes" because they can take the place of nouns. Because pronouns can substitute, or stand in, for nouns in sentences our writing becomes more active and more interesting. Using pronouns helps us avoid repeating the same noun over and over again. In this unit, you will learn the many choices you have in selecting the correct pronoun to convey your ideas.

UNIT OBJECTIVES

When you complete Unit 4, you will be able to:

- identify pronouns and their antecedents.

- understand when to use the masculine, feminine, or neuter pronoun.

- understand the three cases of pronouns—nominative, objective, and possessive.

- choose the correct form of a pronoun in a sentence.

- clarify the difference between who and whom/which and that.

- use interrogative and indefinite pronouns correctly.

- write sentences using the correct pronouns.

LESSON 9 — ANTECEDENTS, NUMBER, AND GENDER

PRONOUNS

Part of Speech A pronoun is a word that takes the place of a noun. It is one of the eight parts of speech.

Pronouns help us avoid repeating nouns; for example:

Chad and his friend, Joe, interviewed their former teacher to gather information for their report.

If we had not used pronouns, the sentence would be quite awkward:

Chad and Chad's friend, Joe, interviewed Chad and Joe's former teacher to gather information for Chad and Joe's report.

There are six classifications of pronouns: personal, interrogative, indefinite, relative, demonstrative, and intensive. The *personal* pronouns are listed below.

I	it	him	my	his	our
you	we	her	mine	her	ours
he	they	us	your	hers	their
she	me	them	yours	its	theirs

CHECKUP 1

Underline the personal pronouns in the following sentences. Then write the pronouns in the spaces at the right.

1. The teacher met with <u>her</u> students in the computer lab.
2. You have my permission to use our copier.
3. Their daughter laughed at the rabbit wiggling its ears.
4. Each of the twins had her ticket for the concert.

1. <u>her</u>
2. _____
3. _____
4. _____

FOLLOW THE LEADER!

A pronoun often follows the noun to which it refers, so we can consider pronouns as followers and nouns as leaders. The noun, or leader, to which the pronoun refers is the *antecedent*.

George likes to run with his dog. *George* is the *leader* or *antecedent*. *His* is the *follower*—the pronoun that refers to and replaces the noun George.

George   his

The noun, or leader, can have more than one pronoun refer back to it.

Jim thought about what he would put in his wagons. *Jim* is the leader or antecedent. The pronouns *he* and *his*, which replace the noun Jim, are the followers.

There can be more than one noun in a sentence that serves as a leader, or antecedent. Make sure you match the pronoun to the correct antecedent.

The corporation paid its stockholders a healthy dividend on their investments. *Corporation* is a leader. *Its* is the follower. *Stockholder* is another leader. *Their* is the follower.

Underline the pronouns and their leaders—the antecedents—in the following sentences. Then write the pronouns and their leaders in the spaces at the right.

1. Mother told her boss about her idea.
2. The student gave his assignment to the professor.
3. Bob used his spreadsheet to complete information on presidents and their cabinets.

1. her, her, Mother
2. _____
3. _____
_____

AGREEMENT—SINGULAR OR PLURAL?

Pronouns, like nouns, have number. They can be either singular or plural. A singular antecedent requires a singular pronoun. A plural antecedent requires a plural pronoun.

All van drivers were asked to wear their uniforms. Both the noun *drivers* and the pronoun *their* are plural.

Each van driver was asked to wear her uniform. Both the noun *driver* and the pronoun *her* are singular.

Do the pronouns in these sentences follow their leaders? Underline any incorrect use of singular or plural pronouns. Write your corrections in the spaces at the right. (*Hint:* The leaders are in italics.)

1. The *dogs* fought to get off his chains.
2. The Hollywood *star* lost their ability to attract large audiences.
3. The *lawyers* forgot to bring his laptop computers.
4. *Cheryl* had their application completed that same day.

1. their
2. _____
3. _____
4. _____

AGREEMENT—MALE, FEMALE, OR NEUTER?

Pronouns also have gender. A pronoun should have the same gender as its antecedent.

The *man* logged onto *his* computer before getting *his* coffee. The word *man* is obviously masculine in gender and requires the masculine personal pronoun *his*.

The *woman* logged onto her computer before getting *her* coffee. The word *woman* is obviously feminine in gender and requires the feminine pronoun *her*.

Some nouns can be either masculine or feminine, or both. These nouns are called *common-gender nouns*. If you know the gender of a common-gender noun by the way it is used in a sentence, then use the appropriate pronoun.

Every *member* of the Girl Scouts turned in *her* order. The common-gender noun *member* is feminine because the Girl Scouts is an all-female group. Use the feminine personal pronoun *her*.

If a common-gender noun can be both masculine and feminine in a particular sentence, use pronouns that reflect both genders.

Every *member* of the group gave *his* or *her* support to the project. A *member* could be male or female; therefore, *his* or *her* is correct.

If a noun is neither masculine nor feminine, it is *neuter* and requires a neuter pronoun. *It* and *its* are neuter pronouns.

When the *printer* is delivered, please take *it* to Ms. Cortez's office. *Printer* is neither masculine nor feminine, but neuter, and requires the neuter pronoun *it.*

Do the pronouns in these sentences follow their leaders? Underline any incorrect use of pronouns. Write your corrections in the spaces at the right. If a sentence is correct, write OK.

1. The manager wanted their employees to wear uniforms.
2. The magnet school was known for its emphasis on the arts.
3. The wireless technology beams their computer signal.
4. Each office assistant said she would be willing to work on the report.

1. his *or* her
2. _____
3. _____
4. _____

EXERCISES

EXERCISE 1 Identify the pronouns in the following sentences by writing them in the spaces at the right. (*Hint:* There may be more than one pronoun in a sentence.)

1. Why did we give the car to them?   1. _____
2. We enjoyed their wedding reception.   2. _____
3. The children begged their parents for a dog.   3. _____
4. Her manager agreed to help him and his assistant with the work.   4. _____
5. The business manager resigned her position when she became ill.   5. _____
6. Ann Marie promised us that we could have the tennis court by noon. 6. _____
7. They want to give the award to you and me.   7. _____
8. We wish we could attend the opening ceremony, but we are already   8. _____
   committed to another engagement.
9. We visited them during the holidays.   9. _____
10. Yes, I will buy several of your tickets tomorrow.   10. _____
11. My problem is that they will not listen to me.   11. _____
12. You and your sisters have given me much comfort during my hospital stay. 12. _____
13. Several people asked him for his autograph.   13. _____
14. They can give you all the help you need.   14. _____
15. Please ask our lawyer to give it to you.   15. _____
16. Shall we have the meeting at your place or at mine?   16. _____
17. Was he the one your supervisor wanted to hire?   17. _____
18. Did Robert and Lori celebrate their anniversary?   18. _____
19. Give us an account of what you did when you were in Washington, D.C. 19. _____
20. Each of the companies had its books audited.   20. _____
21. The actress would often forget her lines.   21. _____
22. He agreed to assist her in her research.   22. _____
23. The package may not reach its destination.   23. _____
24. Our associates were impressed by what their consultants said.   24. _____
25. While his daughter was away, they corresponded by e-mail.   25. _____

EXERCISE 2 Replace the word or words in parentheses with a pronoun. Write the pronouns in the spaces at the right.

1. (*The students*) are required to take algebra.   1. _____
2. (*Lynn*) asked her manager for a raise.   2. _____
3. (*Joe's*) car was in the garage for repairs.   3. _____
4. (*Employees*) wanted to start working on the project immediately.   4. _____
5. (*You and I*) painted (*Bob and Nick's*) apartment.   5. _____
6. Zane gave (*Zane's*) version of the meeting between him and his boss. 6. _____
7. (*The politician*) decided to vote against the bill.   7. _____
8. (*Ms. Rochar and she*) were responsible for preparing the budget.   8. _____
9. I gave (*John*) a graduation gift.   9. _____

10. Are these papers (*Frank's and Mary's*)?   10. _____

11. (*Robert and John*) commuted to college together.   11. _____

12. Have you given (*him and her*) your opinion?   12. _____

13. The graphics done by (*Monica and Jennifer*) were beautiful.   13. _____

14. The assistant told (*Dawn*) about the meeting.   14. _____

15. (*Ashley*) was frustrated when she couldn't access her on-line service. 15. _____

16. Our supervisor promised to notify (*Lois and me*) of any change. 16. _____

17. The president wrote (*the president's*) speech while he was on the plane. 17. _____

18. Bill was the editor of (*Bill's*) high school newsletter.   18. _____

19. Give these copies to (*Jo and Jake*).   19. _____

20. The clerk mailed (*the book*) on Monday.   20. _____

EXERCISE 3 Identify the leaders (the antecedents) of the pronouns in the following sentences by writing the leaders in the spaces at the right. (*Hint:* The pronouns are in italics.)

1. I wanted the security guard to change *his* hours.   1. _____

2. Give the customers what *they* want.   2. _____

3. The students have an opportunity to develop *their* own learning style. 3. _____

4. Dr. Hastings explained the surgery to *his* patient.   4. _____

5. Tina Dawson said *she* would be late for *her* appointment.   5. _____

6. Neither Norm nor Dennis expressed *his* view.   6. _____

7. The council members met weekly to develop *their* plan.   7. _____

8. Have Mr. Shaw and Mr. Patel seen *their* new offices?   8. _____

9. The school plan is ready, but no one has seen *it*.   9. _____

10. The two Senators eventually had *their* bill approved.   10. _____

11. I wanted Floyd to bring *his* report to my class.   11. _____

12. A middle-aged couple bought *their* first house.   12. _____

13. The newly elected mayor announced *her* resignation.   13. _____

14. Legends live on for *their* entertainment and educational value. 14. _____

15. The inexperienced wrestler never thought *he* would win.   15. _____

16. Congress will continue *its* current session until July 4.   16. _____

17. The graduates will be an asset to any college *they* attend.   17. _____

18. Please sign the form and return *it* in the enclosed envelope.   18. _____

19. The young couple were worried about *their* mortgage.   19. _____

20. May I please have my manuscript back after you have read *it*.   20. _____

SHORT STORY Pronouns have not been used correctly in the following paragraph. Circle the pronouns that are used incorrectly and write the correct pronouns in the spaces at the right.

The construction workers carried his lunches to work each day   1. _____
during the summer months and ate her lunches outside. However,   2. _____
when winter arrived he knew the weather would be too cold for   3. _____
him to eat outside. So the workers would eat at a local diner.   4. _____
They specialized in nourishing hot soup and gigantic sandwiches.   5. _____

PRONOUNS AND THEIR CASES

PERSONAL PRONOUNS

Pronouns have number (singular, plural) and gender (male, female, or neuter). Pronouns have one other consideration—*case*. Personal pronouns have three cases: *nominative*, *objective*, and *possessive*. Which case is used depends upon how a pronoun functions within a sentence.

Nominative Case		Objective Case		Possessive Case	
Singular	**Plural**	**Singular**	**Plural**	**Singular**	**Plural**
I	we	me	us	my, mine	our, ours
you	you	you	you	your, yours	your, yours
he		him		his	
she	they	her	them	her, hers	their, theirs
it		it		its	

Notice that the forms *you* and *it* can be either nominative or objective.

NOMINATIVE FORMS OF PRONOUNS

When a pronoun functions as the subject, use the nominative form, or case.

***They* demonstrated the PowerPoint presentation.** *They* is the subject.

CHECKUP 1
Underline the nominative-form pronouns in the following sentences. Then write the nominative-form pronouns in the spaces at the right.

1. <u>He</u> and <u>she</u> arrived at the stadium.
2. I am a doctor.
3. You could be the winner.
4. They think that they will be able to attend.

1. He, she _____
2. _____
3. _____
4 _____

IT IS I! We also use nominative pronouns following the verbs *am*, *is*, *are*, *was*, *were*, *be*, *been*, or any other form of the verb *to be*.

It is *I*. (NOT: It is me.) **The two winners were *we*!** (NOT: us)

CHECKUP 2
Select the correct pronoun from each pair in parentheses, and write it in the space at the right.

1. Judith and (*her, she*) gave the evening devotion.
2. That is (*her, she*) in the movies.
3. Bradley and (*he, him*) wanted to construct the building.
4. It is (*me, I*) who delivered the fax.

1. she _____
2. _____
3. _____
4. _____

OBJECTIVE FORMS OF PRONOUNS

When a pronoun functions as a direct object, an indirect object, or as an object of a preposition, use the objective case. The direct object follows the verb and answers the question *what* or *whom*. The indirect object follows the verb and answers the question *to whom*, *to what*, *for whom*, or *for what*.

The president will buy *him* a computer. Buy *whom* or *what*? A computer (the direct object). For *whom* or *what*? For *him* (the indirect object).

The object of a preposition follows the preposition. Some common prepositions are as follows:

in	on	from	about	after	for	without	except
of	by	under	since	before	like	with	concerning

They need another person like *you*. (NOT: *yourself*). *You* is the object of the preposition *like*.

Now look at these two sentences:

Give the report to *her*. *Her* is the object of the preposition *to*.

Give *her* the report. *Her* is the indirect object.

Since the word *to* is written or stated, it is a *preposition*. The word that follows *to* is the object of the preposition, not an indirect object.

CHECKUP 3

Select the correct pronoun from each pair in parentheses, and write it in the spaces at the right. Make sure you understand *why* your answer is correct.

1. The football player wanted (*they, them*) to continue to play.   1. them
2. Give (*they, them*) whatever they want.   2. _____
3. The principal will give (*him, he*) a second chance.   3. _____
4. We want to work with (*she, her*) on the brochure.   4. _____

POSSESSIVE FORMS OF PRONOUNS

We use the possessive forms of pronouns to show ownership.

my printer   *your* office   *his* idea   *our* firm   *its* quota

As you see, these forms are used *before* nouns. The forms *mine, yours, his, hers, its,* and *theirs* can be used *in place of* nouns. Pronouns that show possession do not use apostrophes.

This jacket is *mine*, but that one is *yours*.   If that copier is *theirs*, then where is *ours*?

CHECKUP 4

Replace the word or words in parentheses with a possessive pronoun. Write the pronoun in the space at the right.

1. Bob and Sue raced to (*Bob and Sue's*) class.   1. their
2. Did Oscar get all of (*Oscar's*) groceries?   2. _____
3. I certainly miss (*Mother's*) cooking.   3. _____
4. The mayor congratulated the boy on (*the boy's*) many honors.   4. _____

PRONOUNS AND GERUNDS

A *gerund* is a verb form that ends in *-ing* and used as a noun. (Remember, nouns are used as subjects, direct objects, indirect objects, objects of a preposition, complements, and appositives.)

Spelling is your hardest course. *Spelling* is a form of the verb *to spell* and is used as the subject of the sentence.

He is majoring in *marketing*. *Marketing* is a form of the verb *to market* and is used as the object of the preposition *in*.

A noun or pronoun used before a *gerund* should be in the possessive case.

I look forward to *his* (NOT: *him*) calling me for an interview.

CHECKUP 5

Replace the word or words in parentheses with a possessive pronoun.

1. I hope you will not mind (*I*) doing the job.   1. my
2. She knows (*you*) taking the lead on the project is a good decision.   2. _____
3. Vladimir objected to (*us*) calling so many people.   3. _____
4. (*Him*) campaigning with us is a good idea.   4. _____

Name _____   Date _____   Score _____

EXERCISES

EXERCISE 1   Select the correct pronoun from each pair in parentheses, and write it in the space at the right.

1. (*You, Your*) ordered the squid for (*us, we*).   1. _____
2. This one is (*my, mine*); that one is (*your, yours*).   2. _____
3. Yes, you and (*me, I*) will answer the phone.   3. _____
4. Bob said that (*she, her*) could buy the office supplies from the new vendor.   4. _____
5. Do you plan to buy dinner for (*we, us*)?   5. _____
6. (*They, Them*) will listen to our concerns at the meeting.   6. _____
7. Janet and (*me, I*) could not stop laughing.   7. _____
8. Please call (*he, him*) at his office before 3 p.m.   8. _____
9. We have scheduled (*they, them*) for an appointment.   9. _____
10. All the workers except (*she, her*) reported on time.   10. _____
11. I don't know why (*she, her*) was chosen to be the chairman.   11. _____
12. (*He, Him*) recommended several people for the job.   12. _____
13. I don't want (*they, them*) to know that I am here.   13. _____
14. (*I, me*) have a plane to catch at two o'clock.   14. _____
15. When will you be able to send (*us, we*) the information?   15. _____
16. (*They, Them*) are arranging our schedules for (*we, us*).   16. _____
17. It was (*they, them*) who collected the data for (*her, hers*) book.   17. _____
18. Are you sure that is (*my, mine*)?   18. _____
19. The computer is (*my, mine*).   19. _____
20. Donald and (*she, her*) will represent the company at the meeting.   20. _____
21. The sewing factory closed (*its, their*) doors when the owner died.   21. _____
22. (*Our, Us*) volunteering to stay late made an impression   22. _____
23. When will Ralph and (*she, her*) be able to come?   23. _____
24. Stern Company announced that (*they, it*) would be moving on July 1.   24. _____
25. Just between you and (*I, me*) I was asked to lead.   25. _____

EXERCISE 2   Correct any pronoun errors in the following sentences. Underline each error. Then write your corrections in the spaces at the right. If a sentence is correct, write *OK*.

1. You will find this subject index useful when you give it to he.   1. _____
2. Them will proceed with their plan for a new office building.   2. _____
3. The festival is important because her child will perform there.   3. _____
4. It was me who reported the election results.   4. _____
5. The dog was loved by she and he.   5. _____
6. Do you object to him being present at the departmental meetings?   6. _____
7. Joan and me loved to hear Johnny and he play.   7. _____
8. The company lost it's lease when new owners bought the building.   8. _____
9. He said that our house would be completed by they.   9. _____
10. Have you heard them speak before?   10. _____
11. I think that the judge should hear you complaint.   11. _____
12. It is me who established the scholarship fund for minority workers.   12. _____
13. You and her seem to be so happy.   13. _____

14. Will you please hand I that letter on Tom's desk.

14. _____

15. Many people do not know that them were authors.

15. _____

16. Are you relying on us finishing the work that you started?

16. _____

17. The mountain range was known for their volcanoes.

17. _____

18. Many of they had explored the possibility of printing a newsletter.

18. _____

19. Them are the people who came from South America.

19. _____

20. Me promised she that me would serve as a moderator.

20. _____

21. Hannah asked they to give her a reason for their actions.

21. _____

22. Have you thought about promoting he?

22. _____

23. The tadpole was for I.

23. _____

24. Check with they before you release the story.

24. _____

25. The company added a new product to their line.

25. _____

26. Have you heard that he will be our new president?

26. _____

27. It is us who will search for the lost pearls.

27. _____

28. He threw the dog it's favorite toy.

28. _____

29. She and I asked he to bring the animals to the shelter.

29. _____

30. Many of them had asked not to work over the Christmas holidays.

30. _____

31. We believe you need to have you're papers filed by April 1.

31. _____

32. Yes, that book over there is our.

32. _____

33. Gretchen and me will staff the Help Desk all week.

33. _____

34. Theirs supply of stationery was very low.

34. _____

35. An ape is an interesting animal because they is so active.

35. _____

36. Neither one of we will be able to furnish the names of the winners.

36. _____

37. Theirs country is in the Caribbean Sea.

37. _____

38. The union resumed their talks with the company representatives.

38. _____

39. The strict laws were repealed by we.

39. _____

40. Between you and I, I think that Henry will get the job.

40. _____

WRITING ACTIVITY Write a sentence for each one of the following pronouns. (Answers will vary.)

1. They _____

2. I _____

3. him _____

4. me _____

5. their _____

6. our _____

SHORT STORY Are the underlined pronouns used correctly? Write the correct form of any incorrectly written pronouns in the spaces at the right. If a pronoun is written in the correct form, write *OK*.

My brother and me decided to go into business together
mowing lawns. Us plan to advertise in the paper and
make some phone calls. Him and me estimate between the
two of us we can cut 50 lawns each week. Mine friends
say it's a great way to earn money, and we agree with them.

1. _____

2. _____

3. _____

4. _____

5. _____

SELECTING THE RIGHT CASE

PRONOUN TROUBLEMAKERS

WHEN WORDS ARE MISSING

Choosing the correct form of a pronoun may be tricky in a sentence like this one:

Howard enjoys Fran more than (*me/I*).

Which pronoun you choose depends on how that pronoun functions in the sentence (direct object or subject). To make your selection easier, imagine, as we have done, where words should be inserted in order to convey the intended meaning of the sentence. Does the sentence mean:

Howard enjoys Fran more than (he enjoys) *me*.

OR does it mean:

Howard enjoys Fran more than *I* (enjoy Fran).

With the missing words in place, select the sentence that expresses the correct meaning. Now determine how the pronoun is used in the sentence you selected—as a direct object or as a subject of the than/as clause? If the pronoun is used as the direct object, use the objective case. If it is used as a subject, use the nominative case.

The general rule is this: When a pronoun follows *than* or *as* in a (comparative) statement, supply the missing words to select the correct form of the pronoun.

	WARNING
	than
	as

CHECKUP 1

Select the correct pronoun from each pair in parentheses and write it in the space at the right. Remember to say the missing words to yourself.

1. Mrs. Pryor shops as much as (*I, me*).
2. Mr. Boetcher has been a manager longer than (*I, me*).
3. I can eat more ice cream than (*he, him*).
4. His talk motivated Charlie as much as (*I, me*).
5. Bruce likes to read books more than (*I, me*).

1. I _____
2. _____
3. _____
4. _____
5. _____

WHEN THERE ARE TOO MANY WORDS

Sometimes we must omit words to make a choice between pronouns. For example:

Sacia and (*I, me*) will go shopping tomorrow. Omit the words *Sacia and* and the choice then becomes simple: *I* will go shopping tomorrow. (NOT: *Me* will go.) A nominative pronoun is needed to be the subject of the verb *will go*.

Let's change the sentence as follows:

Two people, Sacia and (*I, me*), will go shopping tomorrow. *I* is still correct. Omit the beginning words, and you will get *I will go shopping tomorrow*. The nominative *I* is the subject of the verb *will go*. Another example:

Please download the file for Allison and (*I, me*). If you omit the words *Allison and* the choice is clear: download the file for . . . *me*. An objective pronoun is needed to be the object of the preposition *for*.

Select the correct pronoun from each pair in parentheses, and write it in the space at the right.

1. Ask the child or (*him, he*) to lead them.

   1. <u>him</u>

2. Rona asked Marie and (*he, him*) to pack her bags.

   2. _____

3. When you are finished with the journal, please give it to Phyllis or (*they, them*).

   3. _____

4. The minister came to (*her, she*) and Evelyn to offer help.

   4. _____

5. The calculator was used by Kevin and (*I, me*).

   5. _____

6. Because of our experience, Scott and (*I, me*) know the computer better than you.

   6. _____

ANOTHER TROUBLEMAKER!

We must also omit words to choose pronouns correctly in sentences such as these:

   (***We, Us***) **managers are conducting training seminars.**

   They sent invitations to (*we, us*) managers.

Which would you choose, *we* or *us*? In both cases, the choice becomes clear when you omit the word *managers*.

   (***We, Us***) **are conducting training seminars.** Of course, you would not say "*Us* are conducting"! *We* is correct.

   They sent invitations to (*we, us*). Of course, you would not say "sent invitations to *we*"! *Us* is correct here.

Do not be fooled when the pronoun is the object of a preposition:

   All of *us* managers are conducting training seminars. Here, *us* is the object of the preposition *of*, and the object of a preposition is *always an objective form*.

Select the correct pronoun from each pair in parentheses, and write it in the space at the right.

1. (*We, Us*) supervisors are needed in the computer lab.

   1. <u>We</u>

2. Jane said that (*we, us*) teachers should report to school at 7:30 a.m.

   2. _____

3. All of (*us, we*) writers enjoy our jobs.

   3. _____

4. Ask (*we, us*) to do the job, and we will follow through for you.

   4. _____

5. Several of (*we, us*) were invited to the seminar.

   5. _____

6. The people gave it to (*us, we*) women because they wanted it done.

   6. _____

7. They tried to give (*we, us*) samples, but we refused them.

   7. _____

8. Some of (*us, we*) members were asked to represent the Credit Union.

   8. _____

9. Although both of (*we, us*) had been there before, we were eager to go again.

   9. _____

10. (*We, Us*) finance majors are busy preparing our resumes.

   10. _____

11. (*We, Us*) experts could fix almost all computers.

   11. _____

12. They gave the compass to (*we, us*) campers.

   12. _____

LESSON 11

Name   Date   Score

EXERCISES

EXERCISE 1   Select the correct pronoun from each pair in parentheses, and write it in the space at the right.

1. Workers like Mitzie and (*she, her*) were always in demand.   1. _____
2. The recently hired consultant, Jeff Meyerhoffer, is as enthusiastic as (*she, her*).   2. _____
3. After eating the salad, Sharon and (*her, she*) did not eat the fish.   3. _____
4. The report on the Congo was delivered by (*him, he*) and Andrew.   4. _____
5. The land was surveyed by our engineer and (*he, him*).   5. _____
6. My sister and (*I, me*) discussed the matter yesterday.   6. _____
7. Rick and (*I, me*) made plans to travel to Washington, D.C.   7. _____
8. I will dance only with (*her, she*) and Doris.   8. _____
9. The contractor asked Nancy and (*I, me*) to help select the materials.   9. _____
10. I believe that Morris is a better analyst than (*she, her*).   10. _____
11. Mike's departure from our office will hurt the company more than (*we, us*).   11. _____
12. The weather report did not seem to worry Jay and (*her, she*).   12. _____
13. Mr. Parker, our office manager, lets Elaine work more hours than (*I, me*).   13. _____
14. Virginia took Mark and (*he, him*) to the concert.   14. _____
15. Our human resources director needs to remind the computer operators   15. _____
    and (*she, her*) about the approaching deadline.

EXERCISE 2   Select the correct pronoun from each pair in parentheses, and write it in the space at the right.

1. David and (*he, him*) graduated from Princeton.   1. _____
2. We taught Arnie and (*she, her*) how to use word processing software on the   2. _____
   office computer.
3. We brought Alexander and (*he, him*) to the movie lot.   3. _____
4. A complete report needs to be made by either you or (*he, him*).   4. _____
5. Between you and (*I, me*), I suggest that we suspend production for now.   5. _____
6. Dr. Holman and (*he, him*) will advise us about the medical grant.   6. _____
7. The crew and (*he, him*) were friends in high school.   7. _____
8. The three officers and (*they, them*) will investigate the problem and report 8. _____
   back to us.
9. The doctor took care of Betty and (*he, him*).   9. _____
10. The judge called Marya and (*we, us*) to his chambers.   10. _____

EXERCISE 3   Select the correct pronoun from each pair in parentheses, and write it in the space at the right.

1. Julie gave (*they, them*) too much money.   1. _____
2. Having heard our side of the story, do you think they will believe Bruce and (*I, me*)? 2. _____
3. (*Us, We*) nurses need more recognition by the hospital board.   3. _____

4. The little girl wanted Kenneth and (*I, me*) to come to the party.   4. _____

5. Yes, (*we, us*) attorneys promise to let you know when the case comes up in court.   5. _____

6. The petitions were circulated among (*we, us*) voters.   6. _____

7. Fund-raising methods were investigated by (*she, her*).   7. _____

8. Norm said that I should represent David and (*he, him*).   8. _____

9. If someone has to be present, then I recommend that (*he, him*) be our representative.   9. _____

10. Actresses like Tina and (*she, her*) expect star treatment.   10. _____

11. (*I, Me*) now realize that we should have bid higher for the antique desk.   11. _____

12. The PTA meeting was attended by (*we, us*) parents.   12. _____

13. You can send the applications to (*we, us*) reviewers.   13. _____

14. The restaurant served (*they, them*) Chinese food.   14. _____

15. (*We, Us*) librarians were happy to be members of the advising committee.   15. _____

16. Cal's quiet dignity made (*he, him*) popular.   16. _____

17. Mr. Plank said that (*we, us*) workers were doing a fine job of assembling the motors.   17. _____

EXERCISE 4   Follow the directions given for each set.

Write two sentences that illustrate the correct use of a *nominative* case pronoun following the words *than* and *as*. (Answers will vary.)

1. _____

2. _____

Write two sentences that illustrate the correct use of an *objective* case pronoun following the words *than* and *as*. (Answers will vary.)

3. _____

4. _____

Write two sentences that illustrate the correct use of a *nominative* case pronoun preceding a noun. (Answers will vary.)

5. _____

6. _____

Write two sentences that illustrate the correct use of an *objective* case pronoun preceding a noun. (Answers will vary.)

7. _____

8. _____

SHORT STORY   Circle pronouns that are incorrectly used. Write the correct pronoun in the space at the right. If no correction is needed, write *None*.

My mom and me went to the Humane society to adopt a dog for   1. _____

my younger brother and I. The Society supervisors and us toured   2. _____

the pens and looked at many dogs ranging in color and size; it was

very difficult for we to select just one dog. After spending many   3. _____

minutes with the animals, my mom and me decided on a beautiful   4. _____

black lab puppy. We immediately filled out the adoption papers.   5. _____

WHO, WHOM, AND OTHER PRONOUNS

WHO, WHOM, WHICH AND THAT AS RELATIVE PRONOUNS

WHO/WHOEVER, WHOM/WHOMEVER

We may have trouble deciding which form of these pronouns to use because in everyday conversation we tend to use *who* whether it is correct or not. So, let's review some rules.

The pronouns *who/whoever* and *whom/whomever* function in two ways—(1) as interrogative pronouns and (2) as relative pronouns.

> Pronouns are *interrogative* when they ask a question: **Who is going to ride with us?**

> Pronouns are *relative* when they refer back to someone: **Martha is the one who is going with us.**

Like personal pronouns, *who/whoever* and *whom/whomever* have case. *Who/whoever* are in the nominative case and can be used as subjects, complements, and appositives. *Whom/whomever* are in the objective case and can be used as direct objects, indirect objects, and objects of a preposition.

COLUMN 1		COLUMN 2	
NOMINATIVE CASE Who/Whoever		**OBJECTIVE CASE** Whom/Whomever	
Singular	**Plural**	**Singular**	**Plural**
I	we	me	us
he she it	they	him her it	them

> **(*Who/Whom*) is willing to make the cake?**

Substitute a personal pronoun from Column 1: *He* is willing to make the cake.

Substitute a personal pronoun from Column 2: *Him* is willing to make the cake.

The correct substitution is *he* from Column 1 because *he* is the subject of the sentence. Pronouns functioning as subjects have to be in the nominative case. *Who* is in the nominative case and can be a substitute for *he*. The sentence should read as follows:

> ***Who* is willing to make the cake?**

> **The people in town are eager to know (*who/whom*) will be elected mayor.**

Substitute a personal pronoun from Column 1: *She* will be elected mayor.

Substitute a personal pronoun from Column 2: *Her* will be elected mayor.

Since the word selected will function as the subject of the clause, it must be in the nominative case. *She* is in the nominative case. *Who* is also in the nominative case and can be used as a substitute for *She*. The sentence should read as follows:

> **The people in town are eager to know *who* will be elected mayor.**

> **Please make an appointment with *whoever* is listed on your form.** Making a substitution, we could say: *He is listed on the form. He* is in the nominative case.

> **Please make an appointment with *whomever* you want.** Making a substitution, we could say: *make an appointment with him. Him* is in the objective case.

> **Lois Ryan, *whom* I consider the best candidate in the race, said she would withdraw her name.** We could say: *I consider her the best candidate in the race. Her* is in the objective case.

CHECKUP 1

Select the correct word from each pair in parentheses, and write it in the space at the right. If necessary, put the *who/whom* clause in normal order first.

1. (*Who, Whom*) is taller than I?
2. (*Who, Whom*) will be our new supervisor in the plant?
3. Ask the person (*who, whom*) is looking out the window.
4. The custodian (*who, whom*) I married was Larry.

1. Who
2. _____
3. _____
4. _____

WHO, WHICH, THAT

WHO
(essential or nonessential)
▼
person

You already know that *who* is a pronoun, but so are the words *which* and *that*.

Use *who* when referring to a person or to the individuality of a group.

I know *who* is the next award recipient. *Who* refers to an individual person.

WHICH
(nonessential)
▼
place
object
animal

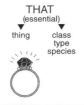

Use *which* when introducing a nonessential clause that refers to places, objects, and animals. Nonessential clauses provide descriptive information that is not necessary to the message of the sentence. (Recall that a clause is a group of related words containing a subject and predicate.)

The estimates, which you sent me last week, are too high. The clause "which you sent me last week" provides nonessential information about the subject, *estimates*. The real message in the sentence is "The estimates are too high." Commas are used around nonessential clauses. (*Hint:* The word *which* always introduces a nonessential clause.)

THAT
(essential)
▼   ▼
thing   class
         type
         species

Use *that* when introducing essential clauses that refer to things, or classes, or types of persons. Essential clauses provide necessary information and are not set off by commas.

The employee survey that I placed on your desk is due tomorrow. The words *that I placed on your desk* provide essential information about the object, *survey*. No commas are used.

CHECKUP 2

Replace each blank in the sentences below with *that* or *which*.

1. The house _____ is for sale is in the historic register.
2. One of the recommendations _____ she made was accepted.
3. You can leave work early, _____ won't disturb me.
4. The appraisal _____ Hank made on the house was accurate.
5. Our office, _____ was painted five years ago, needs to be painted.

1. that
2. _____
3. _____
4. _____
5. _____

CHECKUP 3

Write a sentence using each one of these pronouns. (Answers will vary.)

1. that   The window that was damaged is now repaired.
2. which   _____
3. who   _____
4. whom   _____

CHECKUP 4

Circle any incorrectly used pronouns. Write the correct pronouns in the space. If no correction is needed, write *None* in the blank.

The classrooms (which) were scheduled for renovation this year will be delayed. In talking with Mr. Botts, whom is in charge of the project, I learned the new date has not been set. The renovation, that the school board approved, will use state-of-the-art technology.

1. that
2. _____
3. _____
4. _____

EXERCISES

EXERCISE 1 Select the correct pronoun from each pair in parentheses, and write it in the space at the right.

1. (*Who, Whom*) did you say owned the computer desk?
2. She is the attorney (*who, whom*) is representing Mr. Bartel.
3. Dr. Hayes, (*who, whom*) I met at church, was quoted in the newspaper.
4. They are the ones (*who, whom*) are asking about our services.
5. The children are the ones (*who, whom*) will suffer.
6. Unfortunately, the chairman (*who, whom*) they elected is unable to accept.
7. Give the award to the person (*who, whom*) receives the highest evaluation.
8. Jesse, (*who, whom*) was at the lab, is my partner.
9. He is the one (*who, whom*) will make the decision about the move.
10. To (*who, whom*) is this addressed?
11. Amanda and Jill are the ones (*who, whom*) really know how to write articles for publication.
12. Vance, (*who, whom*) is our advisor, left in a hurry.
13. (*Who, Whom*) do you think we should get to record the minutes?
14. The entertainment industry will give the award to (*who, whoever*) gets the most votes.
15. Nadia Riley, (*who, whom*) I talked to you about this morning, is transferring to the Accounting Department June 1.
16. (*Whoever, Whomever*) registered for the convocation should attend.
17. They chose Barry Carter, (*who, whom*) has worked very hard for the company.
18. (*Who, Whom*) do you think will be my new teacher?
19. (*Whoever, Whomever*) reaches the company quota by the end of the month will receive a $1,000 bonus.
20. He was the actor (*who, whom*) portrayed the alien in the movie.

1. _____
2. _____
3. _____
4. _____
5. _____
6. _____
7. _____
8. _____
9. _____
10. _____
11. _____
12. _____
13. _____
14. _____
15. _____
16. _____
17. _____
18. _____
19. _____
20. _____

EXERCISE 2 Correct any errors in the usage of *who, whom, whoever,* and *whomever.* Underline each error. Then write your corrections in the spaces at the right. If a sentence is correct, write *OK.*

1. None of the nurses, who we knew, were involved in the investigations.
2. Give this manual to whoever is in charge of the computer lab.
3. Many of the celebrities who were from out of town stayed overnight at the Walton Plaza.
4. Jamie, whom believed the soldier, was not at the meeting.
5. Rick Williams, who you introduced us to at the conference, made a very good impression on Mr. Danforth.
6. The man who is sitting next to the keynote speaker is Mr. Shull.
7. We wonder if the auctioneer whom sold the antique was aware of its value.
8. It was she who we thought would be the new coach of our team.
9. The treasurer who we elected is extremely competent.

1. _____
2. _____
3. _____
4. _____
5. _____
6. _____
7. _____
8. _____
9. _____

10. The person who I met at the convention is a candidate for a position   10. _____
    at Carson Corporation.
11. Whom made the tower collapse?   11. _____
12. I think it is wise to support whoever believes in your values.   12. _____
13. Let's ask for nominations from whomever is interested.   13. _____
14. Don gave the invoice to the person whom was in the lobby.   14. _____
15. Who would you recommend?   15. _____

EXERCISE 3   Replace each blank with *which* or *that*. Write the correct answers in the spaces at the right.

1. Where is the cat _____ was lying on the couch?   1. _____
2. Our company, _____ was established 75 years ago, is about to close.   2. _____
3. Most of the boxes _____ he unloaded were from the chemical lab.   3. _____
4. The new journal, _____ contains articles by well-known authors,   4. _____
   has a subscription rate of $50 for the year.
5. The churches _____ were represented at the conference wanted unity.   5. _____
6. His article on the communication process, _____ was published in the   6. _____
   company newsletter, won him an award.
7. The computer _____ I wanted had a printer.   7. _____
8. Chicago, _____ is a large city, has several wonderful museums.   8. _____
9. I wonder if the camp, _____ I attended, was destroyed.   9. _____
10. Our new building, _____ opened in January, was furnished by Howards. 10. _____
11. This is the shampoo _____ I use.   11. _____
12. They sold the car _____ had the most mileage.   12. _____
13. The issue, _____ I think you understand, is up for vote.   13. _____
14. Yours is the recommendation _____ was accepted.   14. _____
15. The group _____ was nominated is from Ohio.   15. _____

EXERCISE 4   Correct any errors in the usage of *which* and *that*. Underline each error. Then write your corrections in the spaces at the right. If a sentence is correct, write *OK*.

1. The television programs which I chose to watch were humorous.   1. _____
2. The petition that Judge Kraft received had more than enough signatures.   2. _____
3. There was something which we thought was not quite right.   3. _____
4. The store which is owned by Mr. Easton is on Washington Road.   4. _____
5. The luxurious car that was in front of Mark's house was not his.   5. _____
6. Unlike most reports that are written at the request of management,   6. _____
   recommendation reports are often initiated by the writer.
7. The horse, that we loved, was sold at the auction.   7. _____
8. Simon's report on health benefits, which I sent you last week, should   8. _____
   answer all your questions.
9. The veto which caused so much anger seemed to be political.   9. _____
10. She is the type of student which will do well in math.   10. _____

13

MORE ABOUT PRONOUNS

INTERROGATIVE, DEMONSTRATIVE, INTENSIVE, AND INDEFINITE PRONOUNS

PRONOUNS IN QUESTIONS

Pronouns used in questions are interrogative pronouns: *who, whom, whose, which,* and *what*.

> ***Who** is using the conference room at 1 p.m.?* *Who* is the subject of the verb *is*.
>
> ***Whom** should I call first?* Normal order: I should call *whom* first. *Whom* is the direct object.
>
> ***Whose** report do you prefer?* *Whose* is a possessive pronoun like *hers* or *his*. Careful! Do not confuse *whose* with the contraction *who's,* which stands for *who is*.
>
> ***What** would you buy?* The word *What* is indefinite—it refers to nothing in particular.
>
> ***Which** brand of toothpaste do you buy?* The word *Which* refers to one particular person or thing.

The words *whose* and *which* are also used as adjectives.

> ***Whose** sweater was left on the chair?* The word *Whose* modifies sweater.
>
> ***Which** cookie do you like better?* The word *Which* modifies cookie.

DEMONSTRATIVE PRONOUNS

This, that, these, and *those* are demonstrative pronouns. They point out what is being referred to. Be sure to remember that *this* and *that* are singular; *these* and *those* are plural.

SINGULAR	PLURAL
this computer, that computer	these printers, those printers

Use *this* and *these* to identify things that are near. Use *that* and *those* for things that are far.

> ***These** boxes are for recycling cans. **Those** boxes (on the counter) are for papers.* *These* identifies the boxes that are closer. *Those* identifies the boxes that are farther away.

This, that, these, and *those* are adjectives when they modify a noun but pronouns when they stand alone.

ADJECTIVES	PRONOUNS
This book is mine. *That* book is yours.	*This* is mine. *That* is yours.

INTENSIVE PRONOUNS

Personal pronouns that end in *-self* (singular) or *-selves* (plural) are intensive. They add emphasis or intensity. The pronouns *myself, yourself, herself, himself,* and *itself* are singular; *ourselves, yourselves,* and *themselves* are plural.

> **I will edit this letter *myself*.** The pronoun *myself* refers to *I*.
>
> **We will answer these letters *ourselves*.** The pronoun *ourselves* refers to *we*.

A pronoun ending in *-self* or *-selves* *must* refer to something in the sentence—its antecedent.

> Wrong: **The officer talked with Karen and myself.** What does *myself* refer to? Nothing.
> Right: **The officer talked with Karen and *me*.**

In sentences where *you* is understood, *yourself* may be perfectly okay.

Please file this *yourself*. *You* is understood: (*You*) please . . .

Beware! There is no such word as *hisself*. Say *himself*. *Theirselves* and *theirself* are also incorrect.

CHECKUP 1 Select the correct pronoun from each pair in parentheses, and write it in the space at the right. *Hint*: Make sure a *self*-ending pronoun has a leader!

1. He (*hisself, himself*) found the missing heir.
2. (*Who, Whom*) do you want to invite?
3. (*What, Which*) one of the printers is a laser printer?
4. I wonder if you would give it to (*whomever, whoever*) asked for it.
5. Keep a copy of the contract for (*yourself, ourselves*).

1. himself
2. _____
3. _____
4. _____
5. _____

INDEFINITE PRONOUNS

EACH* and *EVERY The pronouns *each* and *every* are called *indefinite pronouns* because they refer to persons, places, or things *in general*. They are not specific. NOTE: *No one* is always two words. *Any one* and *every one* are written as two words only when the word *of* follows.

Any one of you can come. BUT: **Anyone can come.** **Every one of the books was new.**

Frequently Used Indefinite Pronouns Indefinite pronouns used most frequently include:

SINGULAR					
Use singular verbs					
anybody	each	every	everything	no one	one
anyone	either	everyone	neither	nothing	someone

PLURAL			
Use plural verbs			
both	few	several	many

SINGULAR OR PLURAL		
all	none	most
any	more	some

Everyone likes his and her schedule. *Everyone* is singular; *likes* is singular. NOTE: *Everyone* is masculine or feminine so we use *his* and *her* and not just *his*.

Both engineers enjoy working overtime. *Both* is plural; *enjoy* is plural.

For a pronoun that can be either singular or plural, look at the word to which it refers to determine whether a singular or a plural verb is needed.

None of the manuscript was mailed. *None* can be singular or plural. The word it refers to, *manuscript*, is singular. Use a singular verb.

None (no one) was hurt. Some of the report was accurate.

None of the cartons were shipped. *None* refers to *cartons*. *Cartons* is plural. Use a plural verb.

None (of the people) were hurt. Some of the reports were accurate.

CHECKUP 2 Circle pronouns used incorrectly in the following paragraph. Write the correct pronoun in the space at the right. If no correction is needed, write *OK*.

Ruby, (whom) opened the door for you, wishes to speak with Anne and yourself regarding your career plans. She knows that each of you has many choices to make and no one can make choices for you. All young persons need to gather as much information as possible for theirselves.

1. who
2. _____
3. _____
4. _____
5. _____

Name _____   Date _____   Score _____

EXERCISES

EXERCISE 1   Select the correct pronoun from each pair in parentheses, and write it in the space at the right.

1. The race car driver (*who*, *whom*) I admired won the race.
2. (*What*, *Which*) have they done with the evaluations?
3. (*What*, *Which*) team won the World Series?
4. (*What*, *Which*) of the two plans do you suggest we use?
5. (*Who*, *Whom*) discovered the South Pole?
6. (*What*, *Which*) did you learn from your historical study of letters?
7. (*That*, *Those*) are the rockets being launched next week.
8. (*That*, *Which*) partner in the firm is more reliable?
9. (*Who*, *Whom*) faxed my resume to IBM?
10. (*Which*, *What*) of you would like to work on the Feinberg account?
11. (*Which*, *What*) dictator chose to lead his country to disaster?
12. (*What*, *Which*) has happened to all the supplies in the cabinet?
13. (*What*, *Which*) appears to be the cause of the illness?
14. (*Who*, *Whom*) are you performing for this evening?
15. We can compare (*this*, *these*) schools to our schools.

1. _____
2. _____
3. _____
4. _____
5. _____
6. _____
7. _____
8. _____
9. _____
10. _____
11. _____
12. _____
13. _____
14. _____
15. _____

EXERCISE 2   Select the correct pronoun from each pair in parentheses, and write it in the space at the right.

1. (*This*, *These*) school has a computer for every three students.
2. (*That*, *Those*) are the transparencies that I need for the presentation.
3. Conservative politicians thought (*this*, *these*) resolution was doomed.
4. (*That*, *Those*) portraits of our founders need to be refinished.
5. We watched the pilot throw (*this*, *those*) cans away.
6. (*This*, *These*) computers were purchased sometime in July.
7. Public radio chose (*that*, *those*) program to receive the funds.
8. (*That*, *Those*) are not the ones that we ordered.
9. The restaurant chose (*that*, *these*) logo.
10. (*That*, *Those*) window was replaced several times already.

1. _____
2. _____
3. _____
4. _____
5. _____
6. _____
7. _____
8. _____
9. _____
10. _____

EXERCISE 3   Select the correct pronoun from each pair in parentheses, and write it in the space at the right.

1. The physical therapist prescribed exercises for him to do by (*hisself*, *himself*).
2. Since no one else was around to help, we had to do all the work by (*ourselves*, *themselves*).
3. The students thought the calculator could work by (*itself*, *themselves*).
4. Many of the participants wanted to try the new technique by (*ourselves*, *themselves*).
5. The report stated that they should decide for (*theirselves*, *themselves*).

1. _____
2. _____
3. _____
4. _____
5. _____

6. Allen saw (*himself, hisself*) on the video. 6. _____
7. We thought the doctor (*himself, hisself*) would give the opening remarks. 7. _____
8. All of us enjoyed (*ourselves, yourselves*) at the centennial celebration. 8. _____
9. The artists painted everything by (*theirselves, themselves*). 9. _____
10. Andy said that he should keep it for (*hisself, himself*). 10. _____

EXERCISE 4   Decide whether a singular or a plural verb is needed to complete each of the following sentences. Select the correct verb from each pair in parentheses, and write it in the space at the right.

1. Anyone in the senior class (*is, are*) eligible for a scholarship. 1. _____
2. Several visitors from foreign countries (*is, are*) on campus. 2. _____
3. If someone (*need, needs*) a ride to the meeting, please let me know. 3. _____
4. Neither Jeanette nor Marcy (*wants, want*) to express an opinion. 4. _____
5. Many of the people (*was, were*) ready to leave after the first act. 5. _____
6. Any one of the colors (*is, are*) acceptable to me. 6. _____
7. Nothing you say (*is, are*) going to make me change my mind. 7. _____
8. Most of the afternoon (*was, were*) spent reading the guidelines. 8. _____
9. Neither of the brokers (*was, were*) willing to lower the commission rate. 9. _____
10. (*Is, Are*) somebody willing to serve as host at the opening session? 10. _____

EXERCISE 5   Correct any pronoun errors in the following sentences. Underline each error. When you have a choice, correct the pronoun rather than another word. Then write your corrections in the spaces at the right. If a sentence is correct, write *OK*.

1. Ron and me were always on good terms. 1. _____
2. Which of these computers has been repaired? 2. _____
3. I wonder whom did this damage. 3. _____
4. This folders are the ones we should consider buying for our seminar participants. 4. _____
5. Each one of the men blamed themself. 5. _____
6. The sisters were angry at themselves for the mistake. 6. _____
7. Would you please tell me whom is the owner of the company. 7. _____
8. They said the bird destroyed himself. 8. _____
9. The letter was addressed to who this may concern. 9. _____
10. Every carpenter should use their own tools. 10. _____
11. Are those your keys? 11. _____
12. The machinist repaired everything by themselves. 12. _____
13. People like themself should be proud of themselves. 13. _____
14. Each child seemed to be taking care of theirselves. 14. _____
15. The team discussed the plays among theirselves. 15. _____

EXERCISE 6   Write a sentence that would illustrate the correct use of each of the following pronouns. (Answers will vary.)

1. Which _____
2. This _____
3. Myself _____
4. Everyone _____
5. Few _____

VERBS

UNIT 5 OVERVIEW

Verbs are essential words because every sentence must have a verb as well as a subject. The subject and verb form a partnership in a sentence. Verbs provide the action for the subject or the state of being or show a relationship between things. In this unit, you will learn how verbs can be used in the sentence, how to make them agree in number with the subject, and how to change their tenses to show different time periods. Also, some of the most frequently confused verbs will be practiced so that you can easily choose the right verb in a sentence.

UNIT OBJECTIVES

When you complete Unit 5, you will be able to:

- identify the difference between transitive and intransitive verbs.

- identify the four uses of verbs in sentences.

- recognize a verb phrase.

- apply the four principal parts of a verb.

- distinguish between the present, past, and future tense of verbs.

- demonstrate the correct use of the verbs *to be, to have, to do, and to go.*

- use the present perfect, past perfect, and future perfect tenses of verbs.

- create subject and verb agreement.

- select the correct verb when given the choices between *lie/lay; sit/set; rise/raise; learn/teach; leave/let; bring/take; affect/effect; borrow/lend.*

14 USES OF VERBS

VERBS

Part of Speech Verb Noun

As you know, a sentence must have both a subject and a verb. Verbs are action words—they make sentences *move*! Notice how the verbs in the following paragraph move each sentence.

> As a student at a Midwestern State University, I *strengthened* my ability to get along well with others and to adapt to new environments. While a first-year student, I *participated* in the Student Volunteer Action Group. As a sophomore, I *organized* and *planned* the Fall Festival. During my junior and senior years, I *joined* several associations.

CHECKUP 1 Underline the verbs in the following sentences. Then write the verbs in the spaces at the right.

1. He <u>expressed</u> his appreciation to the customer. 1. <u>expressed</u>
2. Prepare employment correspondence on high-quality paper. 2. _____
3. She demonstrated the proper lifting technique. 3. _____
4. Many of them agreed to the new regulations. 4. _____

We use verbs to make statements and requests, to give commands, and to ask questions.

> Make statements: **Our churches *held* an ecumenical service.**
>
> Make requests: **Please *complete* the application.**
>
> Ask questions: **Who *returned* the documents?**
>
> Give commands: ***Give* the book to Kartcher.**

Notice that requests use the word *please* but commands do not.

CHECKUP 2 Decide how the verbs are used in the following sentences. Underline each verb. Then state whether the verb is used in a statement, a request, a command, or a question.

1. The manager <u>reviewed</u> the benefits. 1. <u>statement</u>
2. Who requested the Stoner file? 2. _____
3. Tell the children to come inside. 3. _____
4. Dogs bark for different reasons. 4. _____
5. Please ask Will to see me in my office. 5. _____

THE HAVES AND THE HAVE-NOTS

Transitive

The dog shook his tail.

Intransitive

The dog shook.

Direct objects are words that receive the action of the verb. Some verbs have direct objects and others do not. You can see if a verb has a direct object by saying the verb, then asking the question *whom* or *what* after it.

> **He *wrote* the *manuscript*.** The verb is *wrote*. *Wrote* whom or what? The manuscript. *Manuscript* is the direct object.
>
> **Ms. Fontaine applauded.** The verb is *applauded. Applauded* whom or what? Nothing. There is no word to receive the action of the verb—no direct object.

Verbs that have direct objects are said to be transitive; those that do *not* have direct objects are said to be intransitive. Some verbs can be both, depending on how the are used.

Do not confuse an adverb that answers the question *how* for a direct object.

The student behaved poorly. Poorly is an adverb, not a direct object.

CHECKUP 3 Underline the verb in each of the following sentences. Then write the direct object of the verb in the space at the right. If there is no direct object, write *have-not*.

1. Bartley <u>retired</u>.
2. He programmed the computer.
3. Edit the proposal carefully.
4. We fished all day.
5. He hit a home run.

1. <u>have-not</u>
2. _____
3. _____
4. _____
5. _____

HELP!

Sometimes a verb needs help. A verb, its helpers, and intervening adverbs make up a *verb phrase*. Intervening nouns and pronouns are not part of the verb phrase. The main verb is always the last verb in the phrase.

The secretary will always provide the copies for the meeting. *Will always provide* is the verb phrase. *Will* is the helper; *provide* is the main verb. *Always* is the intervening adverb.

Have you cleaned the bathroom yet? The main verb is *cleaned*; the helping verb is *have*. The helping verb is separated from the main verb by the personal pronoun *you*. *You* is not part of the verb phrase.

Helping (Auxiliary) Verbs The most commonly used helping verbs are the various forms of *be*, *have*, *do*, and *can*, as well as the forms of *may*, *must*, *shall* and *will*, which are interchangeable with *can*.

be:	*am, is, are, was, were, been, being*
have:	*have, has, had*
do:	*does, did*
can:	*could, would, will, shall, may, should, must, might* (to express *ability*)
may:	*may, might* (to express *permission*)
must:	*must* (to express *insistence* or *condition*)
shall:	*shall, should* (to express *ought to*)
will:	*will, would* (to express *consent, inclination*, or *determination*)

CHECKUP 4 Underline the helping verbs in the following sentences. Then write the *main* verbs in the spaces at the right.

1. We <u>will</u> receive a bonus.
2. Bob will serve dinner soon.
3. The books are being displayed in the showcase in the lobby.
4. The manager is handling the situation.
5. Several of us have been traveling during the summer.

1. <u>receive</u>
2. _____
3. _____
4. _____
5. _____

CHECKUP 5   Write a sentence using a helping verb. Underline the helping verb in each sentence. (Answers will vary.)

1. has   <u>He has been</u> working at the project all night.
2. must   _____
3. does   _____
4. were   _____

Name   Date   Score

EXERCISES

EXERCISE 1 Find the verbs in the following sentences. Write the verbs in the spaces at the right.

1. The police stopped all traffic.   1. _____
2. We receive over 100 calls per day.   2. _____
3. Jan coordinated all the activities for her office.   3. _____
4. They demonstrated the proper techniques.   4. _____
5. The receptionist assisted the general manager.   5. _____
6. Please fax me your request.   6. _____
7. The company expanded its sales territory.   7. _____
8. Most of us face economic worries.   8. _____
9. We make our decision on Tuesday.   9. _____
10. Our character is a composite of our hearts.   10. _____
11. The speaker caught my attention immediately.   11. _____
12. We both acknowledged the problems in the company.   12. _____

EXERCISE 2 Decide how the verbs are used in the following sentences. Underline the main verb and any helping verbs in each sentence. Then state whether the verb is used in a statement, a request, a command, or a question.

1. Lock the door after 5 p.m.   1. _____
2. The department received new computers today.   2. _____
3. Who examined the merchandise?   3. _____
4. Please turn off the lights.   4. _____
5. Where was the package?   5. _____
6. We review customer comments daily.   6. _____
7. Provide a full explanation for your decision.   7. _____
8. The department lacks consistency.   8. _____
9. Please answer the letter within the next 48 hours.   9. _____
10. Did you read the manager's memo today?   10. _____

EXERCISE 3 Underline the main verb and any helping verbs in each sentence. If the verb *has* a direct object, write the direct object in the space at the right. If the verb *does not have* a direct object, write *have-not*.

1. They disagreed.   1. _____
2. Jon washes his car weekly.   2. _____
3. The rock concert begins at 8 p.m. at Miller Auditorium. 3. _____
4. He greeted the customer with a smile.   4. _____
5. Several of the employees played at the benefit yesterday. 5. _____
6. She behaved properly.   6. _____
7. He gave her a plant as a present.   7. _____
8. Glen collected antique bottles.   8. _____

9. Several people called.

10. We purchased a new car today.

11. Darlene wanted a commitment to quality from her staff.

12. We walked on the beach.

13. Joe plays the drums in the band.

14. By his side stood the little girl.

15. Have you finished the report yet?

9. _____

10. _____

11. _____

12. _____

13. _____

14. _____

15. _____

EXERCISE 4   Underline the *helping* verbs in the following sentences. Then write the *main* verbs in the spaces at the right.

1. The meeting will be postponed until next week.

2. The game has been played very well.

3. Have you fed the dog today?

4. The cherry crop had been ruined by the late frost.

5. The guests might be arriving late.

6. Were you invited to the reception afterwards?

7. Tom is going to the dance.

8. They had planned the event carefully.

9. I would have gone with you to the open house.

10. The employee was given a warning.

11. The plane must have been late.

12. She could be selected for the position.

13. Tim had studied very late last night.

14. They are celebrating their anniversary.

15. The signs were hanging upside down.

1. _____

2. _____

3. _____

4. _____

5. _____

6. _____

7. _____

8. _____

9. _____

10. _____

11. _____

12. _____

13. _____

14. _____

15. _____

EXERCISE 5   Write two verb phrases for each of the following verbs. (Answers will vary.)

1. fall   _____   _____

2. start   _____   _____

3. design   _____   _____

4. collect   _____   _____

5. drive   _____   _____

6. revise   _____   _____

7. try   _____   _____

8. place   _____   _____

9. struggle   _____   _____

10. build   _____   _____

SHORT STORY   Underscore the verbs or verb phrases in the following paragraph. Write the direct object of the verb in the space at the right. If there is no direct object, write *have-not*.

You dream it, and we will build it for you! We can build the house of your dreams at an affordable price. We have been in business for forty years and our reputation for dependability is known throughout this area. You must come to our building center and let one of our experts design the home of your dreams.

1. _____

2. _____

3. _____

4. _____

5. _____

6. _____

VERB PHRASES, VERB PARTS, AND LINKING VERBS

MORE ABOUT VERBS

ADVERBS THAT INTERRUPT

Sometimes in a verb phrase the helping verb (or auxiliary verb) is separated from the main verb by an adverb. In such a case, the main verb follows the adverb. Remember, an *adverb* is a word that modifies a verb, an adjective, or another adverb. Adverbs tell "how," "when," and "where." Some common adverbs are:

always   soon   seldom   not   often   never   very

The company's annual report *is seldom released* in January. *Is seldom released* is the verb phrase. *Is* is the helper; *released* is the main verb because it tells what has been done. *Remember:* The main verb is *always* the last word in the verb phrase. *Seldom* is an adverb that separates the helper *is* from the main verb *released*.

They were badly injured in the accident. *Were badly injured* is the verb phrase. *Were* is the helper; *injured* is the main verb. *Badly* is an adverb that separates the helper from the main verb.

CHECKUP 1

Underline the verb phrases and any adverbs in the following sentences. Then write the main verbs and the adverbs in the space at the right.

1. The population <u>is rapidly declining</u>.
2. The manager was seldom seen in his office.
3. The results were finally announced.
4. Mr. Grant had not been seen for several days.

1. declining, rapidly
2. _____
3. _____
4. _____

PRINCIPAL PARTS OF VERBS

Verbs have four principal parts: *present, past, past participle,* and *present participle.* These *principal parts* are used to make all other forms (or tenses) of the verb. Past participles are formed by adding *d* or *ed* to the present part. Present participles are formed by adding *ing* to the present part. If the verb ends in *e*, drop the *e* before adding *ing* as in *typing.* Verbs that form their past and past participle are called regular verbs.

Here are the principal parts of the regular verb *to walk* (*to walk* is called *the infinitive*):

Infinitive	Present	Past	Past Participle (always needs a helping verb)	Present Participle (always needs a helping verb)
to walk	walk	walked	walked	walking

Verbs that form their past and past participle by completely changing their spelling are called *irregular* verbs. The principal parts of irregular verbs are listed in the dictionary.

Infinitive	Present	Past	Past Participle (always needs a helping verb)	Present Participle (always needs a helping verb)
to begin	begin	began	begun	beginning

Remember, when you use a helping verb with the past participle or present participle, you are creating a verb phrase. The main verb in that verb phrase is always the last verb.

CHECKUP 2 Underline the verb phrases in the following sentences. Then write the main verbs in the spaces at the right. Also, indicate whether the main verbs are present participles or past participles.

1. Samantha <u>had responded</u> to the call from her uncle.
2. They are bringing their dog.
3. Several of our clients were prepared to be witnesses.
4. Robert might be arriving earlier than Lance.
5. We have been running for five minutes.

1. <u>responded, past participle</u>
2. _____
3. _____
4. _____
5. _____

LINKING VERBS

A verb that joins, or "links," its subject to a noun, pronoun, or adjective that follows it (the verb) are called *linking verbs*. Some common linking verbs are:

1. *To be (am, is, are, was, were, be, being, been):*
   We are the cast. *Are* links *we* to *cast.*

2. *To appear:*
   She appears knowledgeable on the subject.

3. *To seem:*
   Dorothy seems enthusiastic about the trip.

4. Verbs of the senses, such as *to feel, to look, to smell, to taste, to hear:*
   I feel wonderful today.

The word that is "linked" to the subject is called a *predicate noun*, a *predicate pronoun*, or a *predicate adjective*. A predicate noun or pronoun is the same as the subject; the predicate adjective describes the subject. A predicate noun or pronoun should be in the nominative case to agree with the subject.

Rachael *is* the lead *singer.* *Singer* is the predicate noun.

The lead singer *is she.* *She* is the predicate pronoun.

Rachael *is great!* *Great* is the predicate adjective.

The linking verb does not show action so it never has a direct object. The function of the linking verb is to "link" the subject with the noun, pronoun, or adjective that follows it.

CHECKUP 3 Underline the predicate nouns, predicate pronouns, or predicate adjectives in the following sentences. Then state whether the underlined words are predicate nouns, predicate pronouns, or predicate adjectives in the spaces to the right.

1. Georgia's car was <u>green</u>.
2. He was nervous about the trip.
3. It was she at the door.
4. Jon is a friend of ours.
5. Kathy is the new manager.

1. <u>predicate adjective</u>
2. _____
3. _____
4. _____
5. _____

Name _____ Date _____ Score _____

E X E R C I S E S

EXERCISE 1 Underline the verb phrases and any adverbs in the following sentences. Then write the main verbs and the adverbs in the spaces at the right.

1. Marie is truly excited about the adventure.
2. Did you really understand what he meant by that remark?
3. The speaker was obviously talking too long.
4. The lawyers had evidently won their case.
5. Jeff has not been studying for days.
6. The investigator had easily solved the case.
7. We were really trying our best to win.
8. Are you not receiving the money from the tenants?
9. They were anxiously waiting for the game to start.
10. I have eagerly responded to the question several times.

1. _____
2. _____
3. _____
4. _____
5. _____
6. _____
7. _____
8. _____
9. _____
10. _____

EXERCISE 2 Write the principal parts of the following regular verbs in the spaces provided. You may use the dictionary to check for the correct spelling.

Infinitive	Present	Past (-*d* or -*ed* ending)	Past Participle (requires helper) (-*d* or -*ed* ending)	Present Participle (requires helper) (-*ing* ending)
to talk	talk	talked	talked	talking

Present	Past	Past Participle	Present Participle
1. create	_____	_____	_____
2. twist	_____	_____	_____
3. install	_____	_____	_____
4. pack	_____	_____	_____
5. learn	_____	_____	_____

EXERCISE 3 Write the correct verb form for each of the verbs in parentheses. Then indicate whether the verb is a past or past participle.

1. The plane has (*taxi*) to a stop.
2. We (*discuss*) the situation.
3. The decorators had (*design*) our office for a showcase.
4. He (*introduce*) the next act?
5. The trustees (*eliminate*) several staff positions.
6. They have not (*announce*) the location of the seminar.
7. The class (*vote*) for the officers last year.
8. Jan has (*suggest*) an alternative plan.
9. Hernandez had (*anticipate*) the outcome.
10. The school (*offer*) the summer sessions once before.

1. _____
2. _____
3. _____
4. _____
5. _____
6. _____
7. _____
8. _____
9. _____
10. _____

Underline the verb phrases in the following sentences. Then write the main verbs in the spaces at the right. Also, indicate whether the main verbs are present or past participles.

1. He was driving over the speed limit.
2. The store had expanded several times.
3. The car had been painted several times.
4. The director was conducting a seminar on ethics.

5. They were gathering up the collection.
6. Jack and John were both generating great sales.

7. They had searched all over for the missing letter.
8. Randy had managed the service station for five years.
9. They had been practicing for days.

10. We were very much interested in the voting results.

1. _____
2. _____
3. _____
4. _____
    _____
5. _____
6. _____
    _____
7. _____
8. _____
9. _____
    _____
10. _____

EXERCISE 5
Underline the predicate nouns, predicate pronouns, or predicate adjectives in the following sentences. Then state whether the underlined words are predicate nouns, predicate pronouns, or predicate adjectives in the spaces to the right.

1. Robert is a master mechanic.
2. It is he who called yesterday.
3. She is anxious to hear their answer.
4. The couple was excited.
5. It is I who made that statement.

1. _____
2. _____
3. _____
4. _____
5. _____

WRITING ACTIVITY
Write sentences using what you have learned in this lesson. (Answers will vary.)

1. Write a sentence that uses the past part of the verb *want*.

    _____

2. Write a sentence that uses the past participle of the verb *want*.

    _____

3. Write a sentence that uses the present participle of the verb *want*.

    _____

4. Write a sentence that uses the present participle of the verb *want*.

    _____

SHORT STORY
Underline the verb phrases in the following sentences. Then write the main verbs and adverbs in the spaces at the right.

Driving in a mall can be dangerous to your health. Cars are coming from all directions and no one wants to stop. People are eagerly looking for a parking space. Most people want that parking space right next to the entrance of the mall. We cannot walk a few steps; we have been badly spoiled!

1. _____
2. _____
3. _____
4. _____
5. _____
6. _____

VERB TENSES—YESTERDAY, TODAY, AND TOMORROW

VERB TENSES

Verbs change their forms to show the time an action occurs. The time of the verb's action is its *tense*. The four parts of a verb—present, past, past participle, present participle—are used to form the tenses. Let's see how the *present, past,* and *future* tenses are formed.

TODAY—PRESENT TENSE

The present tense is the present *part* of the verb. Use the present tense to show that action is happening now or that it is habitual. Present tense verbs can be singular or plural. If the subject of a sentence is singular, use a singular verb; if the subject is plural, use a plural verb.

> **Kelsey obeys the stop sign.** *Obeys* is the present tense of the verb *to obey*. It shows habitual action—Kelsey obeys the stop sign all the time. *Obeys* is singular to agree with *Kelsey*.

The singular and plural present tense forms of the verb *to enjoy* are:

Singular	Plural
I *enjoy*	we *enjoy*
you *enjoy*	you *enjoy*
he, she, it *enjoys*	they *enjoy*

As you see, in the present tense singular we add an *s* when we say *he, she,* or *it enjoys*. Otherwise, the verb does not change.

Beware! Not all verbs that end in *y* will simply add an *s* in the present tense. If a *y* is preceded by a consonant, change the *y* to *i*, then add *es*.

CHECKUP 1 After each pronoun, write the correct present tense *singular*.

1. to sing   he sings   4. to draw   he _____
2. to teach   I _____   5. to manage   he _____
3. to run   she _____   6. to plan   you _____

CHECKUP 2 After each pronoun, write the correct present tense *plural*.

1. to dance   you dance   4. to fax   you _____
2. to announce   they _____   5. to compute   we _____
3. to demonstrate   we _____   6. to compose   they _____

Present Action in Progress! A verb phrase such as *is walking* shows present action that *is in progress*. We call this tense present progressive. Form the present progressive tense with a verb's present participle plus a present tense of the verb *to be—am, is,* or *are*.

> **I *am doing* homework. You *are doing* homework. She *is doing* homework.**

CHECKUP 3 After each pronoun, write the correct present progressive tense.

1. to appear   I am appearing   3. to send   she _____
2. to walk   he _____   4. to examine   they _____

YESTERDAY—PAST TENSE

The past tense is the past *part* of the verb. Use the past tense to show action that was completed in the past.

We *mailed* the package yesterday. *Mailed* is the past tense of the verb *to mail.*

CHECKUP 4 After each pronoun, write the past tense of the given verb.

1. to describe   she described   3. to acknowledge   they _____
2. to reply   he _____   4. to transfer   she _____

Past Action in Progress! Use the past progressive tense to show action that *was in progress* in the past. The past progressive tense is formed with a verb's present participle plus a past tense of the verb *to be—was* or *were.*

She *was playing* baseball while they *were talking.* The verb phrases *was playing* and *were talking* show action that was in progress in the past.

CHECKUP 5 After each pronoun, write the past progressive tense of the verb.

1. to rehearse   he was rehearsing   3. to consume   I _____
2. to fade   it _____   4. to quote   we _____

TOMORROW—FUTURE TENSE

The future tense is formed with the present *part* of the verb plus *will* or *shall*. This tense is used to show action that will happen in the future.

They *will issue* the football tickets *tomorrow.*

CHECKUP 6 After each pronoun, write the future tense of the verb.

1. to arrest   he will arrest   3. to release   they _____
2. to call   she _____   4. to teach   I _____

Future Action in Progress! Use the future progressive tense to show action that *will be in progress* in the future. The future progressive tense is formed with a verb's present participle plus the future tense of the verb *to be—will be* or *shall be.*

Tomorrow he *will be demonstrating* the scanner. *Will be demonstrating* shows action that will be in progress sometime in the future.

CHECKUP 7 After each pronoun, write the future progressive tense of the verb.

1. to brush   he will be brushing   3. to learn   we _____
2. to speak   you _____   4. to lead   they _____

Name _____ Date _____ Score _____

EXERCISES

EXERCISE 1 Underline the verb in each of the following sentences. Then in the space at the right, write *past*, *present*, or *future* for each verb. (*Hint:* A sentence may have more than one verb.)

1. The tire pressure remains low.
2. The manager emphasized team work.
3. Will he go to the Career Fair at the Student Center?
4. She will announce the winners.
5. Edward remembered the talk show host from his high school days.

1. _____
2. _____
3. _____
4. _____
5. _____

EXERCISE 2 For each verb in parentheses, write the form that shows *present* time.

1. The commission *(decide)* the issue today.
2. She *(love)* her new job.
3. He *(call)* the office every day when he is out of town.
4. He *(work)* very hard each day.
5. He *(respond)* to his official mail promptly.
6. We *(believe)* in ourselves.

1. _____
2. _____
3. _____
4. _____
5. _____
6. _____

EXERCISE 3 For each verb in parentheses, write the form that shows *present progressive* time.

1. Jonathan *(advance)* quickly through the company.
2. Gerald *(inspect)* the meat at the food supply warehouse.
3. They *(talk)* too loudly for me to hear my customer.
4. Her staff calls in from all parts of the country when they *(work)* in the field.
5. We *(prepare)* his speech.

1. _____
2. _____
3. _____
4. _____
5. _____

EXERCISE 4 For each verb in parentheses, write the form that shows *past* time.

1. The children *(hug)* the clown good-bye.
2. The Harrisons *(move)* to California about three years ago.
3. I *(open)* the window for some fresh air.
4. Several of them *(suggest)* going out for a sandwich.
5. The doctor *(examine)* the patient carefully.

1. _____
2. _____
3. _____
4. _____
5. _____

EXERCISE 5 For each verb in parentheses, write the form that shows *past progressive* time.

1. The author *(direct)* most of his compliments to his colleagues.
2. We *(arrange)* the flowers in the vase.
3. He *(suggest)* that you take the week off for a well-deserved vacation.

1. _____
2. _____
3. _____

4. The monkey *(imitate)* the little boy.

5. The meteorologist *(predict)* a mild winter.

4. _____

5. _____

EXERCISE 6   For each verb in parentheses, write the form that shows *future* time.

1. She *(present)* the new product to the customers.

2. Incentives *(motivate)* to perform well.

3. She *(fix)* the faulty computer system.

4. He *(propose)* to his girlfriend tomorrow night.

5. Before the end of the day, we *(collect)* enough samples for our survey.

1. _____

2. _____

3. _____

4. _____

5. _____

EXERCISE 7   For each verb in parentheses, write the form that shows *future progressive* time.

1. Several of the students *(apply)* for the one position.

2. We *(outline)* several chapters for the new book on leadership.

3. I think Jane *(arrive)* tomorrow morning.

4. We *(reply)* to your letter within the week.

5. The parents *(supervise)* the children's activities.

1. _____

2. _____

3. _____

4. _____

5. _____

WRITING ACTIVITY   Write a sentence to illustrate the tense of the verb. (Answers will vary.)

1. to pay *(past tense)*   _____

2 to pay *(present tense)*   _____

3. to succeed *(present progressive tense)*   _____

4. to qualify *(future tense)*   _____

5. to lecture *(future progressive tense)*   _____

6. to lecture *(past progressive tense)*   _____

SHORT STORY   Underline each verb or verb phrase used in the following paragraph. Identify the tense of each. Then write the tense of each verb or verb phrase in the space at the right.

I was walking my dog when I saw my good friend.
Al, who was walking his big dog, Charlie.
We often stop and swap stories. This morning Al
told me that he is planning to build a fence around
his yard to contain Charlie. Al described how
Charlie likes to get loose and bother the neighbors.
As Al spoke, Charlie cocked his head and
looked at me for sympathy.

1. _____

2. _____

3. _____

4. _____

5. _____

6. _____

7. _____

8. _____

17 REGULAR AND IRREGULAR VERBS

IRREGULAR VERBS

As mentioned earlier, verbs can be "regular" or "irregular," depending on how their past and past participles are formed. An example of a "regular" verb is *to look:*

Infinitive	Present	Past	Past Participle
to look	look	looked	looked

The past and past participle are formed by simply adding *d* or *ed* to the present part of the verb.

Some verbs are called "irregular" because they do not form their past and past participle forms this "regular" way. An example of an irregular verb is *to choose:*

Infinitive	Present	Past	Past Participle
to choose	choose	choose	chosen

PRINCIPAL PARTS OF SOME IRREGULAR VERBS

INFINITIVE	PRESENT	PAST	PAST PARTICIPLE
to be	am, is, are	was, were	been
to begin	begin	began	begun
to blow	blow	blew	blown
to bring	bring	brought	brought
to buy	buy	bought	bought
to do	do	did	done
to drink	drink	drank	drunk
to eat	eat	ate	eaten
to fall	fall	fell	fallen
to freeze	freeze	froze	frozen
to get	get	got	gotten
to go	go	went	gone
to have	have	had	had
to hide	hide	hid	hidden
to pay	pay	paid	paid
to rise	rise	rose	risen
to show	show	showed	showed, shown
to speak	speak	spoke	spoken
to teach	teach	taught	taught
to tell	tell	told	told
to wake	wake	wake, woke	waked, woken, woke
to write	write	wrote	written

Remember: The past tense *never* has a helper. The past participle *always* has a helper *(have, has, had)*.

There are many more verbs that form their tenses in an "irregular" way. A more complete listing of these verbs is in the *Appendix*.

CHECKUP 1   Write the past and the past participle for each form of the verb.

1. arise   arose, arisen   11. meet   _____
2. begin   _____   12. ride   _____
3. bind   _____   13. hear   _____
4. cling   _____   14. flee   _____
5. fly   _____   15. deal   _____
6. draw   _____   16. blow   _____
7. ring   _____   17. eat   _____
8. am   _____   18. grow   _____
9. hide   _____   19. think   _____
10. take   _____   20. lend   _____

CHECKUP 2   How well do you know the irregulars? In the space at the right, write the past tense of each verb given in parentheses. Check your answers to make sure they are correct.

1. We (*begin*) the meeting nearly two hours late.   1. began _____
2. He (*take*) the trash out this morning   2. _____
3. The wildflowers (*blow*) in the breeze.   3. _____
4. She (*write*) a best-selling novel.   4. _____
5. She (*buy*) a new outfit.   5. _____
6. Are you sure you (*meet*) them before today?   6. _____

CHECKUP 3   Now write the past participle of each verb given in parentheses. Note that there is a helper before each past participle.

1. I have (*choose*) my dance partner.   1. chosen _____
2. I had (*teach*) high school English for several years.   2. _____
3. The boy had (*forgot*) his homework.   3. _____
4. Arlene had (*say*) earlier that she wanted to go to the fair.   4. _____
5. The pipes had (*burst*) overnight.   5. _____
6. The little boys had (*sit*) patiently waiting for their mother.   6. _____

CHECKUP 4   Underline any incorrect use of verbs in the following sentences. Then write your corrections in the spaces at the right.

1. She <u>dream</u> of being an actress.   1. dreamed *or* had dreamt
2. Mark ride his bike to the ballpark.   2. _____
3. He tell the story to each guest.   3. _____
4. Fortunately, no exchange take place in the market.   4. _____
5. Jeffrey ring the doorbell at his aunt's house.   5. _____
6. She tear her favorite sweater.   6. _____

Name   Date   Score

EXERCISES

EXERCISE 1   In the spaces at the right, write the past tense of each verb given in parentheses.

1. I (*watch*) the special movie on television.   1. _____
2. (*Do*) you see any famous movie stars when you were in Hollywood?   2. _____
3. The boy (*runs*) quickly to get help.   3. _____
4. She (*meet*) her friend at the airport.   4. _____
5. We (*flee*) indoors when we heard the thunder.   5. _____
6. He (*pay*) for two tickets for tonight's show.   6. _____
7. After the washer broke, she (*wring*) the clothes by hand.   7. _____
8. He (*win*) the grand prize in the drawing.   8. _____
9. He (*sing*) the national anthem before the game.   9. _____
10. His performance (*steal*) the show.   10. _____
11. I just (*see*) her yesterday at the theater.   11. _____
12. He (*hold*) his fork in his right hand.   12. _____
13. The earthquake (*shake*) the whole town.   13. _____
14. After months of not receiving payment, we (*hire*) a lawyer.   14. _____
15. The witness (*swear*) to tell the truth.   15. _____

EXERCISE 2   In the spaces at the right, write the past participle of each verb given in parentheses. Note that there is a helper for each past participle.

1. The work was (*do*) by noon.   1. _____
2. The boy had (*swim*) the full length of the pool.   2. _____
3. Our parents had (*eat*) dinner by the time we arrived home.   3. _____
4. She had (*lend*) her favorite sweater to her friend.   4. _____
5. The birds had (*fly*) South for the winter.   5. _____
6. I think she had (*bite*) off more than she could chew.   6. _____
7. The couple had (*meet*) several years earlier.   7. _____
8. The children had (*read*) ten books over the summer.   8. _____
9. They had (*lose*) the tournament.   9. _____
10. Are you sure you have (*wear*) this dress before?   10. _____
11. I have (*stand*) in that spot before.   11. _____
12. She had (*hear*) the good news.   12. _____
13. Brenda had (*take*) the contracts to the lawyer herself.   13. _____
14. He had (*throw*) his clothes on the floor.   14. _____
15. Jerry had (*choose*) his new partner.   15. _____

EXERCISE 3   Underline any incorrect use of irregular verbs in the following sentences. Then write your corrections in the spaces at the right.

1. The cat spring from the bushes.   1. _____
2. The leaves have fell early this year.   2. _____
3. The professor has gave me all the assignments I care to do.   3. _____
4. The meeting had began by the time we arrived.   4. _____
5. Yes, we had came earlier, but no one was here yet.   5. _____
6. The furniture that he has chose will be just fine for the living room.   6. _____
7. Didn't you knew about the meeting this afternoon?   7. _____
8. I think we should have wrote to our cousins saying we would be arriving at noon. 8. _____
9. Most of us had keep the ticket stubs as souvenirs.   9. _____
10. After working late, Todd had went to sleep.   10. _____
11. They had tell the truth.   11. _____
12. The parents had hide the presents.   12. _____
13. The man deal the cards.   13. _____
14. I eat my lunch over an hour ago.   14. _____
15. They had break the expensive vase.   15. _____

EXERCISE 4   Underline any incorrect use of irregular verbs in the following sentences. Then write your corrections in the spaces at the right. If the sentence is correct, write *OK*.

1. The wind had blown the trash on the lawn.   1. _____
2. The dog bite the intruder.   2. _____
3. The sun shined on the flowers.   3. _____
4. They were show the collection.   4. _____
5. Lynn was do with the assignment.   5. _____
6. The team thought they could win the game.   6. _____
7. Tom dive from the highest diving board.   7. _____
8. Rick was bind to the agreement.   8. _____
9. Lori throw the ball in the air.   9. _____
10. The snow was go by morning.   10. _____

WRITING ACTIVITY   Write a sentence using each verb tense shown. (Answers will vary.)

1. bite   _____
2. drank   _____
3. ridden   _____
4. torn   _____
5. sat   _____

SHORT STORY   Are the underlined verbs used correctly? If not, write the correct verb on the line to the right. Then write the principal part of the correct verb.

Use of the fax machine has grew in the last few years.   1. _____
I thought people believe the regular mail is too slow—   2. _____
people wants immediate communication. I had buy   3. _____

                                                                _____
a fax machine for my home, and I chosen not to put in a   4. _____
separate phone line. I thinks that was a wrong decision.   5. _____

TO BE AND TO HAVE

TO BE AND TO HAVE AS HELPERS

To be and *to have* are two of the most used verbs in the English language. Both are irregular and all of their parts (present, past, past participle, present participle) can be used alone or as *helpers* for other verbs. When *to be* is used alone it is called a *linking* verb. Since you will be using *to be* and *to have* so much, make sure you know their parts and their tenses.

Infinitive	Present Tense	Past Tense	Past Participle	Present Participle
to be	am, is, are	was, were	been	being
to have	have, has	had	had	having

TODAY—PRESENT TENSE

Use the present tense to show that an action is taking place now or that it is habitual. The present tense of *to be* has three forms—*am, is,* and *are.* The present tense of *to have* has two forms—*has* and *have.*

Present Tense of *To Be*	
I *am*	we *are*
you *are*	you *are*
he, she, it *is*	they *are*

Present Tense of *To Have*	
I *have*	we *have*
you *have*	you *have*
he, she, it *has*	they *have*

I *am* **the manager of catering.** *Am,* when used alone, is a linking verb.

I *am throwing* **the ball.** *Am,* when used with another verb, is a helping verb.

Present Action in Progress! The present tense of *to be (am, is, are)* is combined with a verb's present part to show action presently in progress. Present action in progress is called the *present progressive tense.* See how *to be* and *to have* form their own present progressive tenses:

Present Progressive Tense of *To Be*	
I *am being*	we *are being*
You *are being*	you *are being*
he, she, it *is being*	they *are being*

Present Progressive Tense of *To Have*	
I *am having*	we *are having*
you *are having*	you *are having*
he, she, it *is having*	they *are having*

CHECKUP 1 For each item below, write the correct present progressive tense of the verb in parentheses.

1. my life (*to be*)   is being   3. the family (*to have*) _____
2. they (*to be*)   _____ 4. the guests (*to have*) _____

YESTERDAY—PAST TENSE

The past tense of a verb shows that something happened in the past. Notice that *to be* has only two forms in the past tense—*was* and *were*.

Past Tense of *To Be*	
I *was*	we *were*
you *were*	you *were*
he, she, it *was*	they *were*

Past Tense of *To Have*	
I *had*	we *had*
you *had*	you *had*
he, she, it *had*	they *had*

You *were* late for the meeting.   **They *had* their tickets in their hands.**

Past Tense in Action! To show that action was in progress in the past, use the *past progressive tense* (present participle plus *was* or *were*).

Past Progressive Tense of *To Be*	
I *was being*	we *were being*
You *were being*	you *were being*
he, she, it *was being*	they *were being*

Past Progressive Tense of *To Have*	
I *was having*	we *were having*
you *were having*	you *were having*
he, she, it *was having*	they *were having*

I *was being* stubborn that day.   **The committee *was having* a meeting Saturday.**

CHECKUP 2 After each of the following words, write the correct past progressive tense form of the verb in parentheses.

1. the child (*to be*)   was being   3. the club (*to have*) _____

2. his parents (*to be*) _____   4. it (*to have*) _____

TOMORROW—FUTURE TENSE

To show that action will happen sometime in the future, use the future tense. Form the future tense by using the verb's present part plus *will* or *shall*.

Future Tense of *To Be*	
I *will be*	we *will be*
you *will be*	you *will be*
he, she, it *will be*	they *will be*

Future Tense of *To Have*	
I *will have*	we *will have*
you *will have*	you *will have*
he, she, it *will have*	they *will have*

You *will be* on you way home soon.   **I *will have* time to bake the cake.**

Future Action in Progress! To show that some action will be in progress sometime in the future, use the *future progressive tense*. Form this tense by using a verb's present participle plus *will be* or *shall be*. *To be* does not have a future progressive tense.

Future Progressive Tense of *To Have*	
I *will be having*	we *will be having*
you *will be having*	you *will be having*
he, she, it *will be having*	they *will be having*

We *will be having* company at Thanksgiving.

EXERCISES

EXERCISE 1   Underline the entire form of the verb *to be* in each of the following sentences. Then write the entire form of the verb *to be* in the space at the right. (*Hint:* A sentence may have more than one verb.)

1. My suggestion is the best one of all.   1. _____
2. The music was too loud.   2. _____
3. The boy is being disruptive.   3. _____
4. You are sure that the light was on when you left.   4. _____
5. I am certain the plane will be late.   5. _____
6. The guests will be here any minute.   6. _____
7. The designers were hopeful about winning the contract.   7. _____
8. They are being so helpful to the cause.   8. _____

EXERCISE 2   Select and underline the correct form of the verb *to be* in parentheses. Then write it in the space at the right.

1. I (*am, are*) most happy with the color you chose.   1. _____
2. The woman (*is being, are being*) rude to the host.   2. _____
3. We (*was, were*) thrilled with the results of the voting.   3. _____
4. Jeremy (*is, will be*) ready tomorrow morning.   4. _____
5. Willie (*is, are*) sure that he'll be elected president.   5. _____
6. The employees (*were, will be*) tired of the long hours.   6. _____
7. He (*was, were*) grateful for all the attention he received.   7. _____
8. The buyers (*is being, are being*) very aggressive.   8. _____
9. We (*is, will be*) conservative in our projections   9. _____
10. She (*is, are*) the new salesperson for our company.   10. _____

EXERCISE 3   Replace the question mark in each sentence with the correct present tense form of the verb *to be*. Write your answer in the space at the right.

1. I (?) ready to begin the test.   1. _____
2. You (?) ready to assume responsibility as chairperson.   2. _____
3. Jon (?) anxious to visit his cousin.   3. _____
4. You and he (?) adamant about the changes, aren't you?   4. _____
5. Jennifer (?) happy with her promotion.   5. _____
6. We (?) sure you will agree with us.   6. _____

Now replace the question mark in each sentence with the correct future tense form of the verb *to be*.

7. Bob and Cathy (?) leaving for vacation on Friday.   7. _____
8. Are you sure we (?) out of town when you return?   8. _____
9. The teachers (?) meeting with the parents tomorrow.   9. _____
10. Who (?) the next secretary for the club.   10. _____

EXERCISE 4 Underline the entire form of the verb *to have* in the following sentences. Then write the entire form of the verb *to have* in the space at the right. (*Hint:* A sentence may have more than one verb.)

1. He has a large collection of cards.
2. The classes of 1993 and 1995 were having high school reunions.
3. We will have hamburgers at the cookout.
4. The Klammers are having a fiftieth anniversary celebration.
5. They will be having spaghetti for dinner.

1. _____
2. _____
3. _____
4. _____
5. _____

EXERCISE 5 Select and underline the correct form of the verb *to have* in parentheses. Then write it in the space at the right.

1. Many of us (*is having, are having*) to change our vacation plans.
2. Glen (*has, have*) a high level of patience.
3. Chris (*has, had*) the flu for three days.
4. Meredith (*is having, are having*) fun playing with the new puppy.
5. The family (*will had, will have*) a reunion next week.

1. _____
2. _____
3. _____
4. _____
5. _____

EXERCISE 6 Replace the question mark in each sentence with the correct present tense form of the verb *to have*. Write your answer in the space at the right.

1. You may (?) several questions to ask after the tour.
2. I (?) many requests for a tour of the Fetzer Development Center.
3. Thomas (?) his own business.
4. Who (?) the highest score yesterday?
5. The host family (?) two French students staying at their home.

1. _____
2. _____
3. _____
4. _____
5. _____

WRITING ACTIVITY Write a sentence that uses the forms of *to be* and *to know*. (Answers will vary.)

1. are _____
2. have _____
3. are being _____
4. were _____
5. will be _____

SHORT STORY Underline the uses of the verbs *to be* and *to have*. Then write the tense of each verb in the space at the right.

I am ready to plan my garden for this year. I will be having a variety of flowers and vegetables. It is fun to think of things growing after the long, dull winter. Do you have a love of growing plants from seed? My mother was responsible for my green thumb. She had the real ability to grow almost anything. I recall whenever a club was having a party, they would ask for her flowers to decorate the tables. She would always respond with a "Yes, I will have flowers for you."

1. _____
2. _____
3. _____
4. _____
5. _____
6. _____

7. _____

TO DO AND TO GO

TO DO AND TO GO AS HELPERS

To do and *to go* are two more commonly used irregular verbs.

TODAY—PRESENT TENSE

Use the present tense to show that an action is happening *now*, or that it happens all the time.

The present tense of *to do* has two forms: *do* and *does*. The present tense of *to go* has two forms: *go* and *goes*.

Present Tense of *To Do*	
I *do*	we *do*
you *do*	you *do*
he, she, it *does*	they *do*

Present Tense of *To Go*	
I *go*	we *go*
you *go*	you *go*
he, she, it *goes*	they *go*

I *do* all the stocking of merchandise at night.   **We *go* to school at 7:15 a.m.**

Present Action in Progress! Verbs showing action in progress are in the present progressive tense. The present progressive tense is always formed with a verb's present participle and a present tense helper of the verb *to be—am, is,* or *are*.

Present Progressive Tense of *To Do*	
I *am doing*	we *are doing*
you *are doing*	you *are doing*
he, she, it *is doing*	they *are doing*

Present Progressive Tense of *To Go*	
I *am going*	we *are going*
you *are going*	you *are going*
he, she, it *is going*	they *are going*

We *are doing* our best to be number 1.   **I *am going* now to accept the award.**

CHECKUP 1   In the spaces after each of the following words, write the correct present progressive tense of the verb in parentheses.

1. the client (*to do*)   is doing   4. this project (*to go*)   _____
2. I (*to do*)   _____   5. the men (*to go*)   _____
3. teachers (*to do*)   _____   6. friends (*to go*)   _____

YESTERDAY—PAST TENSE

The past tense of a verb shows that something has happened in the past. Notice that *to do* and *to go* have only one form in the past tense.

Past Tense of *To Do*	
I *did*	we *did*
you *did*	you *did*
he, she, it *did*	they *did*

Past Tense of *To Go*	
I *went*	we *went*
you *went*	you *went*
he, she, it *went*	they *went*

You *did* a kind deed.   **We *went* to the theatre.**

Past Action in Progress! To show that action was in progress in the past, use the past progressive tense (present participle plus *was* or *were*).

Past Progressive Tense of *To Do*	
I *was doing*	we *were doing*
You *were doing*	you *were doing*
he, she, it *was doing*	they *were doing*

Past Progressive Tense of *To Go*	
I *was going*	we *were going*
you *were going*	you *were going*
he, she, it *was going*	they *were going*

They *were doing* their duty.

Ted *was going* to meet you at the airport.

CHECKUP 2   In the spaces after each of the following words, write the correct past progressive tense form of the verb in parentheses.

1. his son (*to do*)   _was doing_
2. the students (*to do*)   _____
3. members (*to do*)   _____
4. Bill and I (*to do*)   _____
5. The supervisors (*to do*)   _____

6. all females (*to go*)   _____
7. one of them (*to go*)   _____
8. Sherry (*to go*)   _____
9. the team (*to go*)   _____
10. Her husband (*to go*)   _____

TOMORROW—FUTURE TENSE

To show that action will happen in the future, use the future tense. Form the future tense of a verb by using a verb's present tense plus the helpers *will* or *shall*. The future tense of *to do* and *to go* has only one form.

Future Tense of *To Do*	
I *will do*	we *will do*
you *will do*	you *will do*
he, she, it *will do*	they *will do*

Future Tense of *To Go*	
I *will go*	we *will go*
you *will go*	you *will go*
he, she, it *will go*	they *will go*

The plumber *will do* the work.

A copy of the book *will go* to all sponsors.

Future Action in Progress! To show that an action will be in progress sometime in the future, use the future progressive tense. Form the future progressive tense by using a verb's present participle plus *will be* or *shall be*.

Future Progressive Tense of *To Do*	
I *will be doing*	we *will be doing*
you *will be doing*	you *will be doing*
he, she, it *will be doing*	they *will be doing*

Future Progressive Tense of *To Go*	
I *will be going*	we *will be going*
you *will be going*	you *will be going*
he, she, it *will be going*	they *will be going*

Clark's Carpets *will be doing* the work.

The drivers *will be going* to their stations early.

CHECKUP 3   After each of the following words, write the correct future progressive tense form of the verb in parentheses.

1. the lawyer (*to do*)   _will be doing_
2. the committee (*to do*)   _____
3. Lisa and Drew (*to do*)   _____
4. he and Janet (*to do*)   _____
5. our company (*to do*)   _____

6. Alice (*to go*)   _____
7. The girls (*to go*)   _____
8. All (*to go*)   _____
9. our family (*to go*)   _____
10. the dentist (*to go*)   _____

LESSON 19

EXERCISES

EXERCISE 1 Underline the entire form of the verb *to do* in each of the following sentences. Then write the entire form of the verb *to do* in the space at the right.

1. What is he doing in the lab?
2. All of the children are doing well in class.
3. Was she doing her share of the workload?
4. What were you doing when we interrupted you?
5. Jason will be doing the budget this year.
6. The twins did all of their homework.

1. _____
2. _____
3. _____
4. _____
5. _____
6. _____

EXERCISE 2 Select and underline the correct form of the verb *to do* in parentheses, and write it in the space at the right.

1. The computer (*am doing, is doing*) the calculations.
2. The research team (*was doing, were doing*) the experiments in the lab.
3. They (*do, does*) that kind of training in the Learning Center.
4. Several of the students (*did, had did*) solve the problems.
5. You six (*will do, will had do*) equations one and two.
6. An accountant (*will being doing, will be doing*) our taxes.

1. _____
2. _____
3. _____
4. _____
5. _____
6. _____

EXERCISE 3 Replace the question mark in each sentence with the correct present tense form of the verb *to do*. Write your answer in the space at the right.

1. Beth (?) work for extra credit.
2. You always (?) the best job for us.

1. _____
2. _____

Now replace the question mark with the correct past tense form of the verb *to do*.

3. The police (?) an extensive investigation.
4. The professor (?) a thorough job of teaching a complex subject.

3. _____
4. _____

Now replace the question mark with the correct future tense form of the verb *to do*.

5. That room (?) nicely for our meeting.
6. The men (?) the yard work.

5. _____
6. _____

EXERCISE 4 Underline the entire form of the verb *to go* in each of the following sentences. Then write the entire form of the verb *to go* in the space at the right.

1. The parents are going to organize a tutoring session.
2. Jack is going on an expedition to Antarctica this December.
3. She was going to the library that evening.
4. Several kids were going to the mall after school.
5. Will you be going to town this afternoon?
6. Am I going to see the President?

1. _____
2. _____
3. _____
4. _____
5. _____
6. _____

EXERCISE 5 Underline the correct form of the verb *to go* from each pair in parentheses, and write it in the space at the right.

1. Rita (*am going, is going*) to Antioch College in Yellow Springs.
2. Joshua (*were going, was going*) to the town meeting.
3. We (*goes, go*) to church every week.
4. The coordinator (*gone, went*) to supervise the student teachers.
5. He and I (*will have go, will go*) to the concert tomorrow.

1. _____
2. _____
3. _____
4. _____
5. _____

EXERCISE 6 Replace the question mark in each sentence with the correct present tense form of the verb *to go*. Write your answer in the space at the right.

1. We (?) to the gym every other day.
2. This chart (?) on the right side of the figures.
3. We (?) to the post office every morning to pick up the mail.

1. _____
2. _____
3. _____

Now replace the question mark with the correct past tense form of the verb *to go*.

4. He (?) to the doctor for a checkup.
5. Many of us (?) to the program out of curiosity.
6. They (?) through the procedures one more time.

4. _____
5. _____
6. _____

Now replace the question mark with the correct future tense form of the verb *to go*.

7. We (?) if you think it would be best for us to do so.
8. Betty (?) to Adams Manufacturing for an interview.
9. Do you think he (?) to the movies with us?
10. They (?) to the sales conference in October.

7. _____
8. _____
9. _____
10. _____

WRITING ACTIVITY Write a sentence for each form of the verbs *to do* and *to go*. (Answers will vary.)

1. does   _____
2. go   _____
3. will do   _____
4. will be doing   _____
5. went   _____

SHORT STORY Write the tense of each underlined form of the verb *to go* or *to do* in the space at the right.

<u>Did</u> you know floors in your house can be beautiful as well as
functional? You <u>will be doing</u> yourself a favor if you
<u>go</u> to your local carpet store and see the variety of choices
for all rooms in your house. Recently, I <u>went</u> to a local
dealer who <u>does</u> installations in many homes to choose a
pattern for my kitchen. To my delight the pattern I wanted
<u>was going</u> on sale the following week. Since we
<u>are doing</u> our kitchen remodeling in stages, I decided to wait
for the sale. I <u>will be going</u> back next week to start
the paper work for the order.

1. _____
2. _____
3. _____
4. _____
5. _____

6. _____
7. _____
8. _____

LESSON 20

JUST PERFECT!
THE *PERFECT* TENSES

THE PERFECT TENSES

The perfect tenses are used to make subtle distinctions between two actions or events, both of which happened in the past or will happen in the future. All perfect tenses are formed by combining a verb's past participle with a tense of the verb *to have*.

THE PRESENT PERFECT TENSE

The present perfect tense is used to denote an action that was started in the past and is continuing into the *present* and maybe beyond. The present perfect tense is formed by combining a verb's past participle with *have* or *has*.

> **I have shopped at their store many times.** The present perfect tense gives a sense of continuation—the action was started in the past but it is not completed as of now. The present perfect tense *implies* that the action is ongoing.

Remember, to express action *started and completed* in the past, use the *past tense*.

> **I shopped at their store many times.** Using the past tense gives a sense of finality—the action was started and completed prior to the present time.

CHECKUP 1 After each pronoun, write the present perfect tense of the verb.

1. to create   <u>they have created</u>   3. to increase   <u>you</u>
2. to supervise   <u>he</u>   4. to walk   <u>she</u>

Now underline the present perfect tense in each of the following sentences. Then write each verb phrase in the space at the right.

5. James <u>has arranged</u> the meeting for tonight.   5. <u>has arranged</u>
6. They have recommended five of us for the award.   6. _____
7. The group has prepared its final report.   7. _____
8. The client has extended his contract for one year.   8. _____

THE PAST PERFECT TENSE

Use the past perfect tense to show a *time relationship* between two *past* actions where one past action happened before another past action or time. Use the past perfect tense for the earlier of the two past actions; use the past tense for the later of the two past actions. The past perfect tense is formed with a verb's past participle plus *had*.

> **I *arrived* after she *had left*.** Two actions took place in the past—arriving and leaving. Which one took place first and how will you indicate this to the reader? Put the earlier of the two past actions (leaving) in the *past perfect tense* (the verb's past participle plus *had*). Put the later of the two past actions (arriving) in the past tense.

> **I *had completed* the task before *3 a.m.*** The past action of *completing* the task took place *before* the time of 3 a.m. Express the earlier past action, *completed*, in the past perfect tense.

After each pronoun, write the past perfect tense of the given verb.

1. to prepare   <u>they had prepared</u>   3. to manage   he _____
2. to audit   <u>he</u> _____   4. to identify   we _____

Now underline the past perfect tense verb in each of the following sentences. Then write each verb phrase in the space at the right.

5. Paul and Jennifer <u>had decided</u> to replace the broken chair.   5. <u>had decided</u>
6. The mayor had addressed the issue of unemployment.   6. _____
7. We had notified them of the changes several weeks in advance.   7. _____
8. The actors had performed very well that afternoon.   8. _____

THE FUTURE PERFECT TENSE

The future perfect tense is used to show a *time relationship* between two future actions where one future action will happen before another future action or time. Use the future perfect tense for the earlier of the two future actions. The future perfect tense is formed with a verb's past participle plus *will have.*

I *will have suggested* the proposal by next week. The future action of *suggesting* the proposal will take place prior to the stated time in the future (*next week*). The earlier future action should be expressed in the *future perfect tense* (a verb's past participle plus *will have*).

By the time I call, you will have gone. The future actions are *calling* and *going. Going* will take place first, so it should be expressed in the future perfect tense.

He will have completed the job by noon tomorrow. The future action of *completing* the job will take place prior to a stated time in the future (*noon tomorrow*).

After each pronoun, write the future perfect tense of the given verb.

1. to learn   1. <u>you will have learned</u>
2. to serve   2. <u>he</u> _____
3. to operate   3. <u>she</u> _____
4. to reach   4. <u>we</u> _____

Now underline the future perfect tense verb in each of the following sentences. Then write each verb phrase in the space at the right.

5. By Friday, we <u>will have processed</u> 1,000 applications.   5. <u>will have processed</u>
6. By noon, the race walkers will have walked over five miles.   6. _____
7. Max will have achieved his goal by the end of this month.   7. _____
8. Martin and Jamal will have gone to Alaska by July 1.   8. _____

In the space provided, indicate the tense (present perfect, past perfect, or future perfect) of each of the italicized verbs in the following sentences.

1. The scientists *will have released* their results by tomorrow.   1. <u>future perfect</u>
2. The students *had listened* carefully to the test instructions.   2. _____
3. The meeting *will have started* prior to your arrival.   3. _____
4. Jake and Sam *had learned* a valuable lesson.   4. _____
5. The witness *has told* several conflicting stories.   5. _____

EXERCISES

EXERCISE 1 After each pronoun, write the present perfect tense of the given verb.

1. to revise   he _____   4. to conduct   they _____
2. to report   she _____   5. to collect   he _____
3. to write   we _____   6. to advise   she _____

Now underline the present perfect tense verb in each of the following sentences. Then write each verb phrase in the space at the right.

7. Dean has disputed the results of the test.   7. _____
8. Judy has asked Jane to be her partner.   8. _____
9. Each of them has worked long hours in the factory.   9. _____
10. Chris has exceeded his own expectations.   10. _____

EXERCISE 2 After each pronoun, write the past perfect tense of the verb indicated.

1. to proceed   he _____   4. to equip   she _____
2. to expire   it _____   5. to arrange   we _____
3. to hire   she _____   6. to eat   he _____

Now underline the past perfect tense verb in each of the following sentences. Then write each verb phrase in the space at the right.

7. The manager had received an announcement from the director.   7. _____
8. The parties had settled out of court.   8. _____
9. Because of her concern, Dan had gone to the doctor.   9. _____
10. The controller had audited all departmental expense accounts. 10. _____

EXERCISE 3 After each pronoun, write the future perfect tense of the verb indicated.

1. to break   they _____   4. to conduct   he _____
2. to notify   she _____   5. to portray   she _____
3. to plan   he _____   6. to predict   they _____

Now underline the future perfect tense verb in each of the following sentences. Then write each verb phrase in the space at the right.

7. Pete will have played the guitar all day.   7. _____
8. Before you arrive, I will have arranged all of the flowers.   8. _____
9. By 3:15 tomorrow, we will have counted the votes.   9. _____
10. When Haren finally arrives, I will have settled things.   10. _____

EXERCISE 4 In the space provided, indicate the tense (present perfect, past perfect, or future perfect) of each of the verbs.

1. had begun _____
2. has created _____
3. will have completed _____
4. had reviewed _____
5. have wrapped _____
6. will have notified _____

7. has left _____
8. will have checked _____
9. had stated _____
10. have skated _____
11. had called _____
12. will have begun _____

EXERCISE 5 In the space provided, indicate the tense (present; past; future; present progressive, past progressive, or future progressive; or present perfect, past perfect, or future perfect) of each of the italicized verbs.

1. Jeremy *had located* the missing part to the system.
2. You *have obligated* yourself to this fund raiser.
3. By this time next week we *will have answered* most of the inquiries.
4. The guide *showed* us how to correctly steer the raft.
5. Gene *sings* in the choir every week.
6. Everyone *will participate* in the project.
7. The chief executive officer *is convincing* us that the company will remain independent.
8. The company *will be hiring* more employees next month.
9. Tim *was teaching* his son how to fish.
10. The lumber company *had supplied* us with scraps to build our stage props.

1. _____
2. _____
3. _____
4. _____
5. _____
6. _____
7. _____
8. _____
9. _____
10. _____

WRITING ACTIVITY Write a sentence using the verb tense shown. At the end of your sentence, write the tense of the verb. (Answers will vary.)

1. have helped _____
2. will have walked _____
3. had moved _____

SHORT STORY In the spaces provided at the right, indicate the tense of each of the underlined verbs.

Based on experience, we have estimated we will receive 550 calls a day to our Help desk line. Connie is one of the few people who staff the Desk. Connie had been abrupt with customers, so I recommended that she enroll in a seminar on customer service skills. After she completed the seminar, Connie agreed this was a good idea. Connie realized in the seminar that she had not been friendly with customers. She managed to create ill will with people who had called for help. The seminar made her realize the importance of speaking with a smile on the phone. With the help of the seminar, Connie has achieved the ability to create a win-win situation with her customers.

1. _____
2. _____
3. _____
4. _____
5. _____
6. _____
7. _____
8. _____
9. _____
10. _____
11. _____

SUBJECT AND VERB AGREEMENT

FOLLOW THE LEADER AGAIN!

Like the pronouns we discussed in Lesson 9, verbs must also follow their leader (the subject) in person and number (singular or plural).

I *prefer* to pay my bills by check. In this sentence, the verb *prefer* agrees in number (singular or plural) with its subject *I*.

	Singular	**Plural**
First Person	I *prefer*	we *prefer*
Second person	you *prefer*	you *prefer*
Third person	he, she, it *prefers*	they *prefer*

Looking at the table, you can see that I is first person singular. Therefore, use the first person singular verb, *prefer.*

SUBJECTS AND VERBS MUST AGREE

The general rule is this: *A verb must agree with its subject in person* (first, second, or third) *and in number* (singular or plural). Thus, *I* and *prefer* agree. Let's look at a few more examples:

Mark *is* our manager. The verb *is* agrees (in number) with its subject, *Mark.*

The office system *majors are* hosting a "PC" Day. Nouns are always considered third person. They can be third person singular or third person plural. Since *majors* is plural, the verb must be plural. The verb *are* is plural.

CHECKUP 1 Select the correct verb in parentheses, and write it in the space at the right. Make sure your choice agrees with its subject!

1. Ricky (*walk*, *walks*) two miles each day.
2. The nurses (*need*, *needs*) your help today.
3. Carl (*move*, *moves*) into his new apartment the first of the month.
4. The new book (*has*, *have*) over 500 pages.

1. walks
2. _____
3. _____
4. _____

COLLECTIVE NOUNS AND COMPOUND SUBJECTS

Do you remember collective nouns from Lesson 6? They take singular verbs when the group acts as *one*; plural verbs when the members act as individuals.

The *committee plans* to reconvene at 1 p.m. The committee is acting as a group. It is singular and requires a singular verb. The verb *plans* is singular and agrees with the collective noun *committee.*

The *committee were* divided in their opinions. Because *committee* refers to the committee members acting as individuals, the plural verb *were* is used.

Compound subjects, as you know, have two or more nouns or pronouns. If the parts of the compound subject are joined by *or* (or *nor*), the verb must agree in number (singular or plural) with the subject that *follows* the word *or* (or *nor*).

Neither the supervisors nor the *assistant has* the authority to approve the change. The singular noun *assistant* follows the word *nor*. Use the singular verb *has*.

But watch what happens when the sentence is changed.

Neither the assistant nor the *supervisors have* the authority to approve the change. Now the plural noun *supervisors* follows the word *nor*. Use the plural verb *have*.

If the parts of the compound subject are joined by *and*, the subject is plural and requires a plural verb.

Alexander and Yana are traveling to Europe. The plural verb *are* agrees with the compound subject *Alexander and Yana*.

Exception! Two subjects joined by *and* are still considered singular if they are modified by the indefinite pronouns *each* or *every*.

Every woman and child *was* given preference. The singular verb, *was,* is correct because *every* means every single one.

Each man and child *was* identified with a name tag. The singular verb, *was,* is correct because *each* means each one person.

CHECKUP 2 Select the correct verb from each pair in parentheses, and write it in the space at the right.

1. Neither the pen nor the papers (*was, were*) on the desk.   1. _were_____
2. Only a few of the students (*is, are*) paying attention.   2. _____
3. Every boy and girl (*has, have*) a pair of mittens.   3. _____
4. Each of the students (*has, have*) an assignment to complete.   4. _____
5. Dan and Bob (*is, are*) managing the departments.   5. _____

OTHER PROBLEMS

When a sentence is not in normal order, the correct verb may not be clear. Change the sentence to normal order: Subject first, then verb.

Where (*is, are*) my box of nails? Normal order: My box of nails is where? The subject *box* is singular and requires a singular verb. *Is* is singular.

Somewhere in the house (*is, are*) the missing contracts. Normal order: The missing contracts are somewhere in the house. The subject *contracts* is plural and requires the plural verb *are*.

A sentence that begins with *there* may also cause problems because its subject follows the verb. In such sentences, *there* is an expletive. *There* is never used as a subject of a sentence.

There (*is, are*) several candidates. The subject is *candidates*, a plural noun requiring a plural verb. *Are* is plural.

(*Is, Are*) there a doctor in the house? The subject is *doctor*, a singular noun requiring a singular verb. *Is* is singular. Thus: *Is* there a doctor in the house?

There are other indefinite pronouns in addition to *each* and *every* that cause trouble. Recall from Lesson 13 that some indefinite pronouns are always singular, some are always plural, and some others may be singular or plural.

Either of the two employees *is* welcome. *Either* is always singular.

Both of the assistants *are* here today. *Both* is always plural.

Most of the printing *is* finished. *Most* is singular here; it refers to the singular noun *printing*.

Most of the terminals *are* down. *Most* is plural here; it refers to the plural noun *terminals*.

EXERCISES

EXERCISE 1	Select the correct verb form from each pair in parentheses, and write it in the space at the right. Make sure your choice agrees with its subject!

1. Who (*is, are*) the new director?   1. _____
2. (*Does, Do*) either of you know where my files are?   2. _____
3. There (*is, are*) some administrative assistants who always do well.   3. _____
4. Not one of the managers (*was, were*) available yesterday.   4. _____
5. Many on the commission (*wants, want*) more time to read the report.   5. _____
6. There (*is, are*) one more report left to complete.   6. _____
7. The status of the patients (*was, were*) given by Dr. Smith.   7. _____
8. Here (*is, are*) the list of names that you requested.   8. _____
9. Either Harry or his assistants (*is, are*) supervising the installation.   9. _____
10. All of the students (*is, are*) prepared for the test.   10. _____
11. Each of the reports (*require, requires*) scrutiny.   11. _____
12. The two of you (*is, are*) needed in the principal's office.   12. _____
13. Either Jon or Greg (*has, have*) the file you are missing.   13. _____
14. Both (*is, are*) delighted to hear of the good news.   14. _____
15. You and he (*has, have*) been selected as contest judges.   15. _____
16. Each of the soldiers (*run, runs*) ten miles per day.   16. _____
17. His responses to the attorney's questions (*was, were*) very clear.   17. _____
18. Something about these forms (*seem, seems*) strange.   18. _____
19. Much time and money (*was, were*) devoted to this project.   19. _____
20. Rebecca, like many in her family, (*is, are*) an artist.   20. _____

EXERCISE 2	Underline any error in subject-verb agreement in the following sentences. If there is an error, correct the verb, not the subject. Write your correction in the space at the right. If there is no error, write *OK*.

1. Do Pat or Maggie know the score of the game?   1. _____
2. Not one of the applicants were recommended for the position.   2. _____
3. Have each of the procedures been reviewed.   3. _____
4. The instructor demonstrated how to reboot the system.   4. _____
5. One of the customers were complimenting our staff.   5. _____
6. Babysitting the girls under these conditions are exhausting.   6. _____
7. Four people from the center has agreed to help.   7. _____
8. Is any of the terminals operating properly?   8. _____
9. Very few residents was happy with the proposal.   9. _____
10. There were a list of items to be repaired on the bulletin board.   10. _____
11. The quest for health and wealth were her main concern.   11. _____
12. A handful of items was left for people to purchase.   12. _____
13. The papers for the speech was left at the office.   13. _____
14. Molly and her twin sister was writing articles for a national magazine. 14. _____
15. Two-thirds of the athletes were on time for the track meet.   15. _____

16. The wind and cool air causes the flowers to freeze.   16. _____
17. John Earhart, our corporate lawyer, review about ten new cases a day.   17. _____
18. The stock market reports shows a rapid decline in value.   18. _____
19. The poor-tasting and overpriced meal were not what we expected.   19. _____
20. Most of the people in the audience was pleased with the performance.   20. _____

EXERCISE 3   For each of the following phrases, underline the subject and identify it as singular or plural by writing *singular* or *plural* in the space provided.

1. a few members of the cast   1. _____
2. each member of the senator's staff   2. _____
3. all of the offices   3. _____
4. one of the women   4. _____
5. the group of men, women, and children   5. _____
6. something about these letters   6. _____
7. the mailing costs for the letters   7. _____
8. someone in the office   8. _____
9. every sophomore   9. _____
10. a swarm of bees   10. _____
11. the cheers of the crowd   11. _____
12. the director and the band   12. _____
13. each one of the reports.   13. _____
14. the sole of the shoe   14. _____
15. the average score of the tests   15. _____

WRITING ACTIVITY   Write a sentence using the following **nouns** as **subjects**. Make sure your verb agrees with the subject. (Answers will vary.)

1. freeways   _____
                   _____

2. Monday   _____
3. lectures   _____
4. people   _____
5. one   _____

SHORT STORY   Underline each subject once and verb twice in the following paragraph. If there is an error in subject-verb agreement, write the correct verb.

Has you ever taken a walk on an early spring morning?   1. _____
The birds is making their noises in the fields, especially   2. _____
the red-winged blackbirds. Each of the birds protect its   3. _____
territory. The soft grayish buds of the pussy willow tree
is beginning to show. The smell of freshness are in the   4. _____
air. The rays of the sun is bouncing off each blade of grass.   5. _____
Nature are in her glory.   6. _____

TO *LIE* AND *TO LAY*

USING *TO LIE* AND *TO LAY*

Can you memorize a few words? Memorize the four principal parts of the following verbs, and you will avoid some of the most difficult verb problems in our language. Read them slowly, and look for easy ways to remember these few words.

Infinitive	Present	Past	Past Participle	Present Participle
to lie (recline or remain)	lie	lay	lain	lying
to lay (put or place)	lay	laid	laid	laying

Notice that the past tense of *to lie* is *lay*, which is identical to the present tense of *to lay*. This duplication of words as different tenses causes confusion when selecting *to lie* and *to lay*.

Lie The verb *to lie* means to recline or to remain. It is intransitive and never has a direct object.

lie

My cousin lies on the bed. Lies what? No answer. There is no direct object.

Since the verb *to lie* never has a direct object, its past participle cannot be used with *being* verb helpers.

Lay The verb *to lay* means to put or to place or to cause to lie. It is a transitive verb and always takes a direct object.

lay

Please lay the boards on the ground. Does the verb *lay* have a direct object? Let's see: Please lay (whom or what) on the ground? Lay the *boards* on the ground. *Boards* is the direct object.

CHECKUP 1

Underline the direct objects in the following sentences. Then write the direct objects in the spaces at the right. If a sentence has no direct object, write *have-not*.

1. She laid her <u>papers</u> on the desk.
2. Please lay the carpet in the den.
3. I was lying on the sofa for several hours.
4. Lay your pencils down when time is called.
5. Lie down if you feel ill.

1. _papers_____
2. _____
3. _____
4. _____
5. _____

TO LIE

Read the following tenses of *to lie*. Remember, *to lie* means "to recline or to remain."

TO LIE (*never has* a direct object)

Present Tense	
I *lie*	we *lie*
you *lie*	you *lie*
he, she, it *lies*	they *lie*

The leaves *lie* on the ground now.

Present Progressive Tense (present participle, *lying*, plus *am, is*, or *are*)	
I *am lying*	we *are lying*
you *are lying*	you *are lying*
he, she, it *is lying*	they *are lying*

The leaves *are lying* on the ground now.

Past Tense	
I *lay*	we *lay*
you *lay*	you *lay*
he, she, it *lays*	they *lay*

The leaves *lay* on the ground yesterday.

Present Perfect Tense (past participle, *lain*, plus *have* or *has*)	
I *have lain*	we *have lain*
you *have lain*	you *have lain*
he, she, it *has lain*	they *have lain*

The leaves *have lain* on the ground for days.

TO LAY

Read the following tenses of *to lay* aloud. Remember, *to lay* means "to place something."

TO LAY (*always has* a direct object)

Present Tense	
I *lay*	we *lay*
you *lay*	you *lay*
he, she, it *lays*	they *lay*

I *lay* the newspaper on the table.

Present Progressive Tense (present participle, *laying*, plus *am, is*, or *are*)	
I *am laying*	we *are laying*
you *are laying*	you *are laying*
he, she, it *is laying*	they *are laying*

I *am laying* the newspaper on the table.

Past Tense	
I *laid*	we *laid*
you *laid*	you *laid*
he, she, it *laid*	they *laid*

I *laid* the newspaper on the table.

Present Perfect Tense (past participle, *laid*, plus *have* or *has*)	
I *have laid*	we *have laid*
you *have laid*	you *have laid*
he, she, it *has laid*	they *have laid*

I *have laid* the newspaper on the table.

CHECKUP 2   Select the correct verb from each pair in parentheses, and write it in the space at the right.

1. She and her friends (*lie, lay*) on the beach any chance they get.   1. _lie_____
2. Is the trash (*lying, laying*) on the ground for a reason?   2. _____
3. Will and Andy have (*lain, laid*) the new carpet.   3. _____
4. She (*lies, lays*) her clothes on the rack to dry.   4. _____
5. The painter (*lies, lays*) the portfolio on the counter in the lobby.   5. _____

Name _____ Date _____ Score _____

EXERCISES

EXERCISE 1   Select the correct verb from each pair in parentheses, and write it in the space at the right.

1. Am I to (*lie*, *lay*) the box right side up?   1. _____
2. Maria (*layed*, *laid*) the mail on the kitchen table.   2. _____
3. Each afternoon, Norman (*lies*, *lays*) down to take a nap.   3. _____
4. The tree was (*laying*, *lying*) in the middle of the road.   4. _____
5. Have these printouts been (*lying*, *laying*) here all day?   5. _____
6. The attorney had (*lain*, *laid*) the contracts aside for the time being. 6. _____
7. Where had the manager (*lain*, *laid*) the annual report?   7. _____
8. Some items (*lay*, *laid*) covered in dust.   8. _____
9. The portraits had (*laid*, *lain*) in the attic for several years.   9. _____
10. The papers had (*laid*, *lain*) here for about a week.   10. _____
11. The baby had (*lain*, *laid*) in the crib waiting for the nurse to bathe her. 11. _____
12. Who (*lay*, *laid*) these proposals on my desk?   12. _____
13. Be careful to (*lay*, *lie*) it in a safe place.   13. _____
14. These dogs have (*lay*, *laid*) around all day.   14. _____
15. The workers have finished (*lying*, *laying*) the tile.   15. _____

EXERCISE 2   Replace the question mark with the correct form of *to lie* or *to lay*. Write your answers in the spaces at the right.

1. After back surgery, Ron (?) on his stomach for several weeks.   1. _____
2. The manager had (?) the checks on his desk.   2. _____
3. Will you (?) the paper down and come here?   3. _____
4. Did you get that tan from (?) in the sun or from working in the garden? 4. _____
5. The dancers (?) their outfits in the dressing room.   5. _____
6. The new schedules were (?) on the supervisor's desk.   6. _____
7. The courier was (?) the envelopes in the bin.   7. _____
8. The new schedules were (?) on the desk by Stan.   8. _____
9. Rick's sport jacket is (?) on the bed.   9. _____
10. Would you please (?) those file folders on the cabinet.   10. _____
11. The keys were (?) on the dresser.   11. _____
12. He (?) the towel over the rail to dry.   12. _____
13. Sean (?) down the rules.   13. _____
14. How long have these towels been (?) here?   14. _____
15. How long have you been (?) the towels here?   15. _____

EXERCISE 3   Correct any errors in the use of *to lie* or *to lay* in the following sentences. Underline each error. Then write your corrections in the spaces at the right. If a sentence is correct, write *OK*.

1. You certainly are able to laid carpet down easily.   1. _____
2. The strategists were busy lying plans for the campaign.   2. _____

3. They had been lying around all afternoon. 3. _____
4. You may lay down anytime you feel like doing so. 4. _____
5. Our manager just lies the schedules on our desks. 5. _____
6. The boy has layed there for several hours. 6. _____
7. Irene thought that she had layed them there several hours ago. 7. _____
8. Is Lisa still lying on the hammock? 8. _____
9. Martha said the pictures are laying on the table. 9. _____
10. Ben will lie the sign-up lists on the hallway table. 10. _____
11. Did you say you will be lying on the couch or the bed? 11. _____
12. She layed the books on the shelf. 12. _____
13. Don't lie the books on my desk! 13. _____
14. Has Toby laid there all day? 14. _____
15. I see those books lying on my desk again! 15. _____

EXERCISE 4 In each space below, write a sentence using each of the following verbs correctly. (Answers will vary.)

1. lay _____
2. lays _____
3. have lain _____
4. have lain _____
5. lays _____
6. is laying _____
7. lies _____
8. have laid _____
9. laid _____
10. has lain _____
11. lays _____
12. lies _____
13. lie _____

WRITING ACTIVITY Write the following sentences. (Answers will vary.)

1. Compose a sentence that correctly uses some form of the verb *to lie*.

_____

2. Compose a sentence that correctly uses some form of the verb *to lay*.

_____

SHORT STORY Are the forms of *to lie* and *to lay* used correctly in the following paragraph? Underline any form that is incorrect and write the correct form of the verb in the space at the right.

When spring break comes along, college students from around
the country flock to the sunny beaches of the southland to
lay on the beach and get a glorious tan. They ignore medical 1. _____
advice that says laying in the sun is bad for one's health. 2. _____
So they lie their towels on the sand to lay on their 3. _____
backs and then to lay on their tummies. If they 4. _____
have laid too long in the sunshine, red, burning skin 5. _____
will be their memories of spring break.

23 SIT AND SET; RISE AND RAISE

USING *TO SIT* AND *TO SET*

Look at the parts and tenses of the verbs *to sit* and *to set*. Study them carefully.

Infinitive	Present	Past	Past Participle	Present Participle
to sit	sit	sat	sat	sitting
to set	set	set	set	setting

Sit *To sit* means "to rest, recline, or take a seat." It is intransitive and never has a direct object.

> **Everyone must *sit* toward the front of the bus.** *Sit* whom or what? Nothing, so no direct object.

Set *To set* means "to place, or to establish." It is transitive and always has a direct object.

> **The child *set* the table.** *Set* whom or what? The table—the direct object.

TO SIT (*never has* a direct object)

Present Tense	
I *sit*	we *sit*
you *sit*	you *sit*
he, she, it *sits*	they *sit*

Present Progressive Tense (present participle, *sitting*, plus *am, is,* or *are*)	
I *am sitting*	we *are sitting*
you *are sitting*	you *are sitting*
he, she, it *is sitting*	they *are sitting*

Past Tense	
I *sat*	we *sat*
you *sat*	you *sat*
he, she, it *sat*	they *sat*

Present Perfect Tense (past participle, *sat,* plus *have* or *has*)	
I *have sat*	we *have sat*
you *have sat*	you *have sat*
he, she, it *has sat*	they *have sat*

TO SET (*always has* a direct object)

Present Tense	
I *set*	we *set*
you *set*	you *set*
he, she, it *sets*	they *set*

Present Progressive Tense (present participle, *setting*, plus *am, is,* or *are*)	
I *am setting*	we *are setting*
you *are setting*	you *are setting*
he, she, it *is setting*	they *are setting*

Past Tense	
I *set*	we *set*
you *set*	you *set*
he, she, it *set*	they *set*

Present Perfect Tense (past participle, *set,* plus *have* or *has*)	
I *have set*	we *have set*
you *have set*	you *have set*
he, she, it *has set*	they *have set*

CHECKUP 1 Select the correct verb from each pair in parentheses, and write it in the space at the right.

1. We plan to (*sit, set*) next to the groom's family.
2. The children have (*sit, set*) the table.
3. They (*set, sat*) in the top row during the concert.
4. By noon, the waiters were (*sitting, setting*) the tables.

1. sit
2. _____
3. _____
4. _____

USING *TO RISE* AND *TO RAISE*

To rise and *to raise* are two more troublesome verbs. Study the parts and tenses carefully.

Infinitive	Present	Past	Past Participle	Present Participle
to rise	rise	rose	risen	rising
to raise	raise	raised	raised	raising

Rise *To rise* means "to get up, to move upward by itself." It is intransitive and never has a direct object.

Rivers *are rising* to flood stages. *Are rising* whom or what? Nothing, so no direct object.

Raise *To raise* means "to increase or to bring up." It is transitive and always has a direct object.

Sean raised a question after the speech. *Raised* whom or what? A question—the direct object.

TO RISE (*never has* a direct object)

Present Tense	
I *rise*	we *rise*
you *rise*	you *rise*
he, she, it *rises*	they *rise*

Present Progressive Tense (present participle, *rising*, plus *am*, *is*, or *are*)	
I *am rising*	we *are rising*
you *are rising*	you *are rising*
he, she, it *is rising*	they *are rising*

Past Tense	
I *rose*	we *rose*
you *rose*	you *rose*
he, she, it rose	they *rose*

Present Perfect Tense (past participle, *risen*, plus *have* or *has*)	
I *have risen*	we *have risen*
you *have risen*	you *have risen*
he, she, it *has risen*	they *have risen*

TO RAISE (*always has* a direct object)

Present Tense	
I *raise*	we *raise*
you *raise*	you *raise*
he, she, it *raises*	they *raise*

Present Progressive Tense (present participle, *raising*, plus *am*, *is,* or *are*)	
I *am raising*	we *are raising*
you *are raising*	you *are raising*
he, she, it *is raising*	they *are raising*

Past Tense	
I *raised*	we *raised*
you *raised*	you *raised*
he, she, it raised	they *raised*

Present Perfect Tense (past participle, *raised* plus *have* or *has)*	
I *have raised*	we *have raised*
you *have raised*	you *have raised*
he, she, it *has raised*	they *have raised*

CHECKUP 2 Select the correct verb from each pair in parentheses, and write it in the space at the right.

1. The sun (*rises, raises*) in the east and sets in the west. 1. __rises__
2. The boys will be (*rising, raising*) in about an hour. 2. _____
3. We will (*rise, raise*) the flag every morning. 3. _____
4. The water (*rose, rised*) to above flood level. 4. _____

EXERCISES

EXERCISE 1   Select the correct verb from each pair in parentheses, and write it in the space at the right.

1. The full moon (*rised, rose*) in the sky.   1. _____
2. They (*sit, sat*) still during the ceremony yesterday.   2. _____
3. Will you (*set, sit*) down and rest a moment?   3. _____
4. The house (*sets, sits*) on the hill.   4. _____
5. He (*sits, sets*) the table every evening for his parents.   5. _____
6. Please (*set, sit*) the thermostat to sixty degrees.   6. _____
7. (*Sit, Set*) the package over here.   7. _____
8. Are your parents going to (*set, sit*) at this table?   8. _____
9. The dog (*sat, set*) on the girl's lap.   9. _____
10. Are you going to be (*sitting, setting*) new prices soon?   10. _____
11. The objection he (*raised, rose*) concerned flextime.   11. _____
12. The defendant (*raised, rose*) to hear the verdict.   12. _____
13. Mother wants to (*raise, rise*) some vegetables in her garden this summer. 13. _____
14. The sun had (*risen, raised*) early that morning.   14. _____
15. Is the bread (*raising, rising*) like it should be?   15. _____
16. Have you been able to (*raise, rise*) enough money for a scholarship?   16. _____
17. His temper (*rised, rose*) during the debate.   17. _____
18. The employees (*risen, raised*) some concerns about the policy.   18. _____
19. (*Raising, Rising*) early to jog each morning takes a lot of discipline. 19. _____
20. Please (*raise, rise*) when the judge enters the room.   20. _____
21. The companies are (*rising, raising*) the prices for gasoline.   21. _____
22. The stock market (*raised, rose*) to a record high.   22. _____
23. The man (*rises, raises*) his own vegetables.   23. _____
24. My respect for him as (*risen, raised*) tremendously.   24. _____

EXERCISE 2   In the sentences below, underline each incorrectly used verb. Then write your corrections in the spaces at the right. If a sentence is correct, write *OK*.

1. Perhaps she would like to set over here.   1. _____
2. Are you sure you want to sit those boxes so close to the heater?   2. _____
3. Will Alan be setting near to Susan?   3. _____
4. They were sitting up the displays.   4. _____
5. Ask Marie to set the table.   5. _____
6. The employee set in his chair and did not work.   6. _____
7. The dog sets when you issue the command.   7. _____
8. Do sit back in your chair and relax for a few minutes.   8. _____
9. The student sit in the front row of the classroom.   9. _____
10. Have the guidelines for the project been sit yet?   10. _____
11. She was setting on the porch swing.   11. _____

12. Would you like to sat near the stage?   12. _____
13. Please raise and sing our national anthem.   13. _____
14. Everyone raises when the bride walks down the aisle.   14. _____
15. The cost of living rises every year.   15. _____

EXERCISE 3 In each space below, write a sentence using each of the following verbs correctly. (Answers will vary.)

1. sit   _____
2. sitting   _____
3. sat   _____
4. set   _____
5. setting   _____
6. sets   _____
7. rise   _____
8. raise   _____
9. raising   _____
10. rose   _____
11. rise   _____
12. set   _____
13. raised   _____
14. sat   _____
15. rising   _____

WRITING ACTIVITY Can you write a short paragraph that uses the forms of *to sit* and *to set* correctly? A challenge—can you use at least two forms of *to sit* and two forms of *to set* in your paragraph? Underline the forms of *to sit* and *to set* in your paragraph. (Answers will vary.)

_____

_____

_____

SHORT STORY Underline any incorrect uses of the forms of the verbs *to raise* and *to rise*, and *to set* and *to sit*. Write the correct word in the space at the right.

Marcus thought it was time to sit some direction in his life.   1. _____
He had been reared by parents who encouraged him to raise   2. _____
early, to work hard, and to enjoy life. He oftentimes set   3. _____
in his room thinking about the future, but these times were
fruitless. He could not sat goals for himself. Even on   4. _____
days when he raised early in the morning to think about his   5. _____
future, his mind just seemed to shut down. He read stories
of people who risen to fame, sometimes because of sheer   6. _____
luck, but mostly because they raised to meet high goals they had   7. _____
set for themselves. Marcus would sigh and say, "Well, maybe
if I set here just a little longer, I'll come up with my life's plan."   8. _____

MORE TROUBLESOME VERBS

SELECTING THE CORRECT VERBS

LEARN AND TEACH

Simply put, *learn* means "to acquire knowledge." *Teach* means "to instruct." Never say, "He *learned* me." Say instead, "He *taught* me."

Ms. Zahn *taught* me how to delete a file. I learned how to delete a file from Ms. Zahn. She taught; I learned. Never say, "Ms. Zahn *learned* me."—No one can learn you!

Mr. Carrone *taught* me how to write computer programs. I *learned* how to write computer programs from Mr. Carrone. He taught; I learned. Never say, "*learned* me how to write computer programs."

LEAVE AND LET

If you ever confuse *leave* and *let*, just remember that *leave* means "to depart or go away" and that *let* means "to permit or allow." Do not use *leave* or its past tense *left* for *let*.

He *let* me watch television. (NOT: He *left* me watch television.) *Let* means "allow." He allowed me to watch television.

Let me show you how. *Let* means "allow." Allow me to show you how.

I do not want to *leave* you alone in the house. Leave means "depart." I do not want to depart from the house.

Leave sometimes can also mean "to deliver or place," as in the sentence below:

If I were you, I would *leave* a note saying where I was going.

CHECKUP 1   Select the correct verb from each pair in parentheses, and write it in the spaces at the right.

1. When you (*let, leave*), please turn out the lights.
2. Tracy (*let, left*) Jim borrow the car.
3. The teacher (*let, left*) the student use his book.
4. She was (*learned, taught*) the proper lifting technique.
5. I (*taught, learned*) much from past experience.

1. <u>leave</u>
2. _____
3. _____
4. _____
5. _____

BRING TO AND TAKE AWAY

Bring means "to carry something *to* someone." *Take* means "to carry something *away from* someone."

Travis asked Shane to *bring* him a glass of water from the kitchen. (NOT: to *take* him a glass of water.) Shane will carry a glass of water to Travis.

When Denise leaves the office, please have her *take* the books to the library. (NOT: have her *bring* the books with her.) Denise will carry the books away from the office.

CHECKUP 2 Select the correct verb from each pair in parentheses, and write it in the spaces at the right.

1. Will you please (*bring, take*) me the calculator? 1. <u>bring</u>
2. Do you want to (*bring, take*) your lunch to work today? 2. _____
3. It (*brings, takes*) about 30 minutes to walk the two miles. 3. _____
4. We will (*bring, take*) cookies to the party. 4. _____
5. Dad always (*brings, takes*) some candy home for the children. 5. _____

AFFECT AND EFFECT

Affect is a verb that means "to influence or to change." *Effect* can be a verb meaning "to bring about" or a noun meaning "a result or a consequence."

The freeze in Florida will *affect* the price of orange juice in the stores. The freeze will change the price of orange juice.

We must *effect* a dramatic improvement in our sales. We must bring about a change in our sales.

The *effect* was exactly what I had hoped it would be.

CHECKUP 3 Select the correct verb from each pair in parentheses, and write it in the space at the right.

1. The new schedule had a positive (*affect, effect*) on the employees. 1. <u>effect</u>
2. A number of issues were (*affected, effected*) by the company executives. 2. _____
3. Will working late (*affect, effect*) your grades? 3. _____
4. We were all (*affected, effected*) by the team's loss. 4. _____
5. The (*affects, effects*) of the budget cuts were felt by all. 5. _____
6. What was the (*affect, effect*) of the new policy? 6. _____

BORROW AND LEND

Borrow means "to obtain, to take, or to receive something on loan." *Lend* means "to give out or to allow the use of something for a period of time."

I forgot my book; may I *borrow* yours? May I please take your book?

Dad promised to *lend* me his car until mine is back from the garage. Dad promised to allow me the use of his car until mine was back from the garage.

CHECKUP 4 Select the correct verb from each pair in parentheses, and write it in the space at the right.

1. May I (*borrow, lend*) the car tonight? 1. <u>borrow</u>
2. Would you please (*borrow, lend*) me $5? 2. _____
3. Pete had to (*lend, borrow*) Mike's book. 3. _____
4. Dad didn't want to (*borrow, lend*) him the car for the evening. 4. _____
5. You may (*borrow, lend*) my computer this evening. 5. _____

Name   Date   Score

EXERCISES

EXERCISE 1   Select the correct verb from each pair in parentheses, and write it in the space at the right.

1. He needs to (*learn, teach*) how to use a computer.   1. _____
2. Finally, Jimmy (*taught, learned*) how to write a computer program.   2. _____
3. Will you be (*teaching, learning*) at the university this semester?   3. _____
4. I can (*teach, learn*) you how to play the piano.   4. _____
5. (*Teach, Learn*) as much as you can this week.   5. _____
6. You can (*teach, learn*) yourself how to ride a bike.   6. _____
7. Lynn wanted to (*learn, teach*) how to fix a car.   7. _____

EXERCISE 2   Select the correct verb from each pair in parentheses, and write it in the space at the right.

1. Nobody will (*let, leave*) before 5 o'clock.   1. _____
2. Jon chose to (*let, leave*) his book at home.   2. _____
3. Can you (*let, leave*) the dog go outside?   3. _____
4. The system (*lets, leaves*) you create your own resume.   4. _____
5. It is difficult to (*let, leave*) this town behind.   5. _____
6. (*Let, Leave*) Brenda prepare the report for the council meeting. 6. _____
7. Yes, Mr. Tatro (*let, leave*) us use the faculty lounge for our meeting. 7. _____

EXERCISE 3   Select the correct verb from each pair in parentheses, and write it in the space at the right.

1. Will you please (*bring, take*) me a blanket from upstairs.   1. _____
2. We will (*bring, take*) a break in one hour.   2. _____
3. Please (*bring, take*) the mail when you come.   3. _____
4. Father is (*bringing, taking*) home the groceries from the store. 4. _____
5. (*Bring, Take*) a copy of the memo to Ms. Turner.   5. _____
6. (*Bring, Take*) the fax messages to me when you come.   6. _____
7. Please (*bring, take*) a moment to complete this survey.   7. _____

EXERCISE 4   Select the correct verb from each pair in parentheses, and write it in the space at the right.

1. How has the change in plans (*affected, effected*) you?   1. _____
2. Your schedule will (*affect, effect*) how we plan our day.   2. _____
3. Can you (*affect, effect*) a change in the way the work is done?   3. _____
4. What is the (*affect, effect*) of the change?   4. _____
5. What will the (*affects, effects*) be on your production schedule? 5. _____
6. We will all be (*affected, effected*) by the results of the storm. 6. _____
7. How will the new law (*affect, effect*) our company?   7. _____

EXERCISE 5   Select the correct verb from each pair in parentheses, and write it in the space at the right.

1. She is not allowed to (*borrow, lend*) my sweater.
2. You may not (*borrow, lend*) the car this evening.
3. I will (*borrow, lend*) you my tools this week.
4. Try not to (*borrow, lend*) money from your relatives.
5. Would you be willing to (*borrow, lend*) me some money until Friday.
6. Did she ask to (*borrow, lend*) those files from you?
7. Jon wants to (*borrow, lend*) Dan's game for the evening.

1. _____
2. _____
3. _____
4. _____
5. _____
6. _____
7. _____

EXERCISE 6   Have you mastered the troublesome verbs? Let's see. In the space provided write a sentence using the given verb. (Answers will vary.)

1. teach _____
2. leave _____
3. let _____
4. bring _____
5. bring _____
6. borrow _____
7. lend _____
8. learning _____
9. take _____
10. learned _____
11. taught _____
12. bringing _____
13. affected _____
14. borrowed _____
15. leaves _____
16. lend _____
17. took _____
18. effects _____
19. let _____

SHORT STORY   Are the verbs you studied in this lesson used correctly? Underline any verb that is not used correctly. Write the correct verb in the space at the right.

For many years, I knew I wanted to learn children.
Having a mom who was a teacher probably effected
my career choice. She used to take me books to read
about careers in the business world, but the affect
was still the same; I wanted to learn others. I could
picture myself in a classroom leaving students study
subjects that would take them beyond their own environments.
Through a book the student could let his or her own town and
learn about the life of a person living in another country. I am
so pleased I am in a position to learn others.

1. _____
2. _____
3. _____
4. _____
5. _____
6. _____

7. _____

8. _____

UNIT
6

ADJECTIVES

UNIT 6 OVERVIEW

Adjectives are interesting words; they give the reader an opportunity to picture the action taking place in the sentence. Adjectives describe, limit, and qualify nouns and pronouns. When they precede the noun and pronoun in the sentence, they must be punctuated correctly. However, adjectives may also follow the noun and pronoun in which case they may or may not contain marks of punctuation. In this unit you will learn how to punctuate and how to use adjectives creatively and correctly.

UNIT OBJECTIVES

When you complete Unit 6, you will be able to:

- define adjectives as words that modify or limit nouns and pronouns.

- identify descriptive adjectives.

- identify possessive adjectives.

- identify demonstrative adjectives.

- identify quantity adjectives.

- select a comma or a hyphen to separate double adjectives.

- recognize the positive, comparative, and superlative forms of adjectives.

ADJECTIVES TO DESCRIBE, POSSESS, AND LIMIT

ADJECTIVES

Part of Speech

Adjectives modify or limit a noun or a pronoun. An adjective answers the questions: *which one? how many? what kind?*

An adjective that points out the quality of the noun or pronoun is called a *descriptive adjective*:

a ***bitter*** wind   a ***hot*** day   a ***tasty*** meal

An adjective that places a boundary on a noun or a pronoun is called a *limiting adjective*:

my printer   ***few*** people   ***these*** homes   ***nine*** categories   ***a*** book

DESCRIPTIVE ADJECTIVES

Descriptive adjectives are picture-making words, such as *big* and *small*, *short* and *tall*, *dull* and *lively*, *dark* and *bright*, and so on.

> **The *optimistic* report disclosed *unexpected* profits that were gained from an *exciting new* venture.** *Optimistic, unexpected, exciting*, and *new* are descriptive adjectives.
>
> **The *small, red loose-leaf* manual is the programmer's.**

Do you see how the words *the small, red loose-leaf* help to modify or describe the noun *manual*? These words provide details about the manual, which help bring it into sharper focus. *Small* provided a detail about its size—it is not a large book. *Red* provides a detail about its color—not the green or the blue loose-leaf manual but the *red* one. And *loose-leaf* provides a detail about the way *the small, red* manual is bound.

Beware! Nouns are often used as adjectives to modify other nouns or pronouns. Don't be fooled— look to see *how the noun is used*.

> **The company that bought this factory has its headquarters in *New York*.**
>
> *New York* is a noun (a proper noun, in fact); it names a particular place.
>
> **A *New York* company has bought this factory.** Here, *New York* is used to modify the noun *company*; thus *New York* is an adjective in this sentence.

CHECKUP 1

Underline the descriptive adjectives in each of the following sentences. Then write the total number of adjectives in each sentence in the space at the right.

1. The California trip was the highlight of our carefree summer.   1. _2_
2. Human freedom exists in daily life.   2. _____
3. He writes romance novels.   3. _____
4. Our primary job is to assist the flood victims.   4. _____

ARTICLES

A, an, and *the* are called *articles*. Articles are adjectives because they can limit or clarify the words they modify. Perhaps you never notice, but whenever you use *a* or *an*, you are referring to something *indefinite*. Whenever you use *the*, you are referring to something *definite*.

> **A software package will be demonstrated at the meeting.** *A* package is indefinite. It could be any package.

She is *the* clerk who waited on us. *The* clerk is definite. A specific clerk, *the* clerk (not *any* clerk), waited on us.

Use *a* before words that begin with a consonant (or consonant sound) or with the sound of a long *u* (as in *unit*):

a day	a student	a teacher	a classmate
a uniform	a unicorn	a university	a union

a one-hour class (Do you hear the consonant sound *w* in one?)

Use *an* before all vowel sounds (except the long *u* sound) and before words beginning with a silent *h*.

an apple	an umbrella	an essay	an honor (The *h* is silent.)

CHECKUP 2   Underline the descriptive adjectives in the following sentences, and circle the articles *a*, *an* and *the*.

1. (The) lush mountains reflect beautiful colors in (the) fall.
2. The famous landmarks no longer interested the tired tourists.
3. On a steamy August morning, I took a ten-speed bike for a ride in the downtown park.
4. A student brought an apple for the young teacher.

POSSESSIVE ADJECTIVES

The personal pronouns *my*, *his*, *her*, *our*, *your*, *their*, *its*, and the relative pronoun *whose* are adjectives whenever they modify nouns.

My office is on the fifteenth floor. His office in on the tenth floor.

My and *his* are possessive adjectives.

DEMONSTRATIVE ADJECTIVES

When used alone, *this*, *that*, *these*, and *those* are demonstrative pronouns. When they modify nouns, of course, they are called *demonstrative adjectives*.

Those are Harold's brochures. *Those* is a pronoun—it takes the place of a noun.

Those brochures are Harold's. *Those* is an adjective—it modifies *brochures*.

These were very interesting. *These* is a pronoun—it takes the place of a noun.

These books were very interesting. *These* is an adjective—it modifies *books*.

Each of these books was very interesting. *Each* is a pronoun.

Each book was very interesting. Here, *each* modifies *book*, so it is an adjective.

QUANTITY ADJECTIVES

Quantity adjectives are numbers such as *two*, *ten*, *first*, and *fifth*; but there are also "quantity words," such as *few*, *several*, *all*, *none*, *some*, *any*, and *many*. Obviously, they tell "how much."

Only *three* rooms were repainted. *Three* is a quantity adjective.

Very *few* people were present. *Few* is a quantity adjective.

CHECKUP 3   Underline once any possessive adjectives. Underscore twice any quantity adjectives. Circle the demonstrative adjectives, *this*, *that*, *these*, and *those*.

1. My cousin will be attending the computer workshop (this) month.
2. His work load increased this year for several reasons.
3. That hat is not mine.
4. This computer belongs in his room.

EXERCISES

EXERCISE 1	Decide how many adjectives are in the following sentences. Underline each adjective, and circle each article (*a*, *an*, or *the*). Then write the total number of adjectives (including articles) in each sentence in the space at the right. (*Hint:* Be sure to include possessive adjectives, such as *my* and *our*, and quantity adjectives, such as *two*, *tenth*, *few*, and *all*.)

1. A reasonable compromise was needed for a peaceful resolution of the problem.   1. _____
2. One day at lunch our ecumenical group of doctoral students discussed the Sunday sermon.   2. _____
3. My college students asked if I would base their grades on relative performance instead of raw scores.   3. _____
4. The popular zoo had some unusual and dangerous animals.   4. _____
5. We hope that many students will have excellent computer skills.   5. _____
6. Few students had to take final exams because of the new grading policy.   6. _____
7. Many large dogs were being kept behind the wire fence near the brick house.   7. _____
8. By early June, the rich fields of winter wheat sprouted lush carpets of grain.   8. _____
9. An exciting new cure for the dreaded disease of diabetes may have been found.   9. _____
10. A desolate highway median became a setting for colorful wildflowers.   10. _____
11. The small boy heard his aged father say that he was starting an exercise program.   11. _____
12. Freshmen athletes know the importance of making healthful choices and avoiding reckless behavior.   12. _____
13. The versatile artist was able to paint vibrant flowers as well as abstract portraits.   13. _____
14. Two red pencils were lying on the oak desk.   14. _____
15. The music must be quick and upbeat before my handsome son shows any interest.   15. _____

EXERCISE 2	Underline only the demonstrative adjectives (*this*, *that*, *these*, and *those*), possessive adjectives, and quantity adjectives in the following sentences. Then write the total number of demonstrative, possessive, and quantity adjectives in each sentence in the space at the right.

1. That actress had several lines added to her script.   1. _____
2. Many athletes will appear at several events for their favorite charities.   2. _____
3. A few of these language classes will be taught by your former teacher.   3. _____
4. His first sermon was given to only a few members.   4. _____
5. My comments were made to only one person during that famous trial.   5. _____
6. Whose disk was lying by that keyboard on my desk?   6. _____
7. I remember putting that book under my desk in the first row.   7. _____
8. Her subordinates have won these awards two years in a row.   8. _____
9. This panel consists of five women who work with my mom.   9. _____
10. Their boss ordered ten new computers for the office.   10. _____
11. I wanted that car to be in my garage so my three sons would be impressed.   11. _____
12. That opinion was expressed by his colleagues only a few weeks before the research paper was published.   12. _____
13. Was that your first experience with voice mail?   13. _____
14. These people baked many fruitcakes for our community.   14. _____
15. A million American children are too heavy, but we think our children are too thin.   15. _____

Use each word listed below in a sentence. Make sure that you use each as an adjective, not as a noun or as a verb. (Answers will vary.)

1. personal _____
2. friendly _____
3. first _____
4. legal _____
5. those _____
6. special _____
7. enclosed _____
8. healthy _____
9. his _____
10. efficient _____
11. storage _____
12. commercial _____
13. interest _____
14. college _____
15. minute _____
16. hazy _____
17. large _____
18. public _____
19. New York _____
20. several _____
21. lengthy _____
22. Chicago _____
23. their _____
24. small _____
25. her _____

SHORT STORY Underline the adjectives in the following paragraph. Then write, in the space at the right, the kind of adjective (descriptive, article, possessive, demonstrative, and quantity) each one is.

Have you noticed the many colorful calendars that
are produced? Some of them depict beautiful flowers
or cuddly animals. A few review history, some have a
theme that is carried out with brilliant colors in the pictures
or with descriptive statements. A calendar can be expensive,
but many calendars are free. Businesses tend to give these
calendars to their customers in the late months of the year.

1. _____
2. _____
3. _____
4. _____
5. _____
6. _____
7. _____
_____

PROPER ADJECTIVES AND DOUBLE ADJECTIVES

USING PROPER ADJECTIVES AND DOUBLE ADJECTIVES

PROPER ADJECTIVES

Proper adjectives are words formed from proper nouns; for example, *Shakespearean* (from the proper noun *Shakespeare*), *Platonic* (from the proper noun *Plato*), *English* (from *England*), and *American* (from *America*).

CHECKUP 1   After each proper noun, write the proper adjective formed from it.

1. Mexico   <u>Mexican</u>   3. Canada   _____
2. Japan   _____   4. China   _____

DOUBLE ADJECTIVES

Sometimes two or more adjectives may be used to describe a word. For example, to describe a leather briefcase that is new, you would probably say, "a new leather briefcase." To describe an office that is large and modern, you would say, "a large, modern office." And to describe a building that is ten stories high, you would say, "a ten-story building."

Did you notice that nothing separates *new* and *leather*, that a comma separates *large* and *modern*, and that a hyphen joins *ten* and *story*? Let's see why.

When to Use a Comma Use a comma between adjectives that modify the *same noun*. As a test, see if you could say *and* between the adjectives and reverse the order of the adjectives without changing the meaning of the description.

> **a *large, modern* office** Both *large* and *modern* modify the same noun, *office*. You could say "an office that is *large* and *modern*"; thus the comma is correct. You can also reverse the order of the adjectives and say "an office that is modern and large."

You cannot say "a new *and* leather briefcase" because it makes no sense. The reason is simple: *leather* modifies *briefcase*, but *new* modifies both *leather* and *briefcase*. Thus, no comma is used.

CHECKUP 2   Decide if you would use a comma at the point marked (?) in each of the following sentences. Write *Yes* or *No* in the space at the right. (*Remember:* If *and* is not appropriate, then a comma is not appropriate either.)

1. The beautiful (?) gracious hostess enjoyed entertaining.   1. <u>Yes</u>
2. The story of his long (?) dull journey put everyone to sleep. 2. _____
3. Upon her return from the war, a warm (?) enthusiastic crowd   3. _____
   greeted Mary at the airport.
4. We saw the old (?) project house ruined by vandals.   4. _____
5. Myles works on a large (?) isolated ranch in Wyoming.   5. _____

When to Use a Hyphen We frequently look for shortcuts—even in our speech. Thus we usually say "a 2-foot ruler" rather than the longer, "a ruler that measures two feet"; we say "a 3-gallon container" rather than "a container that holds 3 gallons"; and so on. When we build up adjectives and place them before nouns, we usually need a hyphen to show that the words work together as *one unit*, as in *2-foot ruler* and *3-gallon container*. But we do not always need the hyphen when the words *follow* the noun, because the words usually read clearly without the hyphen:

BEFORE THE NOUN	AFTER THE NOUN
a *two-piece* suit	a suit that has *two pieces*
third-party rule	ruled by a *third party*

Compound adjectives placed before nouns need hyphens to make them read clearly. Some combinations of words form compound adjectives that are always hyphenated—whether they are used before or after the noun they modify.

BEFORE THE NOUN	AFTER THE NOUN
an ice-cold drink	a drink that is ice-cold
a broken-down car	a car that is broken-down
a soft-spoken friend	a friend who is soft-spoken

Notice that many of these compounds have past participles; for example, *broken* and *spoken*.

Compound adjectives that are always hyphenated appear in the dictionary as hyphenated. They are also identified as adjectives. This is important to remember because the same combination of words may be used as a compound adjective in one sentence but not in another. When this happens, the rules of hyphenation do not apply. For example, the words *up to date* appear in the dictionary as hyphenated when identified as an adjective. Thus, when used as an adjective, this combination of words should always be hyphenated.

BEFORE THE NOUN	AFTER THE NOUN
my up-to-date list	my list is up-to-date

However, in another sentence *up to date* may not be functioning as an adjective. When this combination of words functions as something other than an adjective, it is not hyphenated. In the sentence below, *up to date* functions as a prepositional phrase.

I promise to bring my list *up to date*.

Always check first to confirm that the compound words are used as an adjective—then you can decide whether or not they should be hyphenated.

CHECKUP 3   Decide if you would use a hyphen at the point marked (?) in each of the following sentences. Write *Yes* or *No* in the space at the right. Use a dictionary if your instructor permits.

1. The fourth(?)state convention will be held in November.   1. <u>No</u>
2. She is a well(?)known person in our community.   2. _____
3. The worn(?)out equipment will be replaced by May.   3. _____
4. The funny(?)looking clown brought peals of laughter.   4. _____

Exceptions, Exceptions, Exceptions! Do *not* use hyphens to join proper adjectives:

a *New Jersey* law firm	*North American* ski resorts
the *Supreme Court* decisions	a *San Antonio* school
many *United States* companies	three *Rodeo Drive* stores

Hyphens should not be added to compound words that are normally written without hyphens. Consult your dictionary to see if a compound word should be hyphenated. These compound words would not be hyphenated even when they precede the noun they modify.

a *high school* reunion	*off year* politics	two *real estate* offices
social security payments	a *12 percent* raise	*word processing* center
public relations person	*money market* account	

EXERCISES

EXERCISE 1   Decide if you would use a comma at the point marked (?) in each of the following sentences. Write *Yes* or *No* in the space at the right. (*Remember:* If *and* is not appropriate, then a comma is not appropriate either.)

1. The baseball player signed a million (?) dollar contract.   1. _____
2. The long (?) tiring trip through the mountains left us exhausted.   2. _____
3. Please use the second (?) business envelope for mailing those contracts.   3. _____
4. The old (?) coal furnace was still being used in the elementary school.   4. _____
5. His primary (?) care provider was not on the approved list.   5. _____
6. Are you sure you want those three (?) electric mowers moved to the basement?   6. _____
7. The obnoxious (?) loud client wanted to see our manager.   7. _____
8. An excellent (?) exciting movie is now playing at United Artists.   8. _____
9. The video (?) conferencing was frequently used at the university.   9. _____
10. The largest internet network was introduced by a local (?) computer company.   10. _____

EXERCISE 2   Decide if you would use a hyphen at the point marked (?) in each of the following sentences. Write *Yes* or *No* in the space at the right. Use a dictionary if your instructor permits.

1. Are you interested in getting part(?)time help for the summer?   1. _____
2. Kyle signed a contract for four(?)years.   2. _____
3. Had you heard that he signed a four(?)year contract with the Dodgers?   3. _____
4. The new(?)computer system is ready for installation.   4. _____
5. Calvin, our life(?)insurance agent, has been with Surety Insurance for many years.   5. _____
6. The tall(?)bounty hunter chased the fugitive across three states.   6. _____
7. My short(?)masonry apprenticeship was extremely enjoyable.   7. _____
8. The doctor stated that a five(?)step program should be followed.   8. _____
9. The soft(?)spoken lawyer appeared to be completely confident.   9. _____
10. The cute(?)little poodle appeared at the door of the barn.   10. _____

EXERCISE 3   Insert hyphens where necessary in each of the following sentences. Then write the hyphenated word in the space at the right. If a sentence is correct, write *OK*.

1. The long term goal was to return all the patients to society.   1. _____
2. The extensive information highway on the internet can be overwhelming.   2. _____
3. The well adjusted adolescent was willing to discuss his choices.   3. _____
4. The three bedroom beach house was given to the family by an uncle.   4. _____
5. Unfortunately, she was the lowest paid employee.   5. _____
6. An interest free loan was available to the tornado victims.   6. _____
7. The football game was played in 100 degree heat.   7. _____
8. The real estate office is closed on weekends.   8. _____
9. The friendly looking clerk had received the Outstanding Salesperson Award.   9. _____
10. We were given step by step instructions on how to operate the machine.   10. _____

EXERCISE 4   Rewrite each word group so that it is a hyphenated compound adjective.

1. A house with two bedrooms   _____
2. A contract for six years   _____
3. A job for only part time   _____
4. A plan for eight years   _____
5. A professor who is well known   _____
6. A person who is well organized   _____
7. A boy with brown eyes   _____
8. Slippers that are worn out   _____
9. A building of ten stories   _____
10. A report that is organized well _____
11. A person who is trained well   _____
12. A meeting held at a high level _____
13. A sale that will last for one day _____
14. A book that is written well   _____
15. An improvement that is much needed _____

EXERCISE 5   Use each of the following adjectives or adjective phrases in a sentence. Be sure to use each as an adjective. (Answers will vary.)

1. long-term   _____
2. one-quart   _____
3. gorgeous, red   _____
4. two-dollar   _____
5. well-mannered   _____

WRITING ACTIVITY   Use each of the following word groups in a sentence with a comma or a hyphen to separate the adjectives. (Answers will vary.)

1. hot wet   _____
2. small angry   _____
3. old fashioned   _____
4. heart shaped   _____
5. easy care   _____

SHORT STORY ACTIVITY   Place the correct punctuation marks (hyphen or comma) between adjectives in the following paragraph. Circle your marks of punctuation.

The well manicured lawn of the small farm was filled with a brilliant display of multicolored blooming flowers and shrubs. The several buildings, painted in white with green trim, furnished a background that a skilled artist could truly appreciate. The large stocky horse grazed in the lush green pasture; the long eared donkeys frolicked in their fenced area, and several cats of assorted colors dozed in the bright warm sunshine. The two large collie dogs could be seen wandering in the wet corn field. This picturesque scenery brought tears to the boy's eyes when he realized everything he loved had survived the raging high waters of the flood.

COMPARING ADJECTIVES

A MATTER OF DEGREE

Adjectives allow us to describe things. They also allow us to *compare* our descriptions:

a *later* delivery   **the *latest* delivery**

Forms such as *late/later/latest* represent the three forms of comparisons of adjectives. *Late* is the positive form—it describes *one* thing. *Later* is the comparative form—it compares *two* things. *Latest* is the superlative form—it compares more than two things. Let's look at each comparison.

THE POSITIVE DEGREE

Late describes *one* thing—it is the positive degree.

They attended a *late* meeting. The word *late* describes one meeting.

THE COMPARATIVE DEGREE

Together, *late* and *later* (or *late* and *less* late) allow us to compare the degree of lateness between two things.

Marge was late for the conference, but Raúl was later. *Later* is used to compare *two* degrees of lateness. In this case, the comparative is a higher degree of lateness.

But . . .

Both Marge and Raúl were late for the conference, but Marge was less late.

Less late is used to compare two degrees of lateness. Here, the comparative is a *lower* degree of lateness.

Forming the Comparative Degree Most adjectives form the higher comparative degree by adding *er* to the positive form:

Two Big Books –
Higher Degree Of Comparison

Start ——— big book   bigger book ——→

old + er = older   mild + er = milder   neat + er = neater   young + er = younger

Of course, adjectives that end in *e* or *y* are "special":

close + er = closer (drop one *e*)   happy + er = happier (change *y* to *i*, then add *er*)

Most adjectives of two syllables or more do not "sound right" if *er* is added to the positive form. For these adjectives, we use the word *more* instead of *er* to express the comparison.

Beth was *more cheerful* than Russ. (NOT: cheerfuler)

Two Big Books –
Lower Degree Of Comparison

←——— less big   big book ——— Start

Use *less* to express the *lower* degree of comparison.

Beth was less cheerful than Russ.

THE SUPERLATIVE DEGREE

Together, *late*, *later*, and *latest* (or *late*, *less late*, and *least late*) allow us to compare three or more things.

José was *late*. Dorothy was *later*. Honey was the *latest*.

Three Big Books –
Higher Degree Of Comparison

big book   bigger book   biggest book
Start ——————————→

Forming the Superlative Degree Most adjectives form the higher superlative degree by adding *est* to form the positive form, but some adjectives use the word *most* instead. Use *least* to express a lower degree of comparison.

Three Big Books –
Lower Degree Of Comparison

POSITIVE	COMPARATIVE	SUPERLATIVE
fast	fast + er = faster	fast + est = fastest
cheerful	more cheerful	most cheerful
eager	less eager	least eager

least big   less big   big book Start

All were late, but José was the *least late*.

CHECKUP 1 Decide which adjective form is correct: positive, comparative, or superlative. In the spaces to the right, write the correct form of the adjective given in parentheses.

1. The crust on this pie is (*flaky*) than the crust on that pie.   1. flakier
2. Please purchase the (*coarse*) sandpaper available in the store.   2. _____
3. That document is of (*poor*) quality than the one you have.   3. _____
4. You are (*famous*) for your ideas on management techniques.   4. _____

Beware! Some adjectives cannot be compared in the regular sense because they are absolute; that is, they already express the most extreme degree. Examples of such words are *alive, alone, complete, correct, dead, empty, final,* and *unique*. Absolute adjectives may show comparison by using *more nearly* or *most nearly*.

This glass is *more nearly* full than that one.

THE IRREGULARS

Some adjectives do not form the degrees of comparison in the regular way by adding *er, est, more, most, less,* or *least* to the positive degree. These adjectives show degrees of comparison in an *irregular* way—they change their spelling. Here are some examples:

POSITIVE	COMPARATIVE	SUPERLATIVE
good	better	best
bad	worse	worst
far	farther	farthest
little	less	least
many	more	most
much	more	most

DOUBLE TROUBLE

As you've seen, some adjectives add *er* to make their comparative forms; others use the word *more* (or *less*). Never use both *er* and *more* (or *less*) together for the same word.

He lives a *healthier* life since going on his diet. (NOT: *more healthier* life)

Likewise, never use both *est* and the word *most* (or *least*) for the same word.

We need the *latest* price list. (NOT: the *most latest* price list)

CHECKUP 2 Select the correct adjective form. Write it in the space.

1. The grain in this piece of wood is (*finer, more fine*) than that piece.   1. finer
2. Of the three, the first one is the (*better, more better, best*).   2. _____
3. This sample of cloth is (*unique, more unique, most unique*).   3. _____
4. This is by far the (*easy, more easy, easiest*) task of all.   4. _____

Name   Date   Score

EXERCISES

EXERCISE 1   In the spaces at the right, write the comparative form of the adjective given in parentheses.

1. My house was (*close*) to the road than my neighbor's house.
2. We arrived (*late*) than we planned.
3. The girl seemed (*friendly*) than her sister.
4. I think I get (*fast*) service here than at the old store.
5. We need to give (*good*) service than our competitor.
6. Of these two letters he had written, the first one was (*bad*).
7. Which of the two watches is (*small*)?

1. _____
2. _____
3. _____
4. _____
5. _____
6. _____
7. _____

EXERCISE 2   In the spaces at the right, write the superlative form of the adjective given in parentheses.

1. We need the (*light*) cord possible for our kite.
2. She appeared to be the (*smart*) of all five children.
3. He always bought the (*expensive*) shoes for his son.
4. Mrs. Pryor was the (*kind*) teacher in the school.
5. He felt that the (*high*) grade that he could make would be an 85.
6. Are you the (*young*) in your family?
7. The professor asked for the (*current*) magazine available.

1. _____
2. _____
3. _____
4. _____
5. _____
6. _____
7. _____

EXERCISE 3   Decide which adjective form is correct—positive, comparative, or superlative. In the space at the right, write the correct form of the adjective given in parentheses.

1. Everyone agreed that Barry's recommendation was (*good*) than Angela's.
2. He happens to be the (*kind*) person I know.
3. The (*old*) building in the city is now up for sale.
4. Which of the two typewriters is in (*bad*) shape?
5. The prices of our products are not (*high*).
6. Today is the (*warm*) day of the year.
7. This is the (*bad*) grade that I have ever received.

1. _____
2. _____
3. _____
4. _____
5. _____
6. _____
7. _____

EXERCISE 4   In the space at the right, write the correct form of the adjective given in parentheses. Absolute adjectives may be used in your answers.

1. Did John or Robert have the (*many*) popular name at school?
2. This is the (*easy*) job that I ever had.
3. The farmer's tractor was (*big*) than his son's.
4. The children thought he was the (*mean*) man in town.
5. The two boys tried to figure out who got the (*good*) price.
6. Of all the alternatives given, Andrew's was the (*creative*).
7. I would like to buy something that is (*strong*) than what I have now.

1. _____
2. _____
3. _____
4. _____
5. _____
6. _____
7. _____

Write the comparative and superlative degrees for the following adjectives.

POSITIVE	COMPARATIVE	SUPERLATIVE
1. bad	_____	_____
2. low	_____	_____
3. attractive	_____	_____
4. talented	_____	_____
5. correct	_____	_____
6. fine	_____	_____
7. tall	_____	_____

WRITING ACTIVITY Can you write a sentence that contains both the positive and the comparative forms of each adjective? (Answers will vary.)

1. thick, thicker   _____
   _____

2. adept, more adept   _____
   _____

3. calm, calmer   _____
   _____

Can you write a sentence that contains the positive and the superlative forms of each adjective? (Answers will vary.)

1. thin, thinnest   _____
   _____

2. clean, cleanest   _____
   _____

3. early, earliest   _____
   _____

Can you write a sentence using these "irregulars"? (Answers will vary.)

1. little, less   _____
   _____

2. far, farther   _____
   _____

SHORT STORY Are the positive, comparative, and superlative adjectives used correctly in the following paragraph? Underline any errors you find in the use of these adjectives. Write the correct form of the adjective in the space at the right. If there are no errors, write *OK*.

The happy day of my life was when I graduated from
high school. My beautiful mother stood and applauded
louder than anyone else in the auditorium. I will never
forget her smile. It was the big smile that I had ever
seen. She knew I had been successfuler in high school
than my older brother and she had confidence that I
would achieve greatest success after high school than
my brother. My mom was probably more happier than
I on that graduation day.

1. _____
2. _____
3. _____
4. _____
5. _____
6. _____
7. _____
8. _____
9. _____

UNIT 7

ADVERBS

UNIT 7 OVERVIEW

An adverb performs descriptive and limiting functions in a sentence like an adjective; however, an adverb can only modify a verb, an adjective, or another adverb. The adverb answers these questions: *how? when? where? why? how much? how often? to what degree? in what manner?* and *to what extent?* It can be a single word, a phrase, or a clause. The adverb may also serve as a conjunction to connect two independent clauses. Often an adverb will end in "ly" but some adjectives do, too. Confused? You will learn in this unit how to distinguish between the adverb and the adjective and have lots of practice using adverbs in these many different ways. Adverbs, like adjectives, make our writing clear, vivid, and interesting!

UNIT OBJECTIVES

When you complete Unit 7, you will be able to:

■ define an adverb.

■ distinguish adverbs from adjectives.

■ use the positive, comparative, and superlative degrees of adverbs.

■ place modifiers in their correct position in a sentence.

■ recognize and use conjunctive adverbs.

■ make the correct selection when given words that create trouble.

LESSON 28 ADVERBS: THE *-LY* WORDS

ADVERBS

Part of Speech Adverbs are another one of the eight parts of speech. An adverb modifies a verb, an adjective, or other adverbs. An adverb answers the questions *how? when? where? why? how much? how often? to what degree? in what manner? to what extent?* An adverb can be a word, a phrase, or a clause.

> **Sarah *frequently* misses her appointments.** *Frequently* tells us how often Sarah misses her appointments. The adverb *frequently* modifies the verb *misses*.

> **Acme Company will give you a *really* good buy on a new computer.** *Really* tells us to what degree the buy is good. The adverb *really* modifies the adjective *good*.

CHECKUP 1 Underline the adverb in each of the following sentences. Then in the space at the right, write the word that the adverb modifies.

1. She <u>anxiously</u> waited by the phone.
2. Mr. Bailey wanted to sign the letters immediately.
3. They often played baseball in the park.
4. Don proceeded through the woods cautiously.

1. waited
2. _____
3. _____
4. _____

THE *-LY* WORDS

Did you notice that many of the adverbs in Checkup 1 ended with *ly*? Not all *-ly* words are adverbs, but most of them are. Adverbs (like *usually, finally,* and *completely*) modify verbs and adjectives.

> **The sales representatives *finally* finished their reports.** *Finally* modifies the verb *finished*.

> **We solved these *unusually* difficult problems.** *Unusually* modifies the adjective *difficult*.

HOW? WHEN? WHERE?

Let's see how adverbs answer the questions *how, when, where, why, how much, how often, to what degree, in what manner,* and *to what extent*.

How? Some of the adverbs that answer the question *how* are q*uietly, quickly, loudly, carefully,* and *efficiently*. Most of these adverbs end in *ly*.

> **We *carefully* repaired the lines.** Repaired how? *Carefully. Carefully* modifies the verb *repaired*.

> **The shoppers walked *quickly*.** Walked how? *Quickly. Quickly* modifies the verb *walked*.

When? Most of the adverbs that answer the questions *when* or *how often* do not end in *ly*: examples are *often, once, twice, always, late, never,* and *seldom*.

Always call first. *Always* modifies the verb *call*. You should call first how often? *Always!*
We *meet frequently*. *Frequently* modifies the verb *meet*. We meet when? *Frequently*.

Where? Many of the adverbs that answer the question *where* also do not end in *ly*; examples are *everywhere* and *anywhere, forward* and *backward, up* and *down, above* and *below,* and so on.

> **Turn left at the stop sign.** Turn where? *Left.* The adverb *left* modifies the verb *turn*.

How Much? Adverbs that answer the questions *how much* or *to what degree* usually modify adjectives and other adverbs; examples are *almost, exceedingly, fully, most,* and so on.

> I *fully* **understand.** *Fully* modifies the verb *understand* and explains the extent of understanding.

CHECKUP 2 Underline the adverb in each of the following sentences. Then in the space at the right, write the questions that the adverb answers.

1. We <u>rarely</u> hear from our relatives in Sweden.
2. I desperately wanted to go to the party.
3. He was always late for his dental appointments.
4. That was the most exciting book I've read.
5. Our group meets often to honor the deadline.

1. <u>when (*or* how often)</u>
2. _____
3. _____
4. _____
5. _____

ADJECTIVE OR ADVERB?

Some adjectives and adverbs have the same forms. In the examples below, note how each adjective modifies a noun and how each adverb modifies a verb:

ADJECTIVE	ADVERB
a *late* train	he arrived *late*
he reads a *daily* paper	she runs *daily*
an *early* bus	she came *early*

Words that end in *ly* may look like adverbs, but some adjectives end in *ly* too:

friendly receptionist   *elderly* men   *costly* items   *timely* tips

Use your dictionary whenever you are not sure.

Beware! Several frequently used adverbs have two acceptable forms.

fair, fairly	Grade fair or grade fairly.
deep, deeply	Cut deep or cut deeply.
direct, directly	Ship direct or ship directly.
quick, quickly	Come quick or come quickly.
slow, slowly	Drive slow or drive slowly.
loud, loudly	Talk loud or talk loudly.

INTERROGATIVE ADVERBS

The adverbs *how, why, where,* and *when* are called interrogative adverbs because they introduce questions.

> *How* **did you know it was me?** *How* introduces a direct question.

> **He asked *how* you knew it was me.** *How* introduces an indirect question.

CHECKUP 3 Underline the adverbs in each of the following sentences. Circle each interrogative adverb. Then in the space at the right, indicate whether each adverb modifies a verb (*V*), an adjective (*ADJ*), or another adverb (*ADV*). (*Hint:* Some sentences have more than one adverb.)

1. He was <u>very</u> <u>seldom</u> prepared for a presentation.
2. Bruce speaks too loudly on the phone.
3. Ginger works efficiently and competently.
4. How was your day with the new tutor?
5. Do you attend these meetings very often, Darlene?
6. The badly burned furniture had to be discarded.

1. <u>ADV, V</u>
2. _____
3. _____
4. _____
5. _____
6. _____

EXERCISES

EXERCISE 1   Underline the adverbs in the following sentences. Then write the adverbs in the spaces at the right.

1. The service department will be open tomorrow.
2. The Dean wrote a beautifully worded letter in my behalf.
3. The manager distinctly said that we could leave at 4 o'clock.
4. Don was fully aware of the consequences of his actions.
5. Please be sure to quote us the stock prices accurately.

1. _____
2. _____
3. _____
4. _____
5. _____

EXERCISE 2   Underline once the adverbs in the following sentences. Underline twice the word modified. Circle the interrogative adverbs. Then, in the space at the right, indicate whether each adverb modifies a verb (*V*), an adjective (*ADJ*), or another adverb (*ADV*).

1. Our service will give you a spotlessly clean home.
2. Never had I heard such a long commencement address.
3. We offer a highly qualified staff of accountants to conduct audits.
4. We will leave tomorrow for Tucson.
5. How did you know to memorize that very difficult material?
6. I was at the barbershop yesterday for a haircut.
7. Sandy graciously accepted the flowers.
8. It was a very convenient time to take the week off.
9. How did you learn to get rid of the virus?
10. Janice is always very prepared for her seminars.

1. _____
2. _____
3. _____
4. _____
5. _____
6. _____
7. _____
8. _____
9. _____
10. _____

EXERCISE 3   Underline the adverbs in the following sentences. Then in the spaces at the right, indicate whether the adverb modifies a verb (*V*), an adjective (*ADJ*), or another adverb (*ADV*).

1. We will arrive shortly.
2. His very hard coughing kept me awake.
3. I carefully planned my lesson before entering the classroom.
4. The very naughty dog was put in a cage.
5. Suzie goes this afternoon to the doctor.

1. _____
2. _____
3. _____
4. _____
5. _____

EXERCISE 4   Select the correct word from each pair in parentheses, and write it in the space provided.

1. I (*quick, quickly*) put on my coat and ran outside.
2. Are you (*real, really*) sure you can finish the report by noon?
3. The (*new, newly*) installed word processor works just fine.
4. Move (*cautious, cautiously*) through the construction area.
5. The (*intricate, intricately*) woven design was unique.

1. _____
2. _____
3. _____
4. _____
5. _____

EXERCISE 5 Use each of the following adverbs in a sentence. (Answers will vary.)

1. frequently   _____
2. effectively _____
3. tastefully   _____
4. considerably _____
5. efficiently _____

EXERCISE 6 After each adjective, write the adverb formed from it.

1. deep   _____   6. eager   _____
2. direct _____   7. personal   _____
3. hard   _____   8. sure   _____
4. high   _____   9. alphabetical _____
5. frank _____ 10. slow   _____

WRITING ACTIVITY Use the following adverbs to modify a verb in a sentence. (Answers may vary.)

1. slowly   _____
2. immediately _____

Use the following adverbs to modify an adjective in a sentence. (Answers will vary.)

3. terrifically _____
4. seriously   _____

SHORT STORY Insert an adverb wherever you see a rule. Then in the space at the right, indicate if the adverb modifies a verb (*V*), an adjective (*ADJ*), or another adverb (*ADV*). (Answers may vary.)

Summertime activities are filled _____ with   1. _____
fun-time activities that are done _____ and chores   2. _____
that are done _____ when necessary. What do   3. _____
you do in the summer? Perhaps trips taken _____   4. _____
_____ to a baseball game occupy your time, or perhaps 5. _____
you sit _____ reading books in your _____   6. _____
spare time. Do you take trips _____ to the golf   7. _____
course_____ and practice_____ at getting a   8. _____
_____ exact swing? Maybe you_____ often do nothing 9. _____
except to listen to the _____blowing wind that   10. _____
makes trees sway _____ _____in the breeze.   11. _____

COMPARING ADVERBS

THE THREE DEGREES

Like adjectives, adverbs have three degrees of comparison: the positive, the comparative, and the superlative degrees.

> Positive: **Dustin rollerblades *fast*. He maneuvers *efficiently*.**
>
> Comparative: **Clara rollerblades *faster* than Dustin. She maneuvers *more efficiently* than he.**
>
> Superlative: **Kirsten rollerblades the *fastest*. She maneuvers *most efficiently*.**

The three degrees of the adverb fast are *fast, faster,* and *fastest*. The three degrees of the adverb *efficiently* are *efficiently, more efficiently,* and *most efficiently*. The three degrees of adverbs are formed in the same way the three degrees of adjectives are formed (see Lesson 27).

THE POSITIVE DEGREE

The adverbs *fast* and *efficiently* are positive— they describe; they do not compare.

> **Dustin rollerblades *fast*. He maneuvers *efficiently*.** *Fast* and *efficiently* are positive forms that describe how Dustin rollerblades.

THE COMPARATIVE DEGREE

Let's look at the adverbs *fast* and *efficiently* as examples. Together, *fast* and *faster* or *efficiently* and *more efficiently* allow us to compare two things.

> **Dustin rollerblades *fast*. Clara rollerblades *faster*.** *Faster* is used to compare two degrees of fast.
>
> **Dustin maneuvers *efficiently*. Clara maneuvers *more efficiently*.** *More efficiently* is used to compare two degrees of efficiently.

Forming the Comparative Degree We form the higher comparative degree for adverbs just as we do for adjectives. We add *er* to the positive form.

> **fast + er = faster   slow + er = slower**

For adverbs of two syllables or more, we use the word *more* to express a higher degree of comparison and the word *less* for the lower degree of comparison.

> **more cheerfully   or   less cheerfully   more amusing   or   less amusing**

All -*ly* adverbs use the words *more* or *less*. None of them can add *er* without sounding strange. Also, never add both *er* and *more* (or *less*) to a word.

> **loud   louder** (NOT: more louder)   **more loudly   less loudly**

CHECKUP 1   In the space at the right, write the comparative form of the word given in parentheses.

1. Employees work (*hard*) when given an incentive.   1. <u>harder</u>
2. The seniors watched the game (*closely*) than the freshmen did.   2. _____
3. She seems (*supportive*) than the others.   3. _____
4. She spoke (*assertively*) to the store clerk than her mother did.   4. _____

THE SUPERLATIVE DEGREE

Together, *fast*, *faster*, and *fastest* allow us to compare three or more things. Also, *efficiently*, *more efficiently*, and *most efficiently* allow us to compare three or more things.

> **Dustin rollerblades *fast*, but Clara rollerblades *faster*. However, Kirsten rollerblades the *fastest* of them all.** Three things are being compared. *Fastest* is the superlative form.
>
> **Dustin maneuvers *efficiently*. Clara maneuvers *more efficiently*. However, Kirsten maneuvers the *most efficiently*.** Three things are being compared. *Most efficiently* is the superlative form.

Forming the Superlative Degree Just as you add *er* to form the comparative, you add *est* to form the superlative.

POSITIVE	COMPARATIVE	SUPERLATIVE
high	higher	highest
loud	louder	loudest

Likewise, whenever you use *more* (or *less*) to form the comparative, use *most* (or *least*) to form the superlative.

POSITIVE	COMPARATIVE	SUPERLATIVE
cheerfully	more cheerfully	most cheerfully
	less cheerfully	least cheerfully

THE IRREGULARS

Remember the adjectives *good/better/best*? Now make sure you know *well/better/best* and the other adverbs that are "irregulars."

POSITIVE	COMPARATIVE	SUPERLATIVE
badly	worse	worst
far	farther	farthest (referring to actual distance)
far	further	furthest (extent or degree; figurative distance)
little	less	least

DOUBLE TROUBLE

Be sure that you don't "double" your comparisons by saying things like "most best," "more better," "more louder," "more sooner," "more faster," "more slower," "more earlier," or "more softer."

CHECKUP 2

Select the correct forms for the adverbs in parentheses. Write the correct forms in the spaces.

1. Of all the machines in this room, this one works (*badly*) of all.

    1. <u>worst</u>

2. Marcia writes well, but Harvey writes (*well*).

    2. _____

3. Tim complains about the additional work (*much*) than Rick does.

    3. _____

4. Are you sure he can run (*fast*) than you?

    4. _____

5. You wrote that last paragraph very (*clear*).

    5. _____

EXERCISES

EXERCISE 1   In the spaces at the right, write the comparative form of the adverb given in parentheses.

1. Rusty drives (*recklessly*) than the other competitors.
2. In departmental meetings, Susan speaks (*softly*) than Michiko.
3. Tracy reacted (*quickly*) than her colleagues.
4. He behaves (*well*) with each passing day.
5. His cold sounds (*badly*) today than it did yesterday.
6. Andrew calculated the percentages (*rapidly*) than I expected.
7. Frank arrived (*late*) than Arnold for the meeting with Mr. Thompson.

1. _____
2. _____
3. _____
4. _____
5. _____
6. _____
7. _____

EXERCISE 2   In the spaces at the right, write the superlative form of the adverb given in parentheses.

1. Of all the new employees, Charlene works (*hard*).
2. Sonita is the (*fast*) typist we have in the office.
3. This car runs (*smoothly*) of all our rental cars.
4. This program (*well*) supports our office needs.
5. Peter had sold the (*much*) cars for the month.
6. Kelly's skills were the (*badly*) of all the applicants.
7. This gift was wrapped (*carefully*) of all the gifts.

1. _____
2. _____
3. _____
4. _____
5. _____
6. _____
7. _____

EXERCISE 3   Decide which adverb form is correct—positive, comparative, or superlative. In the spaces at the right, write the correct form of the adverb given in parentheses.

1. Daniel worked (*well*) with his colleagues than Peter did.
2. She answered the questions (*completely*) than Paula.
3. You seem to wrap the gifts (*fast*) than Janet.
4. She fell from the ladder, but she was not (*serious*) injured.
5. She waited (*nervous*) for the test results.
6. He jumped (*far*) than the first athlete.
7. The broken water pipe ruined the (*real*) expensive furniture.

1. _____
2. _____
3. _____
4. _____
5. _____
6. _____
7. _____

EXERCISE 4   In each sentence, replace the question mark with an adverb. Write the adverb in the space at the right. (Answers will vary.)

1. Her supervisor spoke (?) of her work.
2. (?) we'll be able to leave for San Francisco.
3. The company publishes the report (?).
4. Jake ran (?) to answer the phone.
5. The men worked (?) to complete the job by dusk.
6. The employees (?) agreed with the new policy.
7. (?) is the day that we will start production of the new model.

1. _____
2. _____
3. _____
4. _____
5. _____
6. _____
7. _____

8. She (?) travels out of town for seminars.
9. I believe that Bob is a (?) worker than Jorge.
10. Several workers made a (?) hasty decision to leave.

8. _____
9. _____
10. _____

EXERCISE 5   Write the comparative and superlative degrees for the following adverbs.

POSITIVE	COMPARATIVE	SUPERLATIVE
1. little	_____	_____
2. aggressively	_____	_____
3. nervously	_____	_____
4. rarely	_____	_____
5. hard	_____	_____
6. badly	_____	_____
7. patiently	_____	_____
8. well	_____	_____
9. much	_____	_____
10. bright	_____	_____
11. often	_____	_____
12. intimately	_____	_____
13. hastily	_____	_____
14. quick	_____	_____
15. quickly	_____	_____

WRITING ACTIVITY   Write a sentence using the following adverbs. (Answers will vary.)

1. vigilantly   _____
2. more flagrantly   _____
   _____
3. rigorously   _____
4. least   _____
5. truly   _____
6. more adversely   _____
   _____

SHORT STORY   Insert an appropriate adverb in the parentheses. Write your word in the space at the right. (Answers will vary.)

I (?) knew what to say when Judy told me she would not go
(?) to the doctor. She had cut her hand (?) with
the (?) sharp glass. She needed to go (?) to the emergency
room where (?) made stitches could be inserted. I tried my
(?) to convince her, but she (?) turned to me and said "no."
Judy is (?) afraid of doctors and even with the (?) injury, she
would refuse help. I (?) wanted to do something, but what?

1. _____
2. _____
3. _____
4. _____
5. _____
6. _____
7. _____

LESSON 30 SOME TROUBLEMAKERS

USING ADVERBS CORRECTLY

PLACEMENT OF WORDS

Place modifiers close to the words they modify. A misplaced adjective or adverb can change the meaning of a sentence or be confusing to the reader. Pay particular attention to the words *almost, ever, first, hardly, merely, last, just, only, nearly, scarcely, too*, and *also*.

> *Only* I told Ann about the announcement. *Only* I—no one else told Ann about the announcement.
>
> I told *only* Ann about the announcement. I told *only* Ann—not Bill, not Harry, not Bob.
>
> I told Ann about the announcement *only*. I told Ann about the announcement *only*—not about anything else.

CHECKUP 1 Rewrite the sentences below to eliminate misplaced modifiers or unnecessary repetitions.

1. I want only chocolate ice cream and nothing else. _I want only chocolate ice cream._
2. We lost the Oldani account almost. _____
3. Did you see ever such a sight! _____
4. I told him only the secret. _____
5. The parent was there for the only child. _____

AVOID DOUBLE NEGATIVES

Surely you remember the rule about double negatives: Do not use two negatives (*no, not, never, none, nowhere, don't, doesn't, won't*, and so on) together in a sentence. But do you remember that the words *scarcely, rarely, hardly, but*, and *barely* have negative meanings?

> She could *barely* lift the heavy package. (NOT: She *couldn't barely* lift the heavy package.)
>
> He could *hardly* wait to hear the news. (NOT: He *couldn't hardly* wait to hear the news.)
>
> I have *no* markers to use. (NOT: I *haven't got no* markers to use.)
>
> We *haven't* heard anything in the room. (NOT: We haven't heard nothing in the room.)

Rather than use *none* or *nothing* with negative expressions, use the positive words *any* or *anything*. Remember that two negatives cancel each other and make a positive statement.

AVOID UNNECESSARY REPETITIONS

Do not use an adverb to express a meaning already contained in the verb. Here are a few common redundancies (the adverb in parentheses in each case is unnecessary):

clear (off)   drop (down)   finish (up)   recline (back)   refer (back)   first (begin)

CHECKUP 2 These sentences contain double negatives or unnecessary repetitions. In the space provided, rewrite each sentence to eliminate the double negative or unnecessary repetition. (Answers will vary.)

1. I couldn't hardly stop laughing. _I could hardly stop laughing._
2. Please finish up your work, or you'll be late. _____

3. Please repeat again what you said.   _____

4. I haven't no money for you.   _____

5. I haven't got no complaints.   _____

ADVERB OR ADJECTIVE?

Sometimes you may wonder whether to say "She looked *angry*" or "She looked *angrily*." Which is correct, the adjective *angry* or the adverb *angrily*? To help you decide, substitute a form of the verb *to be* (*am, is, was, were*) for the verb in the sentence.

She is *angry*. OR **She is *angrily*.** Which makes more sense? Obviously, the adjective *angry*, not the adverb *angrily*.

Whenever a form of the verb *to be* can be substituted for a sense verb such as *look, taste, feel, smell, sound*, or the verbs *seem appear*, and *grow*, an adjective (not an adverb) must follow.

The pie *tastes* (delicious, deliciously). The pie *is* (delicious, deliciously). *Delicious* is correct.

CHECKUP 3

Decide if the adjective or the adverb in each pair in parentheses is correct. Write the correct word in the space at the right. (Remember to substitute a "being" verb to help you make your choice.)

1. Greg seems to be very (*slow, slowly*) today.   1. __slow_____

2. He looked quite (*angry, angrily*) after the call.   2. _____

3. These apples taste (*sweet, sweetly*) to me.   3. _____

4. The storm arrived (*quick, quickly*) yesterday.   4. _____

5. Elizabeth sounds (*nervous, nervously*) about her decision.   5. _____

SURE AND *SURELY*; *BAD* AND *BADLY*

Sure and *bad* are adjectives that modify nouns and pronouns. They should not be used as adverbs. *Surely* and *badly* are adverbs modifying verbs, adjectives, and other adverbs.

Here's a *sure* way to fix it. The adjective *sure* modifies the noun *way*.

She was *surely* excited about the trip. The adverb *surely* modifies the verb *excited*.

Use *bad* with the verbs *look* and *feel* in expressions such as these:

She feels *bad* about the move. (NOT: She feels badly.)

She looked *bad* after the accident. (NOT: She looked badly.)

BUT: **She was *badly* hurt after the accident.** *Badly* is an adverb modifying the verb *hurt*.

CHECKUP 4

Select the correct word from each pair in parentheses, and write it in the space at the right.

1. Our controller looked (*sad, sadly*) after she announced the cutbacks.   1. __sad_____

2. Jennifer was (*sure, surely*) happy to see Matt and Nancy.   2. _____

3. Charles felt (*bad, badly*) that he could not help you.   3. _____

4. The children sang (*bad, badly*) the first time.   4. _____

5. I feel (*sure, surely*) about my decision.   5. _____

Name _____ Date _____ Score _____

EXERCISES

EXERCISE 1   Rewrite each of the following sentences two times. Each time, change the position of the word *only* so that you also change the meaning of the sentence. (Answers will vary.)

1. Only our president can approve the proposal.

   _____

2. Only the supervisor attended the meeting in the morning.

   _____

3. Only the employees can suggest regulations for this department.

   _____

   _____

EXERCISE 2   Rewrite the sentences below to eliminate any misplaced modifiers or any unnecessary repetitions.

1. Sandy was chosen to head up the department.

   _____

2. The young man tried to understand the speaker's point of view hard.

   _____

3. Please lower down the podium for the next speaker.

   _____

4. The director spoke to the customer assertively on the phone.

   _____

5. Several of the respondents returned the questionnaires immediately.

   _____

6. He referred back to his opening statement several times.

   _____

EXERCISE 3   Rewrite each of the following sentences so that each sentence contains only one negative element. (*Remember:* Avoid two negatives in one sentence.) (Answers will vary.)

1. You do not have no obligation to buy this product.

   _____

2. I haven't no respect for him.

   _____

3. She would not never cheat on a test.

   _____

4. I can't hardly tell that you made a mistake.

   _____

5. I can't never do the math problems right.

   _____

EXERCISE 4 Decide which word in parentheses is correct—the adjective or the adverb. Write your choice in the space at the right. (Remember to substitute a "being" verb to help you make your choice.)

1. Nadia did very (*good, well*) on her final examinations.   1. _____
2. Your drawings are (*incredible, incredibly*).   2. _____
3. You (*sure, surely*) want to have at least two alternatives.   3. _____
4. The music is too (*loud, loudly*).   4. _____
5. I felt (*bad, badly*) that I could not attend the meeting.   5. _____

EXERCISE 5 Select the correct word from each pair in parentheses, and write it in the space at the right.

1. There hadn't been (*no, any*) calls for me.   1. _____
2. We received (*good, well*) information from the accountant.   2. _____
3. I am (*sole, solely*) responsible for the incident.   3. _____
4. He (*would, wouldn't*) rarely offer his help to anyone.   4. _____
5. Phillip proofread the report very (*careful, carefully*).   5. _____

EXERCISE 6 Underline any modification errors in the following sentences. Then write your corrections in the spaces at the right. If a sentence is correct, write *OK*.

1. Does this well water taste *peculiarly* to you?   1. _____
2. You are *sure* mistaken about that teacher.   2. _____
3. Eddie is *positive* the best player on the team.   3. _____
4. They haven't had *no* luck in getting people to join their organization. 4. _____
5. They were not badly hurt in the accident.   5. _____

WRITING ACTIVITY Use the following adjectives or adverbs in a sentence. (Answers will vary.)

1. sure   _____
2. bad   _____
3. bitter   _____
4. surely   _____
5. badly   _____
6. excitedly _____

SHORT STORY Find the errors in word use in the following paragraph. Underline the incorrect adverb or adjective. Write the correct form of the word in the blank at the right. If there are no errors, write *OK*.

When the delightfully smell of spring fills the air,   1. _____
I am ready to get out the year catalogs and place my   2. _____
order for beautiful flowering bulbs, heat-tolerantly   3. _____
vegetable seeds, and gorgeous flowering plants.   4. _____
Lucky, I can subdue that urge to order immediately   5. _____
by thinking to only last year. The ads in the catalog were   6. _____
enticing written. I quick ordered lots of things.   7. _____
And guess what? None of those lusciously flowers   8. _____
or tall, bright colored bulbs grew for me. I easy wasted $50. 9. _____

MORE TROUBLEMAKERS

SELECTING THE RIGHT WORD

USE *OTHER* OR *ELSE*!

In many comparisons we use the word *than* with the comparative degree.

> ***This* job is better *than* any *other* I have had.** This job is better *than* all the other jobs I have had.

Use *other* or *else* when comparing one thing with a group of which it is a part. Without *other* or *else*, the sentences have different meanings:

> **She keys faster *than* anyone in our class.** Without *else*, the sentence means that she is *not* in "our class."
>
> **She keys faster *than* anyone *else* in our class.** With *else*, the sentence means she is in the class.
>
> **She keys faster than all the other students in our class.** Without *other*, the sentence means that she is *not* in "our class."

The words *other* and *else* show that the person or thing is being compared *with others of the same group*. Without *other* or *else*, we show that we are comparing someone or something with a person or thing from a *different* group.

CHECKUP 1 Use a caret ($\wedge$), as shown in the first sentence, to show where you should insert the words *other* or *else* in the following sentences. Then write the correct word in the space.

1. Our branch office is larger than any$_\wedge$branch office.
2. Randy is quieter than the boys in his class.
3. There is no one to play the part.
4. She earns a larger salary than anyone in the company.
5. She helps employees more than any manager in the company.

1. <u>other</u>
2. _____
3. _____
4. _____
5. _____

REAL AND REALLY

All of us hear people say "That was a *real* good show" or "Irma just bought a *real* nice coat." *Real* is wrong in such sentences because *real* is an adjective; you should say "*really* good," "*really* nice." Why? Because the adverb *really* is needed to modify the adjectives *good* and *nice*.

> **We *really* wanted your opinion on the debate.** (adverb)
> **The recipe calls for *real* butter.** (adjective)

I FEEL *WELL*

You have already learned that *good* is an adjective and that *well* is an adverb. True—but there is an exception. When referring to health, use *well*, not *good*:

> **Marcy has not felt *well* since the surgery.** (NOT: felt *good*)
> **Hi! How do you feel today? I feel *well*, thank you.** (NOT: I feel *good*)

CHECKUP 2

Underline any incorrect uses of *good/well* or *real/really* in the following sentences. Then write your corrections in the spaces at the right. If a sentence is correct, write *OK*.

1. Matt can speak <u>good</u> on any topic.
2. Gretchen is real excited about your upcoming visit.
3. The electricians worked really hard rewiring the old house.
4. She felt good enough to return to work.
5. We attended a real important meeting with the officers.

1. _well_
2. _____
3. _____
4. _____
5. _____

ADVERBS THAT JOIN

Conjunctive adverbs join two independent clauses. (An independent clause has a subject and a verb and can stand alone as a complete sentence.) Some of these adverbs are *however, therefore, nevertheless, hence, moreover, otherwise,* and *consequently.* When a conjunctive adverb immediately follows the first independent clause, precede it with a semicolon and follow it with a comma.

The seamstress promised to finish by Tuesday; however, she did not. Two independent clauses are joined by the conjunctive adverb *however.* Precede the conjunctive adverb with a semicolon and follow it with a comma.

When these special adverbs are not functioning as conjunctions, they may appear elsewhere in a sentence. When they do, set them off with commas to indicate a pause; do not set them off with commas if a pause is not needed.

Mr. Anderson agreed to pay our airfare; we offered, *therefore*, to pay the registration fee. A semicolon separates the two independent clauses. *Therefore* is not functioning as a conjunctive adverb in this sentence. Two commas separate the adverb *therefore* to indicate a slight pause.

Mr. Anderson agreed to pay our airfare to the convention; we *therefore* offered to pay the registration fee. A semicolon separates the two independent clauses, but no commas separate the adverb *therefore* because it should be read *without a pause.*

The conjunctive adverbs *then* and *thus* usually need no commas.

Muriel has been a member of our department for twenty years; thus it is appropriate for us to host a retirement party. No comma is needed after *thus.*

Many adverbs join independent clauses. Here are some of the more commonly used ones:

accordingly	consequently	likewise	otherwise
nevertheless	furthermore	yet	thus
however	moreover	then	therefore
hence	notwithstanding	besides	also

CHECKUP 3

Decide which conjunctive adverb best replaces the question mark. Write your choice in the space at the right, and be sure to include the necessary punctuation before or after it. (*Note:* More than one answer may be correct.)

1. We didn't sell enough boxes (?) we were not eligible for the award.
2. I didn't study (?) I will probably fail the test.
3. They want to come (?) they have some errands to run first.
4. First, remove the cover (?) add the toner cartridge.
5. Please respond by noon (?) we will select another candidate.

1. _; consequently,_
2. _____
3. _____
4. _____
5. _____

EXERCISES

EXERCISE 1 The words *other* or *else* are missing from these sentences. Use a caret (∧) to show where you should insert the appropriate word. Then write the correct word in the space at the right.

1. Grant has read more books than everyone in the class.
2. Detroit is larger than any city in Michigan.
3. Her phone rings more often than any phone in this office.
4. Jon displays more maturity than any employee.
5. Todd had better grades than anyone in his class.
6. That book sold better than any book on gardening.
7. Paul is more prepared than any lawyer in the firm.
8. I have received more free samples than anyone in the office.
9. Sonja transcribes faster than all the employees in the department.
10. She runs faster than anyone on the team.

1. _____
2. _____
3. _____
4. _____
5. _____
6. _____
7. _____
8. _____
9. _____
10. _____

EXERCISE 2 Underline any incorrect uses of *good/well* or *real/really* in the following sentences. Then write your corrections in the spaces at the right. If a sentence is correct, write *OK*.

1. Whatever Joel does, he does good.
2. Are you real interested in buying the property on Gull Lake?
3. The old mansion held up fairly well.
4. The apples we bought at the orchard were extremely well.
5. Mom always used real butter when she made her Christmas cookies.
6. Bob Meyers is a real good writer of proposals and contracts.
7. This is the real version of the incident.
8. He says he does not feel good today.
9. That was a real nice thing you did for him.
10. I will do the job as good as I can.

1. _____
2. _____
3. _____
4. _____
5. _____
6. _____
7. _____
8. _____
9. _____
10. _____

EXERCISE 3 Decide which conjunctive adverb best replaces the question mark in each of the following sentences. Write your choice in the space at the right, and be sure to include the necessary punctuation before or after it. (*Note:* More than one answer may be correct.)

1. Marla wanted to go skating (?) she was not feeling well.
2. We achieved our goals (?) we celebrated by going out to dinner.
3. First, complete your homework (?) you may play outside.
4. I need an answer by tomorrow (?) I will ask someone else.
5. I researched the company thoroughly (?) I am prepared to interview.
6. We only need four people (?) we decided to hire five.
7. Five of us wished to attend the meeting (?) our manager said only three of us could go.
8. No one on the committee wished to be the chairperson (?) the senior member appointed someone.
9. They finally decided to go (?) it was too late.
10. It was past the deadline when she returned her reservation (?) she did not get a good seat.

1. _____
2. _____
3. _____
4. _____
5. _____
6. _____
7. _____
8. _____
9. _____
10. _____

Underline any errors in the following sentences. Then write your corrections in the spaces at the right. If a sentence is correct, write *OK*.

1. The young children were behaving very bad in the grocery store.   1. _____
2. She played her favorite song soft on the piano.   2. _____
3. The high school soccer team played extremely good today.   3. _____
4. Jan was persistent that she be given a second chance.   4. _____
5. Tim said that he would be able to finish the report easy within the hour. 5. _____
6. You are being irresponsibly with your finances.   6. _____
7. The company made her a real good offer and she accepted it.   7. _____
8. I would feel better if we could discuss this in person.   8. _____
9. They complained very loud to the manager   9. _____
10. He was injured very bad on the job.   10. _____
11. We can complete this task real quickly if we start now.   11. _____
12. It is a concept that is easily understood.   12. _____
13. The class was confident awaiting the results.   13. _____
14. We can complete this task really quick if we start now.   14. _____
15. He behaved so bad that I refuse to watch him anymore.   15. _____

WRITING ACTIVITY Use each of the following conjunctive adverbs in a sentence. Be sure to punctuate the sentences correctly. (Answers will vary.)

1. furthermore   _____
                 _____
2. yet   _____
3. thus   _____
4. therefore   _____
5. accordingly   _____
6. also   _____
7. likewise   _____
8. nevertheless _____
9. hence   _____
10. however   _____

SHORT STORY Underline any incorrect uses of *good/well* or *real/really* in the following paragraph. Then write your corrections in the spaces at the right. Decide which *conjunctive adverb* or which word (*other* or *else*) best replaces the question mark and write your choice in the space at the right. Be sure to include the necessary punctuation before or after the conjunctive adverb. (*Note:* More than one answer may be correct.) If the line is correct, write *OK*.

I was feeling real good about passing the exam   1. _____
that was real hard. I had studied every   2. _____
night (?) I knew the material real well.   3. _____
The instructor said my score was higher than that of 4. _____
any (?) person in class. Was I excited to hear   5. _____
that! My friend, Vicky, did not do good (?)   6. _____
she is real down in the dumps. She said she was   7. _____
not feeling good before the test (?) she would   8. _____
she would have scored higher.   9. _____

PREPOSITIONS, CONJUNCTIONS, AND INTERJECTIONS

UNIT 8 OVERVIEW

The preposition, conjunction, and interjection are three of the eight parts of speech that you will study in this unit. They are important because they give clarity and interest to your writing. Prepositions and conjunctions are connectives that express a relationship or a connection between two things.

A preposition uses nouns and pronouns to create a phrase that is linked to the rest of the sentence by the preposition itself. Prepositional phrases modify nouns, adjectives, and verbs; therefore, they can function as an adjective or an adverb.

Conjunctions are connectors. They connect things of equal grammatical weight such as adverbs and adverbs, adjectives and adjectives, and clauses and clauses. The conjunction helps to provide coherence and transition to the sentence.

An interjection is a word, a phrase, or an exclamation made to express emotion. Most of the time an exclamation mark follows an interjection, such as Wow! Help! Ouch!

UNIT OBJECTIVES

When you complete Unit 8, you will be able to:

■ identify prepositions and prepositional phrases.

■ distinguish between prepositional phrases used as adjectives and those used as adverbs.

■ eliminate repetitious prepositions.

■ recognize prepositional errors.

■ use coordinating and correlative conjunctions appropriately.

■ place conjunctions and punctuation appropriately in sentences.

■ write with parallel structure.

■ use a variety of interjections to show emotions.

PREPOSITIONS AND THE PREPOSITIONAL PHRASE

PREPOSITIONS

Part of Speech Words such as *in* and *to*, *from* and *by*, *around* and *about*, and *between* and *among* are prepositions. The prepositions most frequently used are:

at	by	far	from	in	of	on	to	with

Other prepositions are (see Appendix A for more):

about	above	across	after	against	among	around
before	behind	below	beneath	beside	between	beyond
down	during	except	into	like	near	off
over	past	through	throughout	toward	under	underneath
until	up	upon	within	without		

CHECKUP 1 Underline the prepositions in each of the following sentences. Then write the total number of prepositions in each sentence in the space at the right.

1. Take the pen <u>on</u> my desk, and sign the letter <u>in</u> his folder. 1. _2_____
2. He placed the cord under the carpet, behind the couch, and around the corner. 2. _____
3. We walked over the bridge, down the path, up the hill and saw the animals standing in the field. 3. _____
4. Please return the library books that are on the shelf, under the table, and against the window. 4. _____
5. We sat beside the managers at the company luncheon. 5. _____

PREPOSITIONAL PHRASES

As you've seen, a noun or a pronoun always follows a preposition: "to *Mrs. Smith*," "except *her*," and so on. Together the preposition plus the noun (or pronoun), and sometimes modifiers, make up a phrase—a *prepositional* phrase. Words may modify the noun or pronoun in a prepositional phrase, but the preposition is always the first word in the phrase and the noun (or pronoun) is always the last:

on your desk—*on* is the preposition; the noun *desk* is the object of the preposition; and *your* modifies the noun *desk*.

Prepositional phrases tell us what the relationship is between things or between people. For example, all of the following sentences have the same subject (*report*) and the same verb (*is*), yet each tells us something different about the relationship between *report* and *desk*. How? By using different prepositions.

The report is *on* the desk. *On* tells us the specific relationship.

The report is *under* the desk. Quite different from *on* the desk!

The report is *in* the desk. *In*—not *on*, not *under* the desk.

Beware! When the word *to* is followed by a verb instead of a preposition, it is an infinitive and not a preposition. Infinitive phrases begin with an infinitive—*to sell* cars, *to score* points, and so on.

> **I wanted *to go home* early, but to no avail.** *To go home* is an infinitive phrase; *to no avail* is a prepositional phrase.

CHECKUP 2 Underline the prepositional phrases in the following sentences. Write the noun or pronoun that is the object of each preposition in the space at the right. Then circle any words that modify the objects of the prepositions. One of the prepositional phrases has two objects. Can you find that phrase? If so, circle the number of the sentence.

1. Except for Monday, the manager will be in the office all week. 1. Monday, office _____
2. Guests of the employees were invited to the picnic. 2. _____
3. Between you and me, I plan to take Monday off. 3. _____
4. He talked about the needed hardware today. 4. _____

How Prepositional Phrases Are Used Prepositional phrases can be used as adjectives and adverbs. They can function as a noun when used as the subject of a sentence.

> **From Columbus to Cleveland is about two hours.** *From Columbus to Cleveland* is the subject of the sentence.

Adjectives modify nouns and pronouns—right? So, if a prepositional phrase modifies a noun or a pronoun, you'll know that the phrase is an *adjective* phrase:

> **Most *of the travelers* were flying South.** Since the phrase *of the travelers* modifies the pronoun *most*, it must be an adjective phrase.

Likewise, if a prepositional phrase modifies a verb, an adjective, or another adverb, you'll know the phrase is an *adverb* phrase because adverbs modify verbs, adjectives, and other adverbs.

> **I was working *in the garden*.** The prepositional phrase *in the garden* modifies the verb *was working*, so the phrase must be an adverb phrase.

CHECKUP 3 Underline the prepositional phrases in the following sentences. Then tell whether each phrase works as an adjective or an adverb by writing *ADJ* or *ADV* in the spaces at the right. Some of the sentences may have more than one prepositional phrase.

1. Many of the files from his office were taken to City Hall. 1. ADJ, ADJ, ADV _____
2. We worked on our exercises this morning, without any instruction. 2. _____
3. Two of the attorneys wanted a trial by jury. 3. _____
4. The programmers are working on the system. 4. _____
5. The instructors of our class are highly trained individuals. 5. _____

CHECKUP 4 Use each of the following prepositional phrases correctly in a sentence. (Answers will vary.)

1. in the closet Please put your coat in the closet. _____
2. through the gate _____
3. after the game _____
4. across the room _____
5. under the umbrella _____
6. to his house _____
7. with the group _____
8. into the garage _____
9. upon a time _____
10. around the corner _____

E X E R C I S E S

EXERCISE 1	Underline the prepositional phrases in each of the following sentences. Then write the total number of prepositions in each sentence in the space at the right. (*Remember:* When the word *to* is followed by a verb, it is an infinitive and not a preposition.)

1. The boys played in the yard until supper time.   1. _____
2. Jake worked on the report and organized the files throughout the day.   2. _____
3. Several of the nurses were on call during the night.   3. _____
4. The members of the jury listened to the instructions of the judge.   4. _____
5. You can divide those papers between you and him.   5. _____
6. After reading the policy, Ken signed on the dotted line.   6. _____
7. They decided to build their house over the hill.   7. _____
8. He placed the key under the blankets that were in the drawer.   8. _____
9. They sat beside the man under the tree.   9. _____
10. Don't forget to come into town and park near the office.   10. _____

EXERCISE 2	Underline the prepositional phrases in the following sentences. In the spaces at the right, write the noun or pronoun that is the object of each preposition. (*Note:* Some sentences may have more than one prepositional phrase.)

1. Only one of the executives is in the office.   1. _____
2. Before dinner, he told the good news to his family.   2. _____
3. After lunch it will be too late to go to the store.   3. _____
4. She went to the seminar and sat in the back row.   4. _____
5. In his retirement speech, he spoke highly of the company.   5. _____

EXERCISE 3	Underline the prepositional phrases in the following sentences. Then tell whether each phrase works as a noun, an adjective, or an adverb by writing *N*, *ADJ*, or *ADV* in the spaces at the right.

1. Without her outline, she could not complete her paper.   1. _____
2. Miriam practices the piano for two hours each day.   2. _____
3. Will you choose from the list or on your own?   3. _____
4. By the ocean is the desired location.   4. _____
5. In his speech, he referenced several of our employees.   5. _____
6. She was ready to go to the shopping mall with her friends.   6. _____
7. Several of the managers commented on my test scores.   7. _____

EXERCISE 4	Use each of the following prepositional phrases correctly in a sentence. (Answers will vary.)

1. around the block   _____
2. to the class   _____
3. behind the chair   _____
4. near the house   _____
5. down the hall   _____

Add a prepositional phrase to act as an adjective modifying the nouns or pronouns listed below. (Answers will vary.)

1. computer _____
2. speech _____
3. river _____
4. litter _____
5. clothes _____
6. house _____
7. printer _____

8. conversation _____
9. convention _____
10. boxes _____
11. shelves _____
12. reviews _____
13. everyone _____
14. cabinet _____

EXERCISE 6
Add a prepositional phrase to act as an adverb modifying each of the verbs listed below. (Answers will vary.)

1. leave _____
2. come _____
3. go _____
4. refer _____
5. arrived _____
6. left _____
7. put _____

8. located _____
9. flew _____
10. wrote _____
11. struggled _____
12. swims _____
13. yelled _____
14. jumped _____

WRITING ACTIVITY
Use each of the following prepositions correctly in a sentence. (Answers will vary.)

1. toward _____
2. down _____
3. between _____
4. among _____
5. through _____
6. except _____
7. past _____

SHORT STORY
Underline the prepositional phrases in the following paragraph. In the space at the right, tell whether each phrase works as an adjective or adverb by writing *ADJ* or *ADV*.

For the last five years, we have lived near the river;
however, until this week we did not own a boat.
Before now we did not have time to go boating
during the week, and on weekends we had only
a few hours. One day our neighbor across the street
persuaded us to take advantage of sales
on boats; and we bought a bright, red boat.
Without our neighbor's advice, we would still be
boatless. We stored the boat behind the garage and
under a canopy to protect it from the weather.
I hope to have lots of fun with the boat
during the hot days of summer.

1. _____
2. _____
3. _____
4. _____
5. _____
6. _____
7. _____
8. _____
9. _____
10. _____
11. _____
12. _____

COMMON PREPOSITION ERRORS

WATCH OUT FOR THESE ERRORS!

ONE TOO MANY

Some prepositions, such as *off*, *up*, *out*, *in*, and *on*, can also function as adverbs. (See Avoid Unnecessary Repetitions in Lesson 30.) Do not add adverbs and prepositions where they are not needed. In each of the following word groups, the preposition functioning as an adverb is not necessary.

> **clear *off*   clean *up*   dust *off*   wipe *off*   off *of*   opposite *to*   near *to*   at *about***
> **The cups fell off *of* the table.** *Of* is not needed; omit it.

Other repetitions to avoid are rise up, fill up, finish up, up above, and down under.

AT THE END

In conversations you may hear people using prepositions at the end of a sentence, but in formal writing you should avoid these expressions.

> **Which page did my logo appear on?** Formal writing should read: On which page did my logo appear?

CHECKUP 1

Underline any incorrect uses of prepositions in the following sentences. Then write *omit* if the preposition should be omitted.

1. Where do you want me to carry the lumber <u>to</u>?   1. <u>omit</u>
2. We need to dust off the furniture before company arrives.   2. _____
3. Stop and we will fill up the car with gasoline.   3. _____
4. Where are you going to?   4. _____

BETWEEN YOU AND ME (NOT *I*)

Pronouns that are objects of prepositions must be in the objective case. Objective case pronouns are *me*, *you*, *him*, *her*, *it*, *us*, and *them*.

> I promised to keep the secret *between you* and *me*. (NOT: *between you* and *I*)
> Give the tickets *to Dan* and *them*. (NOT: *to Dan* and *they*)

AMONG/BETWEEN

Use *between* when speaking of two persons or objects, but *among* when speaking of three or more.

> **They split the winnings *between* the two of them.** Only two people are involved.
> **They split the winnings *among* the five of them.** More than two people are involved.

AT/ABOUT

Use either *at* or *about*, but not both words together.

> WRONG! **Amy takes her break at about 10 a.m.** Take out either *at* or *about*.
> RIGHT! **Amy takes her break about 10 a.m.**   OR   **Amy takes her break at 10 a.m.**

CHECKUP 2

Select the correct word and write it in the space at the right.

1. We have enough money (*among*, *between*) the two of us.   1. <u>between</u>
2. Calvin finishes his job (*at*, *about*) 3:30 p.m.   2. _____
3. Jake came with (*I*, *me*) to interview the plant manager.   3. _____
4. If we are (*among*, *between*) friends, we can share secret stories.   4. _____

FROM (NOT OFF OF)

Off of is always wrong. Sometimes *off* is enough, as you saw earlier; other times, the word *from* is really intended.

> **We obtained our news *from* the Internet.** (NOT: *off of* the Internet)

DIFFERENT FROM (NOT DIFFERENT THAN)

Be careful to use *different from* in sentences such as these:

> **This computer is *different from* the one that was demonstrated.** (NOT: *different than*)
> **This invoice number is *different from* the one recorded in the complaint.** (NOT: *different than*)

BESIDE/BESIDES

Beside means "next to"; *besides* means "in addition to." These words should not be used interchangeably.

> **The president sat *beside* the vice president at the meeting.** (*next to* the vice president)
> ***Besides* the plaque, she was also presented with a $5,000 check.** (*in addition to* the plaque)

COMPARE TO/COMPARE WITH

For in-depth comparisons and an analysis of similarities and differences, use *compare with*. For comparisons that are not in-depth or that merely suggest a similarity, use *compare to*.

> ***Compared to* yesterday's sales total, today's are terrific.** A comparison that is not in-depth.
> **As part of her dissertation, Nadine *compared* teaching methodologies of the 1940s *with* those of the 1990s.** An in-depth comparison.

IDENTICAL WITH (NOT TO)

Be sure to use *identical with*, not *identical to*.

> **The dress pattern should be *identical with* the original design.** (NOT: *identical to* the original)

RETROACTIVE TO (NOT FROM)

Use *retroactive to*, not *retroactive from*.

> **Her salary increase was *retroactive to* July 1.** (NOT: *retroactive from* July 1)

SPEAK TO/SPEAK WITH

Use *speak to* to indicate that you're telling something to someone; use *speak with* to indicate that you're discussing something with someone.

> **The supervisor *spoke to* him about us.** The supervisor *told* him something about us.
> **The supervisor *spoke with* the entire staff about the need to avoid spelling errors.** The supervisor *discussed* this important topic with them.

IN REGARD TO (NOT REGARDS)

Be sure to use *in regard to*, *with regard to*, or *regarding*.

> **I am calling *in regard to* the ad in the newspaper.** (NOT: *in regards to*)

CHECKUP 3 Underline any incorrect uses of prepositions in the following sentences. Write your corrections in the spaces. If a sentence is correct, write *OK*.

1. Compared <u>with</u> yesterday's weather, today is great.   1. <u>to</u>
2. Your edited copy is different from the one I have.   2. _____
3. Merit pay was retroactive from January 1.   3. _____
4. Raymond wanted to borrow a book off of Ms. Towers.   4. _____
5. Her method of teaching is different than his.   5. _____

Name _____   Date _____   Score _____

EXERCISES

EXERCISE 1   Underline any incorrect uses of pronouns or prepositions in the following sentences. Then write your corrections in the spaces at the right. Write *omit* if the preposition should be omitted.

1. Who am I supposed to give the present to?   1. _____
2. Among you and me, I am not prepared for the test.   2. _____
3. The bonus will be split between you, Rick, and me.   3. _____
4. We could not help from wondering who would be chosen.   4. _____
5. Who did Pamela give the medical report to?   5. _____
6. I really don't know where she is at.   6. _____
7. You may take a copy of my report off of the desk.   7. _____
8. Please divide the work among the two of you.   8. _____
9. Have you seen where Jason went to?   9. _____
10. Divide this work between you and he.   10. _____

EXERCISE 2   Select the correct word from each pair in parentheses, and write it in the space at the right.

1. We should (*have, of*) offered to cook dinner.   1. _____
2. It was arranged that the president would sit (*beside, besides*) the philanthropist.   2. _____
3. His version is different (*than, from*) her version.   3. _____
4. The winnings were shared (*among, between*) the five team members.   4. _____
5. I plan to split the profits between you and (*I, me*).   5. _____
6. I would like to speak (*to, with*) you about your lateness.   6. _____
7. The salary increases will be retroactive (*to, from*) last month.   7. _____

EXERCISE 3   Underline any incorrect uses of pronouns or prepositions in the following sentences. Then write your corrections in the spaces at the right. If a sentence is correct, write *OK*.

1. Another employee beside me will be attending the banquet.   1. _____
2. Ask if your salary increase will be retroactive from the first of the year.   2. _____
3. The parents spoke with their child regarding the incident.   3. _____
4. At the reception, John was standing besides Mr. Nolan.   4. _____
5. Between all of us, we should be able to find a solution.   5. _____

EXERCISE 4   Decide if each italicized word is functioning as an adverb or a preposition. (*Remember:* An adverb tells how, when, or where. A preposition shows the relationship between its object and another word in a sentence.) Write *ADV* or *PREP* in the spaces at the right.

1. Will wants to walk *to* the game tonight.   1. _____
2. We had the freedom to move *about*.   2. _____
3. We should know the result *before* noon today.   3. _____
4. After she came *to*, she recognized her parents.   4. _____
5. The Purchasing Department orders supplies *from* DeNoyer Office Supplies.   5. _____

EXERCISE 5   In the spaces provided, complete each sentence by writing a prepositional phrase to modify the italicized word. Remember to include a period in your answer. (Answers will vary.)

1. Please give your *quiz*
2. Give the *certificates*
3. The funds will be *split*
4. Here are the *results*
5. Put the *reports*

1. _____
2. _____
3. _____
4. _____
5. _____

EXERCISE 6   Rewrite the following sentences so the preposition is either used correctly or omitted. (Answers will vary.)

1. Whom are you talking *to*?
2. We couldn't find the boxes that these came *in*.
3. Tell me where you are *at*.
4. When will you finish *up* the project?
5. Where did you see her *at*?

1. _____
2. _____
3. _____
4. _____
5. _____

WRITING ACTIVITY   Use each of the following prepositional phrases in a sentence. (Answers will vary.)

1. for me
2. to the library
3. below the counter
4. between you and me
5. across the street
6. to the group
7. for the day
8. without help
9. near Mr. Wright
10. up the hill
11. except him
12. around the corner
13. within the hour
14. off the deck
15. against the wall

_____
_____
_____
_____
_____
_____
_____
_____
_____
_____
_____
_____
_____
_____
_____

SHORT STORY   Underscore any incorrect uses of pronouns or prepositions in the following paragraph. Write the correct word in the blank at the right. If a word should be omitted, write *omit*. If the line is correct, write *OK*.

Roads are interesting. A country road is different than
a super highway. Some wind through hills and towns;
others skirt the cities and head straight on to someplace.
When you travel on a road, do you sometimes wonder
where is it going to? Beside seeing wild flowers
growing near to the side of the road, maybe you can
catch a glimpse of a deer or fox crossing a field at about
sunset. These are scenes you probably cannot see
in the city; only a trip on a road can offer you nature
at its best. Between you and I, compared with
city driving, I want the country.

1. _____
2. _____
3. _____
4. _____
5. _____
6. _____
7. _____
8. _____
9. _____
10. _____
11. _____

LESSON 34 — CONJUNCTIONS ARE JOINERS!

WHAT DO THEY JOIN?

Part of Speech *Verb* *Noun*

Conjunctions are words that *join*. (Use the word *junction*—a place where two roads join—to remind you that the conjunctions *join*). This lesson covers two kinds of conjunctions—coordinating conjunctions and correlative conjunctions.

COORDINATING CONJUNCTIONS

The seven coordinating conjunctions are *and*, *but*, *or*, *nor*, *yet*, *for*, and *so*. Coordinating conjunctions join two or more of the same grammatical things, such as adjectives with adjectives, adverbs with adverbs, and sentences with sentences. Conjunctions can join words, phrases, or clauses of equal rank.

conjunction

Two or more words:

> **assistants, managers, *and* supervisors** (nouns)
>
> **you, her, *or* me** (pronouns)
>
> **Joanne, Jay, *or* him** (Conjunctions treat nouns and pronouns as the same thing.)
>
> **quick *but* cautious** (adjectives)

Two or more phrases:

> **The job involves proofreading manuscripts, editing documents, *and* revising reports.** (gerund phrases)
>
> **Our manager challenged us to greet the new employees, to visit each department, *and* to call everyone by name.** (infinitive phrases)

Two or more clauses:

> **The track meet was scheduled for today, *but* it was postponed.** (two independent clauses)

Here's a chart to help you decide which coordinating conjunction to use:

USE	FOR	EXAMPLE
and	addition	Tom and Mary will go.
but	contrast	He is fast but sloppy.
or	choice	We can stay or leave.
nor	opposite	I didn't call, nor has he called.

CHECKUP 1

Underline twice the conjunction in each sentence, and write it in the space at the right. Then underline once the items that the conjunction joins.

1. <u>Dan</u> <u>and</u> <u>Jon</u> are the managers of the store.
2. The speaker was witty and charming.
3. You can ask the programmers or the engineers.
4. The fabric was attractive but expensive.
5. Hamburgers and sodas will be provided.

1. _and_____
2. _____
3. _____
4. _____
5. _____

Conjunctions are missing from the following sentences. Use a caret (∧) to show where you should insert each conjunction. Then write the appropriate conjunction in the space at the right. The first one has been done for you.

1. The shoes were comfortable∧not attractive.

2. James Brian are graduating this week.

3. During our lunch hour, we wanted to run to walk.

4. The test was difficult short.

5. Please give this letter to Mr. Baxter his secretary.

1. <u>but</u>

2. _____

3. _____

4. _____

5. _____

CORRELATIVE CONJUNCTIONS

Correlative conjunctions are used in pairs, but once again, they join the same things. Common pairs of correlative conjunctions are *both/and, either/or, neither/nor, not only/but also,* and *whether/or.*

both quickly **and** accurately   *both/and* join two adverbs

judge **either** words **or** actions   *either/or* join two nouns

neither tall **nor** short   *neither/nor* join two adjectives

not only Mary **but also** him   *not only/but also* join a noun and a pronoun

whether under the current **or** over the dam   *whether/or* joins two prepositional phrases

Sometimes *also* is omitted in *not only/but also.* For example:

Not only was Marta late, but she had forgotten to bring the lunch.

Careful! Subjects joined by conjunctions should not cause any problems in verb choice—*if you are careful!*

Either the manager or her assistants have the disk. *Have* is plural to agree with the subject closer to it, *assistants.* (*Her assistants have.*)

Either her assistants or the manager has the key. *Has* is singular to agree with the subject closer to it—*manager.* (*Manager has.*)

Conjunctions are missing from the following sentences. Use a caret (∧) to show where you should insert each conjunction. Then write the appropriate conjunction in the space at the right.

1. Either you∧your partner needs to find the solution.

2. Not only Brian his assistant are gone for the afternoon.

3. The play was neither interesting entertaining.

4. We are not only going shopping going to lunch.

5. We didn't know whether to stop continue driving.

6. See if either Jack Linda is on vacation next week.

7. Not only Jan Mary will be given an award.

1. <u>or</u>

2. _____

3. _____

4. _____

5. _____

6. _____

7. _____

LESSON 34

Name _____   Date _____   Score _____

EXERCISES

EXERCISE 1 Underline twice the conjunction in each of the following sentences, and write it in the space at the right. Then underline once the items that the conjunction joins.

1. Lynn and Jon are planning to visit us.
2. Bob was offered a raise and a promotion.
3. Chris is shy but friendly.
4. You can play basketball or softball.
5. You and he will conduct the presentation.
6. The house was beautiful but expensive.
7. The supervisor or the trainer will help you.
8. We can either go to the zoo or to the beach.
9. Dan or Leslie will return the books to the library.
10. Both Dan and Leslie will return the books to the library.

1. _____
2. _____
3. _____
4. _____
5. _____
6. _____
7. _____
8. _____
9. _____
10. _____

EXERCISE 2 Each of the following sentences needs a pair of conjunctions—but one of the pair is missing from each sentence. Use a caret (∧) to show where the missing conjunction belongs; then write it in the space provided.

1. Either Jan Pat will be promoted.
2. I have neither seen heard from Ramon.
3. We will not only borrow your van fill it with gas.
4. Michael had not decided whether to get a job to start work on a master's degree.
5. Jimmy plans either to work full time to attend school at night.

1. _____
2. _____
3. _____
4. _____
5. _____

EXERCISE 3 Conjunctions are missing from the following sentences. Use a (∧) to show where you should insert each conjunction. Then write the appropriate conjunction in the space at the right.

1. Training is important, it is also long.
2. Martha helped Christy Robin complete the project.
3. The inventor of the new stain remover was not only wealthy friendly.
4. We had planned to go dancing, now we are too tired.
5. Jim Martin is a professor his wife is a surgeon.
6. Winning is good, it isn't everything.
7. Do this assignment pay the consequences.
8. Copying a disk copying a file are not the same thing.
9. Do the work go home.
10. Ordering food eating it at home is fun.

1. _____
2. _____
3. _____
4. _____
5. _____
6. _____
7. _____
8. _____
9. _____
10. _____

Complete the following sentences by adding an appropriate conjunction and a second related group of words. Include the punctuation at the end of each sentence. (Answers will vary.)

1. It was late already, _____
2. Our manager asked people to work overtime, _____
3. We wanted to go to the zoo, _____
4. She wrote her book report, _____
5. The supervisor reviews your performance _____
6. You may stay if you want to, _____
7. He is not home now, _____
8. He can neither stay here tonight _____
9. The assignment will be given to you _____
10. Take either the bus _____

WRITING ACTIVITY Use each of the following conjunctions correctly in a sentence. (Answers will vary.)

1. yet _____
2. for _____
3. so _____
4. whether/or _____
5. not only/but also _____

6. both/and _____
7. both/and _____
8. not only/but also _____
9. so _____
10. whether/or _____
11. neither/nor _____

SHORT STORY Conjunctions are missing in the following paragraph. Use a caret (∧) to show where you should insert each conjunction. Then write the appropriate conjunction in the space at the right. If the line does not need a conjunction, write *OK*. (Answers will vary.)

Do you give quality time to yourself? By this I mean,   1. _____

you take time to read fun things to sleep when you   2. _____

wish. Not only do you choose the time to read to   3. _____

sleep, you determine how much time each   4. _____

activity will take. Perhaps taking a walk watching   5. _____

the birds is more your style. You a friend might   6. _____

sit talk for hours at a time. Both you your friend could   7. _____

swap stories that are both silly crazy. You could choose   8. _____

either an indoor activity an outdoor activity each day of   9. _____

the year. Wouldn't that be fun?   10. _____

COMMON CONJUNCTION ERRORS

AVOID THESE ERRORS

NONPARALLEL FORM

Conjunctions should join items of *like*, or *parallel*, form—two or more nouns, two or more infinitive phrases, two or more dependent clauses, and so on. Avoid construction that is not parallel.

The long pass was thrown *hard* and *with accuracy*. The conjunction *and* joins an adverb (*hard*) to a prepositional phrase (*with accuracy*). Unparallel form.

The long pass was thrown *hard* and *accurately*. Now *and* joins two adverbs—*hard* and *accurately*. This sentence is in parallel form.

It is usually quite simple to make sure that conjunctions join the same things.

The contract was *illegible, lengthy*, and *it is awkward*. *Illegible* and *lengthy*, both adjectives, are joined to *it is awkward*, a simple sentence. Unparallel form.

The contract was *illegible, lengthy*, and *awkward*. Now three adjectives are joined. Much better! This sentence is in parallel form.

These kinds of errors are also often made when pairs of conjunctions are used:

***Either* the clerk delays the materials *or* ships them immediately.** Look at what follows the conjunctions *either* and *or. Clerk* (noun) and *ships* (verb) are not like items—they are not parallel.

The clerk *either* delays the materials *or* ships them immediately. *Either* and *or* are now followed by the same things—verbs! The sentence is in parallel form.

CHECKUP 1 Underline the words that make the sentence unparallel. Correct the sentence so that it is parallel. Write your answer in the space. (Answers will vary.)

1. Either see Jeff or Dawn when you are through working.
2. Mark created, planned, and will implement the strategy.
3. Neither she studies nor listens in class.
4. I agree to discuss neither the terms nor reveal the amount.
5. The radiologist studied the X ray carefully and with competence.

1. See either
2. _____
3. _____
4. _____
5. _____

RUN-ON SENTENCES AND COMMA SPLICES

Learn to use conjunctions correctly to avoid two common sentence errors—the run-on sentence and the comma splice.

Dr. Pesce is retiring we will have a party for him. This is a *run-on sentence*. Two independent clauses run together. A comma and a conjunction should be used between the two clauses.

Dr. Pesce is retiring, we will have a party for him. This is a *comma splice*. The comma should be followed by a coordinating conjunction.

You can correct run-on sentences and comma splices by inserting a semicolon; by inserting a comma and a coordinating conjunction; or by forming two sentences, each beginning with a capital letter and ending with a period. The sentences below are written correctly:

Dr. Pesce is retiring; we will have a party for him. A semicolon joins the two independent clauses.

Dr. Pesce is retiring, *and* we will have a party for him. A comma and a coordinating conjunction join the two independent clauses.

Dr. Pesce is retiring. We will have a party for him. Two separate sentences have been formed.

Indicate whether each of the following groups of words is a sentence with a comma splice, a run-on sentence, or a correct sentence. Write *comma splice*, *run-on*, or *OK* in the space provided.

1. I completed that project I am now starting a new one.   1. _run-on_____
2. We saw the movie last night, it was very interesting.   2. _____
3. Some of us are taking a vacation; we're leaving July 1.   3. _____
4. This is a serious problem, I want and need your help.   4. _____

THAT (NOT *BECAUSE*, *WHY*, OR *WHERE*)

People often incorrectly use *because* and *where* instead of *that* to introduce clauses.

> **The reason is *that* the playing field is too wet for the game.** (correct)
>
> **The reason is *because* the playing field is too wet.** (incorrect)

It is also incorrect to use *why*.

> **The reason *why* is because the playing field is too wet for the game.** (incorrect)

Do not use *where* in place of *that*.

> **I heard *that* you won.** (NOT: I heard *where* you won.)

BECAUSE, SINCE, OR AS (NOT *BEING THAT*)

Never use *being that*. Use *because*, *since*, or *as*.

> ***Because* Ike moved, his address changed.** (NOT: *Being that* Ike moved, his address changed.)

AS I SAID (NOT *LIKE I SAID*)

In business writing and speaking, avoid the expression "like I said." *Like* is a preposition, and a prepositional phrase does not have a verb in it—remember? Use the word *as* instead.

> ***As you said*, I was happy.** (correct)
>
> ***Like you said*, I was happy.** (incorrect—*You said* is a clause because it has a subject (*you*) and a verb (*said*). *Like* is a preposition, and a preposition cannot introduce clauses.)

INTRODUCE A CLAUSE WITH *UNLESS* (NOT *WITHOUT* OR *EXCEPT*)

The words *without* and *except* are prepositions, similar to the word *like*. They should be used to introduce prepositional phrases, not clauses. Use *unless* instead.

> **Rollie will go *unless* I sign the form.** (NOT: Rollie will go *without* I sign the form.)

TRY TO (NOT *TRY AND*)

Try to (plus a verb) forms an infinitive phrase. (An infinitive is the form of the verb preceded by *to*.) Do not use *try and*.

> **Please *try to be* on time for your meeting.** (NOT: Please *try and be* on time for your meeting.)

EXERCISES

EXERCISE 1 Each sentence below has unparallel construction or form. Underline the words that make the sentence unparallel. Correct the sentence so that it is parallel. Write your answer in the space provided. In some cases, tell what word(s) you are omitting. (Answers will vary.)

1. Our physician enjoyed tennis, golf, and playing volleyball.   1. _____
2. Jack edits the reports and has to key them on the computer.   2. _____
3. We were responsible not only for raising the funds but also to distribute them.   3. _____
4. Working in teams is more beneficial than to work alone.   4. _____
5. Today we plan to hike and go swimming.   5. _____

EXERCISE 2 Underline the incorrect words in the following sentences. Then write your corrections in the spaces at the right. If the sentence is correct, write *OK*.

1. The reason I went to London is because I wanted to see Windsor Castle.   1. _____
2. Being that you are here, please help your sister.   2. _____
3. Before you leave tonight, check and see that all the doors are locked.   3. _____
4. I will not go to the picnic except she goes also.   4. _____
5. Will you try and finish by noon?   5. _____

EXERCISE 3 In each of the following sentences, identify the error by writing *run-on* or *comma splice*. Then rewrite the run-on sentences by adding a comma and a conjunction. Rewrite the comma splice sentences by adding a conjunction after the comma. (Answers will vary.)

1. We were tired we wanted to go home.

_____

2. She had no training, she figured out the problem.

_____

3. Last year's model car sold for $15,000 this year's model sells for $18,000.

_____

4. The students wanted to learn, they were willing to study hard.

_____

5. They bought the computer they bought the printer too.

_____

EXERCISE 4 Correct each of the following sentences three different ways: (1) Use a period and a capital letter, (2) use a semicolon, and (3) use a comma and a conjunction.

1. We have plans to sell our home in Indiana we are hoping to buy a condo in Florida.

_____

_____

2. The auditors canceled yesterday's meeting they rescheduled it for Thursday.

_____

_____

3. He is a hard worker he always helps others.

_____

_____

_____

4. Call the repairperson the copier is broken.

_____

_____

_____

EXERCISE 5 Each of the following sentences contains an error in the choice of words or in the placement of conjunctions. Underline the errors, and write the corrections in the spaces at the right. You may add or delete words. (Answers will vary.)

1. Try and beat our prices.   1. _____

2. Like he said, they will not have the time to work on the project.   2. _____

3. Being that it is now 5 p.m., let's go home.   3. _____

4. I read where our company is doing well this year.   4. _____

5. The staff is not only pleasant but they are also efficient.   5. _____

WRITING ACTIVITY Write a sentence using each of the following words. (Answers will vary.)

1. that (to introduce a clause)

_____

2. try to

_____

3. as I said

_____

4. reading, writing, and computing

_____

5. unless

_____

SHORT STORY Underline the errors you find in the following paragraph and write the correct word in the space at the right. If a punctuation mark or word has been left out, insert a caret (∧) where the punctuation or word belongs; then write the correct punctuation or word in the space at the right. If the line has no errors, write *OK*.

The wind has been blowing hard I don't recall   1. _____

a time where the wind has blown for so many   2. _____

days. Like I said, wind usually doesn't blow   3. _____

constantly at this time of year. I even asked   4. _____

the weather people to check and see what their   5. _____

records show. They reported the high winds   6. _____

are not unusual, I don't believe   7. _____

them. Being that I am outside every day, I   8. _____

observe weather. I think the reason why the   9. _____

weather people are wrong is because they stay   10. _____

inside buildings to try and record the weather data.   11. _____

LESSON 36 INTERJECTIONS

WHAT IS AN INTERJECTION?

Part of Speech

An interjection is a word, a phrase, or an exclamation (such as *Wow*, *Ouch*, *Egads*, and *Help*) used to get attention or to express emotion or surprise. Usually, but not always, the interjection is separated from the sentence.

INTERJECTIONS AND PUNCTUATION

When an interjection expresses a strong emotion, punctuate it with an exclamation mark.

> *Great!* **Now we're lost.** A word is used as an interjection.
>
> *Oh, no!* **My lunch is gone.** A phrase is used as an interjection.
>
> *Eureka!* **We found a buyer for our house.** *Eureka* (an exclamation) is an interjection. It shows strong emotion and must be punctuated with an exclamation mark.
>
> *Help!* **I can't shut off the water faucet.** *Help* is an interjection. It shows strong emotion and must be punctuated with an exclamation mark.

CHECKUP 1

Underline the interjections in the following sentences. Then write the interjection and its punctuation mark in the space at the right.

1. <u>Hurrah</u> Summer is coming.
2. Gee whiz Why didn't Eric tell you he is a musician.
3. Voilà Nic put on a suit and looked so handsome.
4. Three cheers Our team will go to the state meet.
5. Good I knew you could do it!

1. <u>Hurrah!</u>
2. _____
3. _____
4. _____
5. _____

Did you notice in the examples so far that the interjection does not have grammatical ties to the sentence? This is true of interjections whether they precede a sentence or follow a sentence.

> **You have been selected as one of two people to run for office. Congratulations!** Notice in this sentence that the interjection, *Congratulations!*, appears after the sentence and is independent of the sentence.

However, sometimes an interjection *is* tied to a sentence. When it is, follow it with a comma. Punctuate the sentence with an exclamation point or a period.

> **Great, we found our way out!**
>
> **Oh, so that's what he meant.**

CHECKUP 2

Underline the interjection in each of the following sentences. Then write the interjection and the appropriate punctuation in the blank at the right.

1. We are holding the winning ticket. <u>Yes Yes</u>
2. There is mud all over my new shoes. Ugh
3. What a party. Wow
4. I finally created a brochure using desktop publishing. Yippee
5. Oh I guess you were right after all.

1. <u>Yes, Yes! *or* Yes! Yes!</u>
2. _____
3. _____
4. _____
5. _____

USING INTERJECTIONS

Interjections are best expressed orally where the emotions can be heard by others. They add a little bit of "flavor" to the words we use. In casual, informal writing, interjections let the reader know the strength of our emotions by the word or phrase we choose to use. However, in formal business writing, we would avoid the use of the interjection.

We are so pleased that your division has the best sales record for this quarter.

In the above example of business writing, the reader knows people are pleased with the performance of the division. The idea has been conveyed through a professional business writing style. We would not say,

***Yippee!* Your division has the best sales record this quarter.**

CHECKUP 3

Underline the interjection in the following sentences. Then at the space at the right, write the interjection and the appropriate mark of punctuation.

1. <u>Well</u> If you won't do the work, then who will do it?
2. Go team go. Rah-rah
3. Oh, no You didn't put bleach in the water.
4. They finally settled their year-long dispute. Amen
5. I can't find my bus pass. Help
6. The plane will take off finally from Gate No. 21. Hurrah

1. <u>Well!</u>
2. _____
3. _____
4. _____
5. _____
6. _____

CHECKUP 4

Write three sentences for each of the following interjections. Place the interjection at the beginning of one of the sentences, tie it to another of the sentences, and place it at the end of one of the sentences. Punctuate correctly. (Answers will vary.)

1. Wow

_____
_____
_____

2. Great

_____
_____
_____

3. Oh, no

_____
_____
_____

4. Egads

_____
_____
_____

5. Eureka

_____
_____
_____

Name   Date   Score

EXERCISES

EXERCISE 1 Decide whether an interjection is used in the following sentence. If the sentence contains an interjection, write *Yes* in the space at the right. If there is no interjection used, write *No* in the space at the right.

1. Golly! Derick deserves a better break than that.   1. _____
2. Read the documentation first.   2. _____
3. Phew! It is hot today.   3. _____
4. When I asked for a new car, my father had one response for me. No!   4. _____
5. We publish catalogs in the summer and in the winter.   5. _____
6. Why do we have to attend every one of the lectures?   6. _____
7. Well! Why am I the last one to know?   7. _____
8. Oops! I guess I was not supposed to tell that story.   8. _____
9. Why in the world can't I balance my checkbook?   9. _____
10. Oh, so that's the way to do it.   10. _____

EXERCISE 2 Underline the interjection used in each of the following sentences. Then write the interjection and the appropriate punctuation in the space at the right.

1. He is sure to see the dent in the car. Woe is me   1. _____
2. Whoops I spilled the juice on the floor.   2. _____
3. By jingo Iris's cake won a blue ribbon at the county fair.   3. _____
4. The sound from the crowd came as one word. Bravo   4. _____
5. Oh, fiddlesticks Just plan to stay overnight at my home.   5. _____
6. My word I have not heard that expression in years.   6. _____
7. Alas What else can I do to help you feel better?   7. _____
8. Egads What do you mean you won't take your test for your driver's license?   8. _____
9. Ouch I have a stiff neck.   9. _____
10. Phooey I just can't keep my eyes open any longer.   10. _____

EXERCISE 3 Write an appropriate interjection to precede each sentence. Provide the appropriate punctuation. (Answers will vary.)

1. You want me to be the lead singer.   1. _____
2. I can't believe you could think of sleeping over 8 hours.   2. _____
3. Did you see how much she packed in that suitcase?   3. _____
4. He hit the ball clear over the left field fence.   4. _____
5. Forgive me for not offering you a cup of coffee right away.   5. _____
6. I can't get up.   6. _____
7. You are the recipient of a $1,000 scholarship.   7. _____
8. We are taking a cruise to the Bahamas this summer.   8. _____
9. Where did I put those keys?   9. _____
10. Mr. Orvela said my resumé was impressive.   10. _____

Write an appropriate interjection to follow each sentence. Provide the appropriate punctuation. (Answers will vary.)

1. My boss gave me an excellent rating in all categories.
2. The coat I have been wanting to buy is discounted 75 percent.
3. Ted didn't have a single error in his 100-page report.
4. Although I was late in arriving at the ticket office, I was able to buy the tickets.
5. Don't shout so loudly.

1. _____
2. _____
3. _____
4. _____
5. _____

EXERCISE 5

Write a sentence using each one of the following interjections. Remember to punctuate correctly. (Answers will vary.)

1. Oops! _____
2. Help! _____
3. Ouch! _____
4. Oh, no! _____
5. Well! _____
6. Hurrah! _____
7. Heavens! _____
8. Wow! _____
9. Yeah! _____
10. Phew! _____

WRITING ACTIVITY

Write a sentence for each interjection. (Answers will vary.)

1. No! _____
2. Voilà! _____
3. Congratulations! _____
4. Hurrah! _____
5. Yes! _____
6. Well! _____
7. My word! _____
8. Hey! _____
9. Yeah! _____
10. Stop! _____

SHORT STORY

Insert an appropriate interjection wherever you see (?) in the paragraph. Write the interjection and the correct punctuation in the blank at the right. (Answers will vary.)

Moths, spiders, caterpillars. (?) You can see all
these critters at dusk. (?) Join the Prairie People
for a hike. (?) We need silence as we meander through
the fields soaking in nature. (?) Maybe we'll see a
giant moth caught in a delicate spider's web. (?)
But don't squash a caterpillar as you gaze. (?)
(?) We hike even if it rains. Only a limited number of
people may register. (?) Call us for more details.

1. _____
2. _____
3. _____
4. _____
5. _____
6. _____
7. _____
8. _____

UNIT 9

CLAUSES AND PHRASES

UNIT 9 OVERVIEW

In this unit you will study clauses and phrases. Phrases and dependent clauses are very much the same; they are not sentences. However, clauses contain a subject and a verb; phrases do not. Our style in writing is developed through the use of dependent clauses, phrases, and words that modify. You will see several examples of how the placement of these items can alter the meaning of sentences. After practicing how to use clauses and phrases to add clarity to your writing, you will learn the importance of writing with parallel structure; that is, writing with a grammatical pattern that maintains consistency among elements in the sentence. After completing Unit 9, you will have many tools at your disposal to make your writing interesting and to give it clarity for the benefit of your reader.

UNIT OBJECTIVES

When you complete Unit 9, you will be able to:

- recognize an infinitive phrase.

- recognize a participial phrase.

- recognize a gerund phrase.

- demonstrate ability to use independent and dependent clauses.

- use subordinate conjunctions to link clauses.

- distinguish among clauses used as nouns, as adjectives, or as adverbs.

- write with parallel structure.

LESSON 37 PHRASES

WHAT IS A PHRASE?

A phrase is a group of related words that does not have a subject and a verb. There are prepositional phrases, infinitive phrases, participial phrases, and gerund phrases. Look at the following prepositional phrase:

to the supervisor There is no verb in this prepositional phrase. *Supervisor* is the object of the preposition *to*.

If a phrase introduces a sentence, follow it with a comma. If a phrase functions as the subject of a sentence, do not follow it with a comma. Set off nonessential phrases with commas.

PREPOSITIONAL PHRASES

Prepositional phrases, like all other phrases, have no subject or verb. Remember, prepositional phrases can be used as nouns, adverbs, or adjectives.

***Under the oak tree* is where I'll be.** The prepositional phrase is used as a noun—subject of the verb *is*.

The woman *with the attache case* is his wife. The prepositional phrase is used as an adjective modifying *woman*.

We will shovel sand *into the wheelbarrow*. The prepositional phrase is used as an adverb—shovel where? *Into the wheelbarrow.*

INFINITIVE PHRASES

To run, to walk, to sit, and *to stand* are infinitives. An *infinitive* is the word *to* plus a verb. An *infinitive phrase* consists of an infinitive and any modifiers it may have. Infinitive phrases can function as nouns, adjectives, and adverbs.

My goal is *to move to the city by winter*. The infinitive *to move* starts the phrase *to move to the city by winter*. This phrase functions as a predicate noun. Note that the complete infinitive phrase includes two prepositional phrases—*to the city* and *by winter*—which modify the infinitive *to move*. Be careful—do not confuse the infinitive in the infinitive phrase with the verb in the sentence.

Beware! Do not confuse an infinitive phrase with a simple prepositional phrase starting with the preposition *to*. Prepositional phrases do not have verbs—*to the park, to my home, to the dog, to the game.* Infinitive phrases have verbs—*to use the computer, to write memos, to dine together.*

CHECKUP 1

Underline the infinitive phrase in each sentence. Write just the infinitive in the space at the right.

1. He wants <u>to plan a cookout</u>.
2. She likes to walk one mile each day.
3. They will show everyone how to fix the printers.
4. Do you have any ideas about how to solve this problem?
5. You said you like to take walks.

1. <u>to plan</u>
2. _____
3. _____
4. _____
5. _____

PARTICIPIAL PHRASES

Remember participles? A participle is a verb part. Words such as *walking* and *running* are present participles. The past participles for these words are *walked* and *ran*. Let's see how phrases that begin with present participles or past participles can be used as adjectives:

> ***Running to the bus stop, Ms. Pulaski caught the 7:15 on time.*** Do you see how *running to the bus stop* describes *Ms. Pulaski*? Because it describes a noun, this phrase works as an adjective. *Running* is a present participle.

> **The accounting records, *inspected by several auditors*, were judged to be accurate.** The phrase *inspected by several auditors* describes *the accounting records*. This phrase works as an adjective. *Inspected* is a past participle.

Beware! To avoid confusion, be sure that when a participial phrase begins a sentence, it is followed by a word that it can logically modify.

> CONFUSING: **Stepping down from the curb, my shoe was splashed with mud.** *Stepping down from the curb* is a participial phrase that introduces the sentence. The phrase is followed by the word *shoe*. However, the shoe was not stepping down from the curb, so the participial phrase cannot logically modify *shoe*.

> CORRECT: **Stepping down from the curb, *I* splashed my shoes with mud.** *I* was stepping down from the curb, so it is logical for the participial phrase to modify *I*. *I* should follow the phrase.

CHECKUP 2 Underline the participial phrase in each of the following sentences. Then write the participle in the space at the right.

1. <u>Emphasizing grammar</u>, the English class was offered to all.　　1. <u>Emphasizing</u>
2. Motivated by the speaker, Ann decided to improve her skills.　　2. _____
3. Persuaded by his parents, Norman applied for admission.　　3. _____
4. Wanting to be a doctor, Julie studies hard throughout college.　　4. _____
5. Given the circumstances, Ellen acted wisely.　　5. _____

GERUND PHRASES

A gerund is a verb form ending in *-ing* that is used as a noun. A gerund phrase consists of a gerund and its modifiers.

> ***Having dinner ready by 6 p.m.* is difficult.** *Having dinner ready by 6 p.m.* acts as a noun—the subject of the sentence. You can substitute a pronoun for this phrase: *It* is difficult.

> **My favorite task at work is *assembling those report figures*.** *Assembling those report figures* acts as a predicate noun. Can you replace the *-ing* phrase *assembling those report figures* with a pronoun? Yes: My favorite task is *this*. Therefore, the *-ing* phrase *assembling those report figures* functions as a noun.

How can you tell the difference between a participial phrase using the present participle (ends in *-ing*) and a gerund phrase? By its function within the sentence. If it functions as an adjective, it is a participial phrase; if it functions as a noun, it is a gerund phrase.

CHECKUP 3 Underline the *-ing* phrase in each of the following sentences. For each *-ing* phrase that works as an adjective, write the word that the phrase modifies. For each *-ing* phrase that works as a noun, write the verb for that noun.

1. <u>Serving his country</u> was an honor.　　1. <u>was</u>
2. Making 32 points was his outstanding achievement.　　2. _____
3. Traveling throughout the West, Donald saw beautiful scenes.　　3. _____
4. Riding horses is her favorite activity.　　4. _____
5. Writing a poem utilizes a person's creativity.　　5. _____

Name   Date   Score

EXERCISES

EXERCISE 1   Underline the infinitive phrase in each of the following sentences. Then write just the infinitive in the space at the right. (*Caution:* Watch for *to* used as a preposition!) Some sentences may have two infinitive phrases. Others may have none—write *none* if this is the case.

1. Are you sure you want to invest that much money in stocks?   1. _____
2. Jill offered to help our family move.   2. _____
3. The surgeon was asked to operate on the patient immediately.   3. _____
4. Please give the report to Ms. Crenshaw before you leave the office.   4. _____
5. We want to save $50 each month.   5. _____
6. What time do you plan to leave tomorrow?   6. _____
7. The women wanted to play bridge; the men wanted to play dominoes.   7. _____

EXERCISE 2   Underline the participial phrase in each of the following sentences. Then write the word that it modifies in the space at the right.

1. Serving on the committee, Jane learned much about local issues.   1. _____
2. Hurrying to catch the bus, Robert fell.   2. _____
3. Reviewing her schedule, Martinez realized she had a test today.   3. _____
4. Walking through the woods, we saw several squirrels.   4. _____
5. Pretending to listen, Hank just kept nodding his head.   5. _____
6. Influenced by her teacher, Mai Ling decided to attend college.   6. _____
7. Earning a college education, Joel had reached his goal.   7. _____
8. Dressed for the part, she applied for the librarian's job.   8. _____

EXERCISE 3   Underline the gerund phrase in each of the following sentences. Then write the verb for that phrase in the space provided.

1. The counselor advises sending applications for financial aid early.   1. _____
2. Flattering the supervisor will not impress anyone.   2. _____
3. Studying the material is the only way you will pass.   3. _____
4. Working for this company requires a college degree.   4. _____
5. Learning about computers challenges Marie.   5. _____
6. Providing children with clothing is very expensive.   6. _____
7. Earning a college education was his main goal.   7. _____
8. Proofreading the manuscript proved easier than she had expected.   8. _____
9. Managing the office demonstrated his leadership style.   9. _____
10. Receiving recognition embarrasses Ken.   10. _____

Underline the infinitive, participial, and gerund phrases in the following sentences. In the space at the right, identify the phrase as an infinitive, a participial, or a gerund phrase.

1. The group decided to meet at the restaurant.   1. _____
2. Faxing the information took a long time.   2. _____
3. Organizing her day, Lucy scheduled her meeting.   3. _____
4. Grabbing her purse, Marcy rushed to the hospital.   4. _____
5. Revising the manual became her top priority.   5. _____
6. Where did you want me to put these items?   6. _____
7. Introducing the employees is first on the agenda.   7. _____
8. Hungry for homemade pie, Jill asked her mom to bake her one.   8. _____
9. Jo asked his employees to submit new ideas.   9. _____
10. Arguing with your parents is not a good idea.   10. _____

EXERCISE 5 Use each phrase given below as the beginning of a sentence. Complete the sentence in your own words, adding punctuation as necessary. (Answers will vary.)

1. Traveling around the world   _____
2. Left in charge of the children   _____
3. Rejecting the proposal   _____
4. Leaving in a hurry   _____
5. Buying a home   _____
6. Preparing for midterms   _____
7. Planning the budget   _____
8. Eliminating other factors   _____

WRITING ACTIVITY Write a sentence using the gerund, participial, or infinitive phrase. (Answers will vary.)

1. to fax the report   _____
2. using charts   _____
3. planning a budget   _____
4. washing the dishes   _____
5. distracted by the noise   _____
6. to rewrite your paper   _____

SHORT STORY Insert an appropriate phrase (infinitive, participial, or gerund) in the (?) parentheses. In the space at the right, write your phrase. Add punctuation if necessary. (Answers will vary.)

Judy asked Fred to complete a project. (?) Fred   1. _____
accepted the challenge. (?) became his first task   2. _____
to complete. Then, (?) was the next task.   3. _____
However, Fred realized he only had one day (?)   4. _____
the work. (?) he asked Judy for an extra day   5. _____
(?) the project. Judy agreed (?). After two days,   6. _____
Fred completed the project.

CLAUSES

TYPES OF CLAUSES

A clause is a group of words containing a subject and a predicate.

INDEPENDENT AND DEPENDENT CLAUSES

Clauses that can stand alone are called *independent clauses;* clauses that do not express a complete thought and cannot stand alone are called *dependent clauses.*

Independent clauses are simple sentences.

An independent clause can function by itself.

A dependent clause cannot function by itself.

Dependent clauses and phrases need to be attached to independent clauses in order to function.

> **Because the grass is tall** is a clause. It has a subject (*grass*) and a predicate (*is*) but does not express a complete thought. It is dependent; it is not a sentence.
>
> **The grass is tall.** This clause can stand alone. It is independent.

Both examples are clauses, yet they are different. What makes one a sentence and the other not a sentence? The answer is the word *because.* The word *because* makes us expect more. It is a conjunction. Its purpose is to join one clause with another clause.

> **Because the grass is tall, you will need to adjust the height of the lawn mower.** Here the clause, *because the grass is tall*, is connected to another clause—*you will need to adjust the height of the lawn mower.* Without that other clause, the *because* clause is incomplete. It is not a sentence. It cannot stand alone. It is a dependent clause. The *because* clause needs help. It needs an independent clause to which it can connect to complete its meaning.

Subordinating Conjunctions Independent clauses are also called main clauses. Dependent clauses are also called subordinate clauses because they are subordinated to an independent clause. *Subordinate conjunctions* connect dependent clauses to independent clauses to form sentences. Listed below are some of the common subordinating conjunctions:

after	although	as	as if	because	before
for	how	if	once	since	so
so that	than	that	though	till	unless
when	whenever	where	whereas	whether	while

Whenever you see these subordinating conjunctions, you will know that they introduce *dependent* clauses.

Beware! A dependent clause does not always appear at the beginning of a sentence.

> **He was tired *after they met for eight hours.*** The dependent clause is used at the end of the sentence, so no punctuation is needed.

Decide if the following groups of words are independent, that is, if they are sentences. If so, write *S* in the space. If not, write *NS* for *no sentence*.

1. Since we were invited.
2. No, we haven't had a chance to see the demonstration yet.
3. Before you leave for work.

1. <u>NS</u>
2. _____
3. _____

Now, underline the dependent clause in each of the following sentences. In the space at the right, write the subordinating conjunction.

4. We were exhausted <u>after we returned from a camping weekend</u>.
5. I will be glad to help you before you take your test.
6. You need training before you can do that job.

4. <u>after</u>
5. _____
6. _____

NOUN CLAUSES

Clauses function in different ways. They can function as nouns, as adjectives, or as adverbs. A clause functions as a noun when it serves as the subject of a sentence, as the object of a verb, and so on.

> **Meg said that *we should all agree.*** Meg said what? *That we should all agree. That we should all agree* is the object of the verb *said*.

> ***That he chose Donna to chair the committee* is a good sign.** *That he chose Donna to chair the committee* is the subject. The verb is *is*.

For an easy way to test whether a clause is a noun clause, just try to replace the clause with a pronoun. Because a noun can be replaced by a pronoun, a noun clause can also be replaced by a pronoun.

> ***This* is a good sign.** The pronoun *this* can replace the noun clause *that he chose Donna to chair the committee*.

ADJECTIVE CLAUSES

Adjective clauses describe—they modify nouns or pronouns. Frequently, adjective clauses begin with the relative pronouns *who, whom, whose, which,* and *that*.

> **Bobby, *who has been with the company for three years,* is our new director**. The clause *who has been with the company for three years* is used as an adjective. It modifies the noun *Bobby*. The clause has its own subject (*who*) and its own verb (*has been*).

ADVERB CLAUSES

Like adverbs, adverb clauses modify verbs, adjectives, and other adverbs. The clause is joined to the word it modifies by a subordinating conjunction, such as *after, although, because,* and *while*.

> **We'll work on that newsletter *when we have time*.** Let's work on that newsletter when? *When we have time.* This adverb clause modifies the verb *work*.

> **They were pleased *although they didn't show it*.** The adverb clause *although they didn't show it* modifies the adjective *pleased*.

Underline the dependent clauses in the following sentences. Then in the spaces at the right identify each dependent clause as a noun clause (*N*), an adjective clause (*ADJ*), or an adverb clause (*ADV*).

1. They hired someone <u>who has several years of experience</u>.
2. Pat said that we should all go to the conference.
3. My assignment, which is due tomorrow, is very difficult.
4. Jason worked on the project when he had time.

1. <u>ADJ</u>
2. _____
3. _____
4. _____

EXERCISES

EXERCISE 1   Decide if the following groups of words are *independent*—that is, if they are sentences. If so, write *S* for each sentence in the space at the right. If the words form a dependent clause, write *NS* for *no sentence.*

1. We'll be free to leave after we finish the work.   1. _____
2. Whenever we have all of the votes.   2. _____
3. Because they had signed the document.   3. _____
4. After the play, we will go to dinner.   4. _____
5. While the medical staff was meeting.   5. _____
6. When you finish your tests.   6. _____
7. Until I hear from my accountant, I will not comment on the case.   7. _____

EXERCISE 2   Underline the dependent clause in each of the following sentences. In the space at the right, write the relative pronoun or the subordinating conjunction that joins the dependent clause to an independent clause.

1. I gave the project to someone else since you did not want it.   1. _____
2. Send me a copy of the list when you have completed it.   2. _____
3. Lisa, who graduated with honors, will attend a private college.   3. _____
4. These are the projects that you researched for us.   4. _____
5. We appreciate the help that you gave our friends.   5. _____
6. I do not know where you left your jacket.   6. _____

EXERCISE 3   Underline the dependent clause in each of the following sentences. Then in the spaces at the right identify each dependent clause as a noun clause (*N*), an adjective clause (*ADJ*), or an adverb clause (*ADV*).

1. Projects that sell well come from the United States.   1. _____
2. Has he told you what the new policy is?   2. _____
3. We are positive that our team had the best scores.   3. _____
4. Please ship that box, which contains the copy paper they ordered. 4. _____
5. He said that the new location will be on Main Street.   5. _____
6. Friends who are like Jean are wonderful.   6. _____
7. Ray played the piano better than Linda did.   7. _____
8. Cars that are very reliable are listed in this consumer newsletter.   8. _____
9. You will be assigned a job unless you volunteer.   9. _____
10. The student, although new to the area, gets along well with others.   10. _____
11. Once you have been here one year, you can apply for promotions.   11. _____
12. Ms. Grossinger manages people much better than Mr. Howard does.   12. _____
13. Call me when you have the financial statements complete.   13. _____
14. Jane, whose test scores are high, will do well in school.   14. _____
15. James stated that he will retire in one year.   15. _____

Each of the following sentences contains an incomplete clause. The first word of each clause is in italics. Complete each clause by writing your answer on the rule provided. Do not add any punctuation. The type of clause required is indicated in parentheses at the end of each sentence. (Answers will vary.)

1. *Who* _____ is a secret at this time. (noun)
2. The reason she received a raise is *that* _____. (noun)
3. We want a new teacher *because* _____. (adverb)
4. Mr. Jones, *who* _____, will be attending the wedding. (adjective)
5. The man, *whom* _____, is the president of the company. (adjective)
6. The vase, *which* _____, is kept in the living room. (adjective)

EXERCISE 5

Use each of the following dependent clauses in a sentence. (Answers will vary.)

1. After I eat lunch, _____
2. Before you answer, _____
3. Because you set goals, _____
4. While you were out, _____
5. If you need help, _____
6. Since you have been gone, _____
7. Although sales have increased, _____
8. While you were consulting with Mr. Porter, _____
9. When you purchased the equipment, _____
10. Because we need additional information, _____
11. Whenever you decide to leave, _____
12. Unless they hear from you today, _____
13. Before a deadline is set, _____
14. Until sales improve, _____

WRITING ACTIVITY

Complete the sentence by adding a dependent noun clause, adjective clause, or adverb clause as indicated. (Answers will vary.)

1. Noun — Jake said _____
2. Adjective — They chose someone _____
3. Adverb — She praises her students more _____
4. Noun — _____ is not always the truth.
5. Adjective — Please give me the box _____

SHORT STORY

Underline any incorrect usage of relative pronouns and subordinating conjunctions you can find in the following paragraph. Write the correct relative pronoun or subordinating conjunction in the space at the right. If the line contains no errors, write *OK*. (Answers will vary.)

Jane, which is my friend, said that a new store is
opening downtown. She read in the paper when
Mr. Bass would be the new owner. Mr. Bass, whom
is a local businessman, is also my neighbor. Being that
I know him well, I asked him about his store. He said what
he was excited about his new venture. I wished him well
and said which I would be in his store again.

1. _____
2. _____
3. _____
4. _____
5. _____
6. _____
7. _____

MISPLACED MODIFIERS AND DANGLING PARTICIPLES

WATCH OUT FOR THESE ERRORS

MISPLACED MODIFIERS

A modifier is misplaced when it modifies the wrong word or phrase in a sentence. A misplaced modifier can be a word, a phrase, or a clause.

Misplaced Words In the following examples, can you see how the placement of one word can dramatically change the meaning of the sentence? You need to be very careful in placing the modifier in the correct position to convey the message you want.

> **Margaret can use *only* mail merge.** Margaret cannot use any other part of the program; she only knows how to use the mail merge.
>
> ***Only* Margaret can use mail merge.** Margaret and no one else is allowed to use the mail merge.

Misplaced Phrases When phrases function as modifiers, place them close to the word they modify.

> ***In a split second*, he had packed his suitcase to follow the circus.** It took him just a split second to pack his suitcase.
>
> **He had packed his suitcase to follow the circus *in a split second*.** He could pack his bags in a split second, but he could not follow the circus in only a split second.

CHECKUP 1 Underline any misplaced words or phrases and use a caret (∧) to show where they should be placed. (You need not show any necessary changes in capitalization or punctuation.)

1. She has <u>only</u> one daughter∧.
2. The supervisor asked Geraldine to write the report twice.
3. Everyone almost elected blue for the team color.
4. Several of the callers asked for red women's dresses.

Misplaced Clauses Clauses also should be placed close to the words they modify. Be careful where you place clauses beginning with the word *that*. Review the following examples:

> **We saw a diamond in the window of a store *that weighed 4 carats*.** What weighed *4 carats*? The *store*? No, the diamond weighed 4 carats. The sentence can be written correctly several ways:
>
> **We saw a diamond *that weighed 4 carats* in the window of a store.**

Or:

> **We saw in the window of a store a diamond *that weighed 4 carats*.** (Notice that the *that* clause is not set off with commas.)

You must also be careful where you place clauses beginning with the word *which:*

> **The calculator has small numerals, *which we had ordered*.** Placing the *which* clause after the word *numerals* incorrectly implies that the numerals were ordered instead of the calculator.
>
> **The calculator, *which we had ordered*, has small numerals.** Here the *which* clause correctly modifies *calculator* as the item that was ordered. *Note:* The *which* clause is set off with commas.

A *that clause* provides information that is essential to the message and *should not* be set off with commas; a *which clause* provides extra information to the message and *should* be set off with commas.

Underline any misplaced clauses in the following sentences. Use a caret (∧) to show where you should insert each misplaced clause. (You need not show any necessary changes in capitalization or punctuation.)

1. Put your clothes∧in the laundry room <u>that need to be washed</u>.
2. Carl ran five miles daily to stay fit wearing a sweat suit.
3. The meeting will be tomorrow that is about the budget.

Replace the question mark in each of the following sentences with either *which* or *that*. Then write the correct word in the space at the right. Use a caret (∧) to indicate where any comma may be needed.

4. There are many CD players from which to choose.
   The mode (?) we recommend is HiFi.   4. _____
5. The reunion (?) we will attend is scheduled for this weekend. 5. _____
6. The car (?) has been for sale was stolen.   6. _____

BEWARE OF DANGLING PARTICIPLES

A participial phrase (see Lesson 37) that begins a sentence should be placed close to the noun or pronoun it modifies. The phrase also must logically agree with the subject of the sentence as the doer of the action expressed by the phrase. The phrase "dangles" if it does not logically agree with the subject of the sentence, or if it is not placed near the word it modifies. To correct a dangling participle, rewrite the sentence to include the correct subject or to place it next to the noun or pronoun it modifies.

> ***Entering the room*, the class gave Dr. Smith a standing ovation.** The subject of the sentence, *class*, is not logically the doer of the action expressed by the introductory participial phrase, *Entering the room.* Logically, *who* would be entering the room? Is the word that identifies *who is entering the room* missing or too far removed from the phrase? Determine who would logically be doing the action expressed in the introductory participial phrase. Then rewrite the sentence to correct the dangling participle.
>
> ***Entering the room*, Dr. Smith received a standing ovation.**

Here is another example:

> ***Having been caught in the rain*, the umbrella was opened by Jane.** The subject of the sentence, *umbrella*, is not logically the doer of the action expressed by the introductory participial phrase *Having been caught in the rain.* Is the correct subject missing or too far removed from the phrase? Determine who or what is the doer of the action expressed by the introductory participial phrase; then rewrite the sentence to correct the dangling participle:
>
> ***Having been caught in the rain*, Jane opened her umbrella.** Now it is logical that the subject of the sentence, Jane, is the doer of the action expressed by the participial phrase.

Rewrite each of the following sentences to correct the dangling modifiers.

1. Carrying a tray of food, Danny's toe caught on the wire.
   <u>Carrying a tray of food, Danny caught his toe on the wire.</u>

2. Lost in the move, we had a box of photographs.

   _____

3. While swatting the wasp, my car went off the road.

   _____

When you look over your writing, always check for any "lost" or 'misplaced" modifiers. Place them close to the words they modify.

EXERCISES

EXERCISE 1 Rewrite each of the following sentences to correct the dangling modifiers.

1. Excited about the trip, my favorite shirt was not packed.

   _____

2. Having been delayed at the airport, the meeting had already begun when we arrived.

   _____

3. Stating his objection, the ceremony was stopped by him.

   _____

4. Running in the hallway, the door hit him.

   _____

5. Frightened by the storm, the blanket was grabbed by her.

   _____

EXERCISE 2 Decide which sentence in each pair shows the correct placement of modifiers, and write the letter of your choice in the space at the right.

1. a. To ensure confidentiality, names were not asked by the supervisor.   1. _____
   b. To ensure confidentiality, the supervisor did not ask names.
2. a. Without proper identification, the license cannot be issued to her.   2. _____
   b. Without proper identification, she cannot be issued a license.
3. a. While I was working on the terminal, the whole system went down.   3. _____
   b. While working on the terminal, it went down by the whole system.
4. a. During the test, the commotion in the hallway broke her concentration.   4. _____
   b. During the test, her concentration was broken by the commotion in the hallway.
5. a. After hearing the appeal, the judge overturned the conviction.   5. _____
   b. After hearing the appeal, the conviction was overturned by the judge.

EXERCISE 3 Each of the following sentences contains dangling modifiers and misplaced words, phrases, or clauses. Rewrite each sentence correctly in the space provided. Be sure to place the modifier as close as possible to the word it modifies. (Answers will vary.)

1. While reading the paper, an article on dogs was found.

   _____

2. The director has been with the company for thirty years will be retiring soon.

   _____

3. Leaving the room, the teacher asked me why I was leaving.

   _____

4. To find the keys, your steps need to be retraced.

   _____

5. Jogging around the park, a squirrel ran in front of me.

   _____

Combine the two sentences in each pair below by using the italicized words in one sentence as a modifier in the other. See the example below. (Answers will vary.)

0. Darlene worked late in the office. She was *editing a manuscript*.
   Editing a manuscript, Darlene worked late in the office.

1. Michael finds the class interesting. He is *listening very closely*.

2. Our teacher uses visual aids to help us understand the concepts. She is *teaching us science*.

3. She understands the author's view. She is *reading the story*.

4. She was *answering the phone*. She let the file fall to the floor.

WRITING ACTIVITY Rewrite the following sentences to correct the dangling modifiers.

1. Sally asked the teacher to help her twice.

2. He is asking a question simply.

3. Running in the hall, his knee was scraped.

4. Startled by the noise, his drink was spilled.

SHORT STORY Underline the dangling participles, and the misplaced words, phrases, or clauses. Rewrite the paragraph to show your corrections. Insert the appropriate punctuation.

Feeling tired, Hank's eyes closed. He was sleeping only for ten minutes when the storm hit. The thunder was extremely loud which rumbled through the sky. Frightened by the noise, the windows were shut by Hank. The rain quickly formed puddles in the yard that was heavy. Hank waited for the storm to end patiently. The fierce storm lasted 15 minutes merely. Delighted to see the sun, the windows were opened again by Hank. Still feeling tired, his eyes closed.

LESSON 40 PARALLEL STRUCTURE

CORRECT PARALLEL STRUCTURE

Parallel structure means that sentence elements are alike in function and in construction. Let's study the following parallel examples:

Subjects:	**men and women were** (NOT: females and men were)
Verbs:	**The highway crew *diverted* cars and *started* construction.**
Infinitives:	**Nicki wants *to shop* and *to eat* dinner at the mall.**
Direct objects:	**The president wanted *a new building* and *a new associate.***
Indirect objects:	**We will buy *him* and *her* each a pen and pencil set.**
Objects of prepositions:	**The coordinator met *with the chef* and *with the baker.***
Adjectives:	***Beautiful* roses and *fragrant* carnations adorned the church.**
Adverbs:	**The landscaper worked *efficiently and competently.***
Phrases:	**The writer looked *on the desk, in the files,* and *in the basket.***
Dependent clauses:	**Call *as you leave work* and *when you get home.***
Independent clauses:	***The driver delivered merchandise to the south side in the morning,* and *he delivered merchandise to the north side in the afternoon.***

CHECKUP 1   Underline the elements in each of the following sentences that should be alike in function and in construction. In the space at the right, indicate whether these elements are used as subjects, verbs, adjectives, adverbs, or objects.

1. I <u>evaluated</u> the situation, <u>located</u> the problem, and <u>presented</u> the solution.
   1. <u>verbs</u>
2. The defense attorney and the prosecuting attorney were called into the judge's chamber.
   2. _____
3. He presented his case passionately and effectively to the jury.
   3. _____
4. The well-written and well-organized procedures manual helped the hospital interns.
   4. _____
5. Amy wanted the red dress and the blue shirt.
   5. _____

WITH CONJUNCTIONS

Conjunctions must be followed by sentence elements of equal rank. Correlative conjunctions—*either/or, neither/nor, not only/but also, whether/or*—should be followed by parallel structure. When *either* is followed by a noun, *or* must be followed by a noun. When *not only* is followed by a verb, *but also* must be followed by a verb. If *neither* is followed by an adjective, then *nor* must be followed by an adjective. Balance nouns with nouns, verbs with verbs, adjectives with adjectives, and so on.

Either the dog *or* the cat may have the bowl of milk. (subjects)

The twins will *neither* write *nor* call. (verbs)

I plan to enter *either* the derby *or* the ice-contest event. (objects)

When *not only* is followed by an infinitive phrase, *but also* must be followed by an infinitive phrase.

She asked *not only* to write the report, *but also* to key it.

IN OUTLINES, LISTS, AND DISPLAYED ENUMERATIONS

Parallelism is especially important in outlines, lists, and displayed enumerations.

OUTLINE:

I.   Kinds of Sentences According to Form
   A.   Simple
   B.   Compound
   C.   Complex
   D.   Compound-complex
II. Kinds of Sentences According to Function
   A.   Declarative
   B.   Interrogative
   C.   Imperative
   D.   Exclamatory

The outline is parallel. The items in roman numerals *I* and *II* are parallel with each other, and each of the subdivisions (*A* through *D*) is parallel with one another.

LIST:	ENUMERATIONS:
Divide the writing process into three steps:	The three elements of effective writing are
Preparing the project	1. Clarity
Researching the subject	2. Conciseness
Organizing the material	3. Courtesy

Both of these lists are parallel. Each item in the first list begins with the present participle of a verb. Each item in the second list is a noun, and all the items in the list are enumerated.

FAULTY PARALLEL STRUCTURE

Faulty parallelism occurs when joined items do not have equal grammatical form. Note the faulty parallelism in the following example.

> **His work in the garden included digging, using the rake, and to plant the seeds.** This is faulty parallelism; *digging* and *using* are present progressive tense and *to plant* is an infinitive.

To make parallel construction clear, repeat an article, a preposition, an infinitive, or a pronoun.

Article:	**We had *a* letter and *a* telegram.**
Preposition:	**Send the letter *to* Mark and *to* David.**
Infinitive:	**She wanted us *to read* and *to critique*.**
Pronoun:	***My* father or *my* mother will take the message.**

CHECKUP 2

In the space at the right, write the word or words that would make each of the following sentences parallel. Use a caret (∧) to show where the missing word should be inserted.

1. It is his privilege to drive and ∧ vote.   1. <u>to</u>
2. Those reports go to the managers in Accounting and Sales.   2. _____
3. Our workshop folders included a pencil, note pad, and an evaluation sheet.   3. _____
4. Do I give this to the manager or director?   4. _____

E X E R C I S E S

EXERCISE 1 In the space at the right, indicate whether the italicized parallel elements are used as subjects, verbs, adjectives, adverbs, direct objects, infinitives, indirect objects, or phrases.

1. The car was *sporty, fast,* and *expensive.*   1. _____
2. I gave *Jane* and *Paul* our new address.   2. _____
3. *Sue* and *I* have been selected for jury duty.   3. _____
4. He *washed* and *waxed* his new car.   4. _____
5. The path goes *down the mountain, around the bend,* and *up the next hill.*   5. _____
6. I advised her to prepare the report *quickly* and *accurately.*   6. _____

EXERCISE 2 Rewrite each sentence so that its elements are parallel. (Answers will vary.)

1. He enjoys reading, running, and to play basketball.

_____

2. These lounge chairs are better for beauty, for appearance, and they are comfortable.

_____

3. Her new job promises to be exciting and a challenge.

_____

4. She advised us to listen carefully, to write notes, and be studying for the test.

_____

5. Revising, revising, and to revise again are essential to good writing habits.

_____

6. If you want to succeed, you need to be a hard worker and self-motivated.

_____

7. George should either make one copy or five copies.

_____

8. Not only turn in the worksheets but also the quizzes.

_____

9. My dilemma is whether to complete it now or save it for later.

_____

10. You should neither contact the judge or the lawyer.

_____

EXERCISE 3 Insert or delete words to make the following sentences parallel. Use a caret ($\land$) to show where words should be inserted. Place in parentheses those words that should be deleted. In the spaces at the right, write the inserted or deleted words. If the sentence is correct, write *OK.*

1. Jay stated that he would call and he would write.   1. _____
2. He paid for not only the trip but for our meals.   2. _____
3. They appreciate the overtime pay and health benefits.   3. _____
4. Either read the chapter or you will have to complete the guide.   4. _____
5. You need to clean your room and put away your clothes.   5. _____

EXERCISE 4 ○   Use each of the grammatical elements listed below in a parallel sentence. (Answers will vary.)

1. nouns

_____

2. verbs

_____

3. direct objects

_____

4. indirect objects

_____

5. adjectives

_____

6. adverbs

_____

7. phrases

_____

8. dependent clauses

_____

9. independent clauses

_____

10. objects of prepositions

_____

WRITING ACTIVITY   Insert an appropriate verb, adverb, adjective, subject, or object in place of the (?) parentheses to make the following sentences parallel. Identify the part of speech you have inserted. Place your answers in the space at the right. (Answers will vary.)

1. The boy (?) a mile, (?) basketball, and (?) in the pool.   1. _____

2. (?) and (?) were invited to attend the wedding.   2. _____

3. He spoke (?) but (?) to the class.   3. _____

4. Her house is (?) and (?).   4. _____

5. He owns a (?) and a (?).   5. _____

SHORT STORY   Underline any faulty parallelism in the following paragraph. Write the correct word or phrase in the space at the right. Where a caret (∧) appears, insert the correct word for parallel structure. Write that word in the space at the right. If the line is correct, write *OK*.

Wendy enjoys walking, reading, and to play the piano.   1. _____

On the weekend, she walks to the park and the library   2. _____

with her friend, Mary. Mary is older, taller, and   3. _____

heavy than Wendy. Talking on the phone,   4. _____

writing notes in class, and to do activities together   5. _____

are a few ways the girls enjoy their friendship. They   6. _____

not only are best friends, but neighbors.   7. _____

PUNCTUATION

UNIT 10 OVERVIEW

Punctuation marks, such as periods, commas, dashes, and colons, signal us as readers to stop, pause, hesitate, or anticipate what is to come. While we may think of these marks as unimportant symbols to use with the written word, we need to recognize that punctuation marks can change the meaning of our words or emphasize or de-emphasize a thought. Punctuation marks are as important as words in conveying a thought. Without them our writing would be confusing or without interest to the reader. Learn the different marks of punctuation and what each one contributes to a message, so you will use them effectively in your writing.

UNIT OBJECTIVES

When you complete Unit 10, you will be able to:

■ correctly identify and use 12 marks of punctuation: question mark, exclamation point, hyphen, comma, semicolon, colon, dash, parentheses, brackets, quotation marks, underscore, and apostrophe.

■ punctuate dependent and independent clauses.

■ use the comma to set off parenthetical elements.

■ distinguish between essential and nonessential appositives.

PERIODS, QUESTION MARKS, EXCLAMATION POINTS, AND HYPHENS

USING PERIODS, QUESTION MARKS, EXCLAMATION POINTS, AND HYPHENS

THE PERIOD

Use a period at the end of a declarative sentence.

You may cast your vote by mail or in person.

Use a period at the end of an imperative command.

Read your e-mail messages frequently.

Use a period after an indirect question.

Our council members asked why a four-lane road is necessary.

THE QUESTION MARK

Direct questions end in question marks, not periods.

How long do you expect to be gone from the office?

Use a question mark to indicate a question within a sentence.

We can come late to the meeting, *can't we***?**

Some sentences sound like questions but are really polite requests or commands. Use periods, not question marks, at the end of such sentences.

Will you please prepare the materials for me. This is not really a question. It's a command—a polite request.

THE EXCLAMATION POINT

In business and formal writing, very few sentences end in exclamation points. Most sentences end in periods; a few will end in question marks. However, use an exclamation point after a word, phrase, clause, or sentence to express strong feelings or emotions.

Your presentation was terrific!   **Wow! What a presentation!**

CHECKUP 1   Insert a period, a question mark, or an exclamation point at the end of each sentence. In the spaces provided, write the names of the punctuation marks.

1. Ken asked Mark to help him with the problem.   1. <u>period</u>
2. Does anyone know where the Curry files are   2. _____
3. Please show Mr. Smith our new system   3. _____
4. That's fantastic, Julie   4. _____

OTHER USES OF PERIODS

Many abbreviations are written with periods, but there are probably as many written *without* periods.

a.m.	Ph.D.	gal	L (for *liter*)	Mrs.	Sr.	lb	km (for *kilometer*)
p.m.	Rev.	qt	cm (for *centimeter*)	Ms.	Esq.	yd	g (for *gram*)
c.o.d.	f.o.b.	pt	m (for *meter*)	Ave.	St.	Blvd.	Apt.
Mr.	Jr.	oz	mm (for *millimeter*)	Jan.	Feb.	Aug.	Sept.

In the list above, note that no extra space is used within abbreviations such as *c.o.d.* and *f.o.b.* because they would be harder to read with extra space. Also note that abbreviations of units of measure, such as pound (*lb*) and centimeter (*cm*), are written without periods. Do not add *s* to their abbreviations to form their plurals; 3 gal (NOT: gal*s*), 4 cm (NOT: cm*s*). In letters and memos, the full words are spelled out; the abbreviations are generally used in tables and in business forms.

Abbreviations in all-capital letters are usually written without periods.

CPA (for certified public accountant)   **WYSIWYG (for what you see is what you get)**
OCR (for optical character recognition)   **MIS (for management information system)**
LAN (for local area network)   **MIPS (for millions of instructions per second)**
UN (for United Nations)   **DTP (for desktop publishing)**

Another use of periods is after initials:

Russell *J.* Hosler, Jr.   **Mr. and Mrs. John *P.* Roland**   **J. O'Connell**

Periods are also used with amounts of money, with percentages, and with decimals.

The price of the oak desk is $325.99.   **Ann was 96.5 percent right.**

OTHER USES OF QUESTION MARKS AND EXCLAMATION POINTS

Question marks and exclamation points, too, can be used elsewhere; their positions are not limited to the ends of sentences.

He gave the supervisor (or was it the manager?) the itemized list of recommendations. Only the clause in parentheses is a question. Thus the question mark goes inside the parentheses.

Please ask Dr. Taylor—isn't she your department chair?—to approve this request.

Where shall we meet for lunch? McDonald's? Repeat the question mark after each question.

Remind her to send the report to our office in Madison, Wisconsin (not Madison, Kansas!). Only the clause within parentheses is an exclamation, so it gets the exclamation point (not the entire sentence).

Not even the principal—imagine!—has the authority to approve your request.

THE HYPHEN

Use the hyphen in compound words, in numbers, and in fractions.

Jules visited his *mother-in-law* on Thursday.
The Browns were celebrating their *forty-third* anniversary.
Over *two-thirds* of the audience agreed with the presenter.

Beware! Most compound adjectives that begin with *well* or *self* are hyphenated whether they precede or follow the noun—*well-adjusted, well-spoken, self-made, self-taught,* and so forth.

Name   Date   Score

EXERCISES

EXERCISE 1   Decide whether a period, a question mark, or an exclamation point belongs at the end of each of the following sentences. Insert the missing punctuation mark in the sentence. In the space provided, write the name of the punctuation mark.

1. Please proofread the contract for the attorney   1. _____
2. What's the difference between Model X and Model Y   2. _____
3. For heaven's sake, stop it right now   3. _____
4. If we finish our work by 3 p.m., may we leave   4. _____
5. Carrie is very interested in math and science   5. _____
6. Congratulations on receiving the Outstanding Nurse Award   6. _____
7. Do you know what you are doing   7. _____

EXERCISE 2   Decide where periods are necessary in the following sentences. Insert the missing periods where they belong, and circle them. In the space at the right, indicate the total number of periods you used in each sentence.

1. Address the letter to Ms R J Smith and family   1. _____
2. Myra received her DDS degree from Michigan State University   2. _____
3. He is Mr B K Noble, Sr and that is his partner   3. _____
4. We ordered nameplates for everyone   4. _____
5. I need to set the alarm for 7 am   5. _____
6. Ms Hilary requested that we send her mail to the following address for Sept and Oct: 204 S Second St, St Paul, MN 55102   6. _____
7. I was surprised to receive a cod package from Mr Hattington   7. _____
8. Rev J T Arnold has a PhD in Theology from St Mary's   8. _____
9. I think Mrs Karingada will be here by 9:15 am   9. _____
10. Send this package cod   10. _____

EXERCISE 3   Decide where question marks and exclamation points are necessary in the following sentences. Insert the missing marks where they belong. In the spaces at the right, indicate the total number of question marks and exclamation points you used in each sentence.

1. Yes We won $5,000 in cash and prizes   1. _____
2. Give this to Mr. Black—isn't he your manager—for him to review.   2. _____
3. William gave the surgeon (or was it the oncologist) the x-rays.   3. _____
4. Wow Look at these diamonds   4. _____
5. Did you see the game last night   5. _____
6. When will you be able to start work on the project for Ms. Okuda   6. _____
7. Fantastic You did it   7. _____
8. Oh, yes We guarantee all our products for one year.   8. _____
9. Won't you at least stay for dinner   9. _____
10. Hey, will you watch where you're going   10. _____

Insert hyphens where necessary in the following sentences. Write the hyphenated words in the spaces provided. If no hyphen is required, write *OK*.

1. Our office is on the twenty second floor.
2. Over two thirds of the class passed the test.
3. Glenn's itinerary was up to date.
4. This is their thirty eighth anniversary.
5. Her comment was made off the record.
6. One half of the members disagreed with the new rule.
7. She is well prepared.
8. The artist's portrait was hanging in the ten story museum.
9. We recommended that a well balanced decision be made.
10. Three fourths of his employees receive monthly bonuses.

1. _____
2. _____
3. _____
4. _____
5. _____
6. _____
7. _____
8. _____
9. _____
10. _____

WRITING ACTIVITY Write a sentence using the word or the phrase given. Provide the correct punctuation in each sentence. (Answers will vary.)

1. mother-in-law _____
2. well-known _____
3. a.m. _____
4. Wow _____
5. LAN _____
6. hot-tempered _____
7. old-fashioned _____
8. why _____
9. Oh, no _____
10. CPA _____

SHORT STORY Decide where a period, a question mark, a hyphen, or an exclamation point belongs in each sentence. Insert the missing punctuation mark, and circle it. In the space provided, write the name of the punctuation mark. Some lines may have more than one punctuation mark.

R Lucy and J Matt went to the park, and they

took their dogs with them You are probably wondering

to yourself, "Why would they take their dogs to a park"

Well, the park is near a large lake The dogs love

the water Lucy would yell, "Go fetch" to her dog

and then Matt would shout "Go get it boy" to his dog

They so enjoyed watching their dogs run and play

Lucy and Matt are well known for their love of animals

1. _____
2. _____
3. _____
4. _____
5. _____
6. _____
7. _____
8. _____

COMMAS: CLAUSES, SERIES, AND INTRODUCTORY ELEMENTS

USING COMMAS

Commas are frequently used in writing—and for good reason. Without them, our writing would be uninteresting, or, sometimes, confusing.

Jesse collects stamps. Jesse receives stamp catalogs. He can order limited edition stamps.

Each sentence above is technically correct. But, with commas the sentences could have been reworded as follows.

Because Jesse is a stamp collector, he receives catalogs from which he can order limited edition stamps.

Of course, it isn't always desirable to write one long sentence instead of three shorter ones, but when it is, you'll need commas.

COMMAS JOIN INDEPENDENT CLAUSES

Independent clauses can be written as individual sentences, or they can be joined as one sentence. One way you can join them is by using a comma and coordinating conjunction after the first independent clause. (See Lesson 35 for more information on joining independent clauses.) Two or more independent clauses joined by a coordinating conjunction (*and, but, or, for, nor, yet,* or *so*) make up a compound sentence.

Dan wrote a research paper on motivation. He submitted it for publication. Two independent clauses.

Dan wrote a research paper on motivation, *and* he submitted it for publication. Compound sentence. (The same two independent clauses are joined by a comma and the coordinating conjunction *and.*)

Beware! Make sure that what follows the word *and* (or any of the other coordinating conjunctions) is indeed an independent clause. If it is not, then do not use a comma.

Dan wrote a research paper and submitted it for publication. No comma is needed because *submitted it for publication* is not an independent clause—it does not have its own subject.

CHECKUP 1 Insert commas where necessary and circle them. Identify the coordinating conjunctions by writing them in the spaces. If a sentence is correct, write *OK*.

1. Martin left the building‚but he will return in one hour.
2. Ms. Horn enjoyed being a juror and she'll be happy to serve again if asked.
3. We can leave here about 10 a.m. or we can leave after lunch.
4. You will need to do your homework and to clean your room.
5. John asked for an application for he wanted to apply for the job.

1. <u>but</u>
2. _____
3. _____
4. _____
5. _____

COMMAS JOIN DEPENDENT CLAUSES TO INDEPENDENT CLAUSES

When a dependent clause is joined to the beginning of an independent clause by a subordinating conjunction, such as *although, unless,* or *since,* a comma is used after the dependent clause. When the dependent clause is at the end of the independent clause, a comma may or may not be needed.

> ***After seeing our catalog,* you will want to place an order.** A comma separates the dependent clause *after seeing our catalog* from the independent clause *you will want to place an order.*

> **You will want to place an order *after seeing our catalog.*** No comma is needed when the dependent clause *follows* the independent clause.

> **Ask her to meet with us when *the manager will be here.*** No comma is needed.

> **Ask her to meet with us at 9 a.m., *when the manager will be here.*** The comma is needed here because the phrase *at 9 a.m.* and the clause *when the manager will be here* say the same thing. The clause is repetitious and not essential to the meaning of the sentence, so we use a comma to set it off from the rest of the sentence.

Dependent clauses can also appear in the middle of sentences. When they do, two commas should be used:

> **I know that Mr. Robertson, *who was elected for his second term,* will do an outstanding job for the city.** Two commas separate the dependent clause from the rest of the sentence.

COMMAS SEPARATE ITEMS IN A SERIES

Notice how we use commas to separate three or more items in a series.

> **Leadership, creative ability, and intelligence are important qualities in getting ahead.** Three items—(1) *Leadership,* (2) *creative ability,* and (3) *intelligence*—are separated by two commas. Note that the last item is preceded by a comma and the conjunction *and.* No comma comes after *intelligence,* the last item in this series. Remember to keep the items joined by the commas parallel.

COMMAS FOLLOW INTRODUCTORY WORDS, PHRASES, OR CLAUSES

Use a comma after introductory words, phrases, or clauses. Use a comma after introductory words such as *yes, no, look, well, in fact, for example, however,* and *therefore.*

> ***No,* we will not issue the parade permits.**

Use a comma after an introductory participial phrase.

> ***Having been awake all night,* I slept through the morning.**

Beware! Do not confuse a gerund (a verb form ending in *-ing* and used as a noun) phrase that is used as the subject of the sentence with an introductory participial phrase.

> ***Running five miles a day* strengthens his legs.** *Running five miles a day* is a gerund phrase functioning as the subject of the sentence. It is not an introductory participial phrase.

Use a comma after an introductory infinitive phrase.

> **To serve everyone quickly, the caterer set up two serving lines.**

Use a comma after a prepositional phrase that has five words or more.

> ***In the spring of next year,* we will start construction on our house on the lake.**

Do not use commas after introductory adverbs that refer to time or place (when, how often, where).

> ***On May 1* we will have our grand opening. *At the meeting* we'll discuss those topics.**

EXERCISES

EXERCISE 1 Insert commas where necessary in the following sentences and circle them. Identify the coordinating conjunction by writing it in the space provided. (*Hint:* Make sure that you check to see if an independent clause follows the conjunction.)

1. I read the letter carefully and I found several glaring errors in it.

   1. _____

2. He wanted to do well in school so he studied each night.

   2. _____

3. I could recommend Harold for the job or I could recommend Lillian.

   3. _____

4. Susan wants to make lots of money but she does not want to work hard.

   4. _____

5. He designed that house and he built that office building.

   5. _____

EXERCISE 2 Complete the following sentences by adding a conjunction and an independent clause in the space provided. (*Hint:* An independent clause can stand alone as a complete sentence.) (Answers will vary.)

1. Samuel understood the question,

   _____

2. Mr. Kelly is our teacher,

   _____

3. We can go to the play at Miller Auditorium,

   _____

EXERCISE 3 Complete the following sentences by adding a dependent clause in the space provided.(*Hint:* A dependent clause contains a subject and a verb but cannot stand alone as a complete sentence.) (Answers will vary.)

1. We volunteered to work on Houses for Humanity

   _____

2. The men watched the game

   _____

3. We were still unable to find the missing documents

   _____

EXERCISE 4 In the following sentences insert commas where necessary to set off dependent clauses. Circle the commas. In the spaces at the right, indicate how many commas are necessary. Also identify the subordinating conjunctions by underlining them. If a sentence is correct, write *OK*.

1. Although we received an invitation to the wedding we were not able to attend.

   1. _____

2. Please see your manager when you are done.

   2. _____

3. While you were sleeping soundly I was tossing all night.

   3. _____

4. Before you can receive the merchandise you ordered please complete the enclosed card to let us know what size you want.

   4. _____

5. After searching for hours we finally found our dog.

   5. _____

6. Unless you have a valid objection this plan will continue.

   6. _____

Look for *three items in a series* in each of the following sentences. Then insert commas where necessary and circle the commas. In the space at the right, indicate how many commas are necessary. If a sentence is correct, write *OK*.

1. The circus is fun for men women and children.

1. _____

2. Despite the angry client the hectic pace and the lack of one employee it was still a good day.

2. _____

3. Your duties include preparing graphics answering phones and printing reports.

3. _____

4. Chris and Michael and Karen were hoping to see the elephants when they were on a safari in Africa.

4. _____

5. During the summer they had the house painted a new garage door installed and the garden expanded.

5. _____

Insert commas where necessary in the following sentences and circle them. In the space at the right, indicate the number of commas you used. If a sentence needs no further punctuation, write *OK*.

1. Actually there may be a new position opening soon.

1. _____

2. Yes I am aware of the problem.

2. _____

3. Seeing the hospital reminded her of her appointment.

3. _____

4. To improve your scores you should study more often.

4. _____

5. By the fall of next year I will have lost ten pounds.

5. _____

Complete the following sentences by adding a conjunction and an independent clause in the space provided. (Answers will vary.)

1. The boy grabbed the ball,

_____

2. The drive to the lake is long,

_____

3. Katie wanted to learn more,

_____

4. Lionel wanted the monogrammed jacket,

_____

Insert commas where necessary in the following paragraph. Circle the commas. In the space at the right, indicate how many commas are necessary. If a line needs no punctuation, write *OK*.

Luke had taken courses in math English science
and history but his favorite class was computers.
When choosing a college he looked at those with
strong computer majors. His plan was to be a
programmer but he had also considered a career
as a consultant. He chose a state college where
he studied hard to succeed in his courses.
Although it was difficult he did not quit and he
graduated with honors. He applied to a large
company and to a small one. Finally a large
company offered him an excellent programmer's
position. Luke accepted it with pleasure and
he became a very successful man.

1. _____
2. _____
3. _____
4. _____
5. _____
6. _____
7. _____
8. _____
9. _____
10. _____
11. _____
12. _____
13. _____

COMMAS: NONESSENTIAL ELEMENTS

LESSON 43

USING COMMAS WITH NONESSENTIAL ELEMENTS

PARENTHETICAL ELEMENTS

Use commas to set off parenthetical elements—words, phrases, and clauses that are not essential to the meaning of the sentence. Parenthetical elements are also called *nonessential elements*. Test whether elements are parenthetical by placing parentheses around the elements. If the sentence makes sense without the elements, then the elements are nonessential and should be set off with commas. If the sentence would not make sense without the elements, then they are essential and should not be set off by commas.

> **Mark, *who completed his MBA degree*, has a job interview today.** The subordinate clause, *who completed his MBA degree*, modifies Mark. Removing it would not affect the meaning of the sentence. It is, therefore, a nonessential clause. Clauses that modify proper nouns are almost always nonessential.
>
> **Walt McLintock, *a technology instructor*, will help the Clausens build their house.** The adjective phrase, *an industrial arts instructor*, modifies Walt McLintock. Removing it would not affect the meaning of the sentence. It is, therefore, a nonessential phrase. Phrases that modify proper nouns are almost always nonessential.

Essential Elements Do not use commas to set off essential elements of a sentence. Essential elements are not parenthetical.

> **John's book *Hatteras* has been on the best-seller list for three months.** If John has many books, then the name of the particular book is essential to the meaning of the sentence and would not be set off by commas. If John has only one book, then the name would be nonessential and would be set off by commas.

CHECKUP 1 Insert commas in the following sentences. Circle the commas. In the space provided, indicate how many commas are necessary. If the sentence is punctuated correctly, write *OK*. Also indicate whether the elements are essential or nonessential.

1. Dawn, a sales manager, received the employee of the month award.

1. 2, nonessential

2. Her brother who was running in the park tripped.

2. _____

3. The student who has the highest score will receive an award.

3. _____

4. His first wife Rita was a great cook.

4. _____

5. The instructor who has the laptop computer was taken to the emergency room.

5. _____

DESCRIPTIVE EXPRESSIONS

Use commas to set off descriptive expressions that provide nonessential information.

> **The skylights, *which were installed last week*, give added light to the room.** Commas set off *which were installed last week* because the clause adds nonessential information.
>
> **Bob Brozowski's latest book, *A Winning Attitude*, has sold over 500,000 copies.** Since *latest* identifies which book, the title is not essential and should be set off with commas.

CONTRASTING EXPRESSIONS

Parenthetical expressions used to show contrast are set off by commas. Generally these expressions begin with *not, but,* or *rather than.*

> **The nurses, *not the doctors*, were requested to attend the lecture.**
>
> **We intend to go to the Midwest Convention, *but not until Friday*.**

CHECKUP 2   Insert commas in the following sentences. Circle the commas. In the spaces provided, write whether the italicized elements are essential or nonessential.

1. John's book *Organizing Your Thoughts* is being used as a textbook.

2. Sue *rather than Sam* will be teaching the class.

3. The cows and the sheep *and not the horses* were grazing on the hillside.

4. Your manager *not your coworkers* will complete your evaluation.

5. You but not Marie can go.

1. _essential_

2. _____

3. _____

4. _____

5. _____

INTERRUPTERS

Notice how commas are used to set off the italicized "interrupters" in the following excerpts. Examples of interrupters are *without a doubt, in other words, of course,* and so on.

> ***Without a doubt*, many of our students are planning to attend college. *Consequently*, we should offer classes that will challenge them. *For example*, we could offer algebra, chemistry, and German. *In addition*, we might consider offering physics, trigonometry, and Russian. We cannot, *of course*, offer all foreign languages. *For this reason*, we need to make some decisions.**

Use one comma for interrupters that introduce a clause; use two commas for those that appear in the middle of a clause.

Introduce a clause:	***In other words*, the deadline is firm.**
Within a clause:	**The deadline, *in other words*, is firm.**

Beware! Sometimes expressions that are commonly used as "interrupters" do not interrupt; they can be important parts of the sentence.

> **Adrian *certainly* knew what he was doing.** No commas.
>
> **They *of course* understood what he had done.** No commas.
>
> ***However* sure you may be, you should still ask.** No comma after *however*.
>
> **There is *no doubt* that we will be awarded the contract.** No commas.

CHECKUP 3   Decide if there are any interrupters in the following sentences. If so, insert commas to show how the interrupters should be separated. Circle the commas. In the spaces at the right, indicate how many commas are necessary. If a sentence is correct, write *OK*.

1. Without a doubt, Harry is the most knowledgeable person.

2. However the decision goes we will be supportive.

3. The candidate said he would obviously withdraw.

4. For example we cannot guarantee interest rates.

5. We should therefore give our opinion before the vote.

1. _1_

2. _____

3. _____

4. _____

5. _____

Name _____   Date _____   Score _____

EXERCISES

EXERCISE 1 Insert commas in the following sentences. Circle the commas. In the spaces provided, indicate how many commas are necessary. If the sentence is punctuated correctly, write *OK*. Also indicate whether the elements are essential or nonessential.

1. It is not wise for you to disobey your parents.
2. Don who is my friend will graduate from college this fall.
3. Those of you who are familiar with the area can drive to the seminar.
4. The concert which is tomorrow night should be great.
5. The students who came to class yesterday met the visiting professor.
6. Employees who have been here one year will receive a raise.
7. My only aunt who works in a candy factory rarely eats candy.

1. _____
2. _____
3. _____
4. _____
5. _____
6. _____
7. _____

EXERCISE 2 Insert commas where necessary in the following sentences. Circle the commas. In the spaces provided, write whether the italicized elements are essential or nonessential.

1. The highlighted paragraph *which is on page one* is of most importance.
2. The students *not the teachers* are participating in the play.
3. The dolphins *not the whales* are also known as porpoises.
4. Steven Spielberg's movie *Schindler's List* is a wonderful documentary.
5. The red wire *not the blue one* should be connected to the yellow wire.

1. _____
2. _____
3. _____
4. _____
5. _____

EXERCISE 3 Decide if there are any interrupters in the following sentences. If so, insert commas to show how the interrupters should be separated. Circle the commas. In the space at the right, indicate how many commas are necessary. If a sentence is correct, write *OK*.

1. Thankfully no one was hurt in the accident.
2. The rain however will not dampen their spirits.
3. Without a doubt this is the best pie I have ever tasted.
4. She will in fact be promoted to supervisor this month.
5. In addition we will need five desks and five chairs.
6. There is no doubt that her children will be successful.
7. Wherever you place it the plant still enhances the room.

1. _____
2. _____
3. _____
4. _____
5. _____
6. _____
7. _____

EXERCISE 4 Write sentences using each of the following interrupters. Insert commas where appropriate. (Answers will vary.)

1. without a doubt

_____

2. for example

_____

3. furthermore

_____

4. in other words

_____

5. after all

_____

6. therefore

_____

7. consequently

_____

8. absolutely

_____

9. lastly

_____

10. in all likelihood

_____

11. in my opinion

_____

12. naturally

_____

13. for this reason

_____

14. as you know

_____

15. however

_____

WRITING ACTIVITY Use the following phrases as nonessential elements in a sentence. Place commas where needed. (Answers will vary.)

1. who is the president

_____

2. which is my favorite

_____

3. not the girls

_____

4. not the sophomores

_____

5. who majors in music

_____

SHORT STORY Insert commas in the following sentences. Circle the commas. In the space provided at the right, indicate how many commas are necessary in the line. If the line is punctuated correctly, write *OK*.

Jane and Marcy who are best friends are attending the   1. _____
same college. They both enjoy math English and   2. _____
science. However Jane not Marcy plans to be a   3. _____
doctor. Furthermore Marcy wants to be a teacher.   4. _____
Both girls who are honor students have made the   5. _____
Dean's list each semester.   6. _____

COMMAS: OTHER USES

USING COMMAS WITH APPOSITIVES

Nouns or noun phrases that rename or explain the immediately preceding noun or pronoun are called *appositives*. Appositives that are not essential are set off by commas. Appositives that are essential do not require commas. In the following sentences, note the deliberate repetitions.

> **Ms. Charlene Karstens, *our office manager*, is well liked by everyone in the office.** Set off *our office manager* with commas because it repeats (in different words) the same information given by "Ms. Charlene Karstens." The expression *our office manager* is an appositive.

> **Both applicants, *Carole Collins and he*, will be interviewed this afternoon.** *Carole Collins and he* is another way of saying *both applicants*, so it is set off with commas. Note that the nominative form *he* is correct because we could say "Carole Collins and *he* will be interviewed this afternoon." The expression *Carole Collins and he* is an appositive.

Beware! Do not set off with commas expressions that are essential to the meaning of the sentence.

> **The word *accommodation* is frequently misspelled.** Since there are many words, it is *essential* to identify which word by naming it. Its name is essential in this case.

> **His book, *Knowing Yourself*, is now on sale.** If he has only one book, it is not essential to name it.

> **His book *Knowing Yourself* is on sale today.** If he has many books, it is essential to name which book.

> **The printer Roy Beck prepared the business cards for us.** There are many printers so it is essential to name which printer.

Do not use a comma to set off closely related and one-word appositives.

> **We teachers agreed with the new schedule.**

Use a comma to separate words that are repeated in a sentence.

> **When you *study, study hard*.** Note the comma in *study, study*.

CHECKUP 1

Decide if any commas are missing from the following sentences. Insert the missing commas in the sentences and circle them. Then write both the word that precedes each comma and the comma itself in the space at the right. If a sentence is correct, write *OK*.

1. My only brother-in-law Jason has been promoted to supervisor.
2. We employees feel that we are not appreciated.
3. When you walk walk with confidence.
4. Both doctors Dr. Graham and she were recommended.
5. The book *The Client* was made into a movie.

1. <u>brother-in-law, Jason,</u>
2. _____
3. _____
4. _____
5. _____

WITH DIRECT ADDRESS

In writing, we use commas to separate the name of the person whom we are addressing from the rest of the sentence. Words used in direct address are parenthetical.

> **Yes, *Ms. Russell*, your appointment is for Tuesday.** Note the commas around the person's name.

IN DATES, ADDRESSES, AND GEOGRAPHICAL ITEMS

In dates, commas help us to separate two consecutive numbers. Use commas to separate the parts of a date when the month, day, and year are given.

Dad signed the first contract on *March 15, 1997*, and the second one on *April 15, 1997*.

Do not use commas to separate only the month and year.

The *December 1997* issue is a special issue that highlights the major events.

Frequently, dates are used as deliberate repetitions:

On Friday, *August 23*, we will have our first meeting.

In addresses, commas help us to identify the parts of the full address.

Mail a copy of the statement to *Mr. Craig Bell, 3432 West Monroe Street, Columbia, SC 29208*, before the end of the month.

In geographic items, use commas to set off the name of a state when it follows the name of the city. Also, use commas to set off counties.

We had hoped to visit relatives in *Reno, Nevada*, while traveling.

The bank considered opening a branch in *Kansas City, Missouri*.

The Olsens would be moving to *Cass County, Michigan*, sometime in May.

TO SEPARATE ADJECTIVES

When two adjectives modify the same noun, use a comma to separate them.

Brianne is a hard-working, loyal employee.

Kelly is an honest, trustworthy employee. Note again that in both examples the word *and* can be used in place of the comma.

They had planned to purchase several new computers. No comma between the two adjectives *several* and *new* (both modify computers). Why? Because you cannot use the word *and* in place of the comma (*purchase several and new computers* does not make sense).

Always test to see whether you can substitute the word *and* for the comma. If you can, then the comma is correct; if you cannot, do not use a comma.

CHECKUP 2

Insert commas where necessary in the following sentences. Circle the commas. In the space at the right indicate how many commas are necessary. If a sentence is correct, write *OK*.

1. No, Sally and Sue, you may not be excused from the table.
2. Mail this to Bob Oliver 200 Main Street Raleigh NC 55502.
3. The March 1991 issue of *Forbes* was not in the library.
4. The new inexpensive desk will be delivered on Tuesday June 15.
5. You can mail this to me in Columbus Ohio.

1. _2_
2. _____
3. _____
4. _____
5. _____

Name _____ Date _____ Score _____

EXERCISES

EXERCISE 1   Decide which sentence in each of the following pairs is punctuated correctly. In the space provided, write the letter of the sentence that is correct.

1. a. Mr. Smith, could you please come into my office?
   b. Mr. Smith could you please come into my office?

2. a. I found Edward's latest book, *Computing Made Easy*, very easy to read.
   b. I found Edward's latest book *Computing Made Easy* very easy to read.

3. a. The new employee is an experienced, sharp individual.
   b. The new employee is an experienced sharp individual.

4. a. The hot, tired marathon runner enjoyed his winning moment.
   b. The hot tired marathon runner enjoyed his winning moment.

5. a. Annie Cook, our new neighbor, owns the local grocery store.
   b. Annie Cook our new neighbor owns the local grocery store.

6. a. Jamie are you planning on going to college?
   b. Jamie, are you planning on going to college?

1. _____

2. _____

3. _____

4. _____

5. _____

6. _____

EXERCISE 2   Decide if any commas are missing from the following sentences. Insert the missing commas in the sentences and circle them. Then in the spaces at the right, indicate how many commas are necessary. If a sentence is correct, write *OK*. (*Hint:* Watch for deliberate repetitions.)

1. We will need one week to complete this project.
2. We are moving to Springfield Illinois before the summer begins.
3. On Monday May 19 we will meet in the conference room.
4. Several of our terminals have had problems.
5. Her brother-in-law Dr. Ted Gomolak recently was hired as the superintendent of schools in Portage.
6. No no that's not the way to make overhead transparencies.
7. Of course Ms. Riley we have the materials ready for you to pick up.
8. Barrien County Michigan is known as the Fruit Belt of the state.

1. _____

2. _____

3. _____

4. _____

5. _____

6. _____

7. _____

8. _____

EXERCISE 3   Insert commas where necessary in the following sentences. Circle the commas. Then in the spaces at the right, indicate how many commas are necessary. If a sentence is correct, write *OK*.

1. The bright aggressive young man achieved his goals.
2. Those two children Jacob and Natalie behave very well.
3. The word *receive* is on the list of frequently misspelled words.
4. Doctors are very very much in demand in a small rural area.
5. Yes Anna I am aware of the situation at hand.
6. Independence Day was noted as July 4 1776 in American history.

1. _____

2. _____

3. _____

4. _____

5. _____

6. _____

Correct the following sentences by inserting commas. Circle the commas. In the spaces at the right, indicate how many commas are necessary. If a sentence is correct, write *OK*.

1. The district manager for Books Inc. Todd Castern is responsible for schools in Ohio Wisconsin Illinois Michigan and Indiana.

2. Her date of birth is June 2 1968 and his is June 2 1969.

3. The September 1996 issue of *Our Town* published an excellent article on the Crosby family.

4. His address is 401 Long Street Bison Maine 22234.

1. _____

2. _____

3. _____

4. _____

Write sentences using the elements specified, and punctuate them correctly. (Answers will vary.)

1. Three or more items in a series using *and*

_____

2. Three or more items in a series using *or*

_____

3. Two dates with consecutive numbers

_____

4. Repetition of *very, very*

_____

5. A request issued to one individual

_____

6. A person's home address using street, apartment number, city, state, and zip code

_____

Write a sentence using the elements specified and punctuate them correctly. (Answers will vary.)

1. creative kind and intelligent

_____

2. December 20 1996

_____

3. 100 Walnut Street Apartment 2C Janesville WI 53545

_____

Correct the following lines by inserting commas. Circle the commas. In the space at the right indicate how many commas are necessary. If a line is correct, write *OK*.

On June 21 1997 we will have our annual company
picnic. There will be games for children activities
for adults and plenty of food. Naturally each employee
can bring guests. Usually the attendance runs close
to 400 people and everyone has a very very good time.
Most people are happy yet tired when they leave.
The activities will include face painting a dunking
booth bingo pony rides and games. No there will
not be a cost to attend. I hope to see all of you there
on June 21 1997 and I promise you will enjoy the day.

1. _____
2. _____
3. _____
4. _____
5. _____
6. _____
7. _____
8. _____
9. _____
10. _____

THE SEMICOLON AND THE COLON

USING SEMICOLONS AND COLONS

THE SEMICOLON

Use a semicolon to join two independent clauses that are not joined by a comma plus a coordinating conjunction.

We do not have enough lightbulbs; someone will have to buy more.

When the second independent clause is introduced by a conjunctive adverb, follow the adverb with a comma.

We do not have lightbulbs; therefore, someone will have to buy more.

When the second independent clause is introduced by a word or phrase, such as *for example, that is, on the contrary,* or *on the other hand,* follow that word or phrase with a comma.

We would like to employ more people; on the other hand, we do not have the funds.

Perhaps by this time you have already asked yourself, "Why not simply make each independent clause into a separate sentence?" Of course, you could do so and avoid using the semicolon, but when you want to show that two ideas are closely related, you may decide that semicolons provide the best means to show that close relationship.

One more case requires semicolons. Use a semicolon to separate items in a series when any of the items already contain commas.

The sales representative's territory includes Providence, Rhode Island; Hartford, Connecticut; and Springfield, Massachusetts. The semicolons clearly separate the three sites.

CHECKUP 1	Insert semicolons and commas where necessary in the following sentences and circle them. Then in the spaces at the right, indicate how many semicolons and commas (total) are necessary.

1. Only Mr. Griffin supported us the others did not.
2. David demonstrates creativity for example he drew the logo.
3. We want Giles for the job however he is taken.
4. I want to leave today Joe wants to leave tomorrow.
5. Send copies of this to the managers in Topeka Kansas Minneapolis Minnesota and Fargo North Dakota.

1. _1_____
2. _____
3. _____
4. _____
5. _____

THE COLON

Colons are used after the salutations in business letters.

Ladies and Gentlemen: Dear Ms. Rockwell and Mr. Osterling:

A colon is also used after an independent clause to show that what follows that clause *further* explains it.

According to the police report, one factor caused the accident: speed. What follows the colon further explains what is meant by *one factor*. A semicolon would not be enough to show a relationship this close.

The semicolon shows that two ideas are related, but the colon shows a much closer relationship. A colon is used when what follows the colon *has already been suggested*. Often the words that appear before the colon are very obvious hints: *the following, as follows, these*, and so on. In general, whatever precedes the colon should be a complete sentence.

> **They needed the following information for their sales presentation: total sales for January, February, and March; estimated sales for April, May, and June; and projected sales for the second half of the year.** The words *the following* will tell you that an explanation or a listing will come after the colon.

> **Please bring the following items with you: warm clothing, walking shoes, and blankets.**

Sometimes the list is typed on separate lines:

> **People communicate for three purposes:**
> **1. to inform**
> **2. to persuade**
> **3. to entertain**

You will also see colons used after words such as *remember, hint,* and *caution*.

> **Caution: The burner remains hot several minutes after the heat is turned off.**

Beware! Do *not* use a colon to interrupt sentences. Never use a colon to separate a verb and its object or a preposition and its object.

> **The regional meetings were held in Boston, Chicago, and Los Angeles.** (NOT: The regional meetings were held in: Boston, . . .)

> **Write to Dr. J. T. Phillips, 103 South Main Street, Sacramento, CA 95819.** (NOT: Write to: Dr. J. T. Phillips . . .)

You are probably familiar with colons used in expressions of time:

> **at 7:30 a.m.   before 5:45 p.m.   after 7:30 p.m.**

CHECKUP 2 Insert colons and commas where necessary in the following sentences and circle them. Then in the spaces at the right, indicate how many colons and commas (total) are necessary.

1. Remember⊙ Our deadline for submitting the proposal is December 1.

    1. _1_____

2. Choose one of the following fruits apples oranges or pears.

    2. _____

3. The meeting was to start at 815 a.m. and to adjourn at 1130 a.m.

    3. _____

4. The person must possess two job requirements computer knowledge and experience.

    4. _____

5. Tell Carmen to bring a lawn chair a place setting and one side dish and to be there by 915.

    5. _____

EXERCISES

EXERCISE 1   Decide which sentence in each of the following pairs is punctuated correctly. In the space at the right, write the letter of the sentence that is correct.

1. a. The seminar was a great success, over 200 people attended.
   b. The seminar was a great success; over 200 people attended.

2. a. The wedding was perfect; not one thing went wrong.
   b. The wedding was perfect, not one thing went wrong.

3. a. Alice has the most experience, she has been here ten years.
   b. Alice has the most experience; she has been here ten years.

4. a. I appreciate your offer; however, I cannot accept it.
   b. I appreciate your offer, however I cannot accept it.

5. a. You should receive your order by February 15, we shipped
      it by National Parcel Service today.
   b. You should receive your order by February 15; we shipped
      it by National Parcel Service today.

1. _____

2. _____

3. _____

4. _____

5. _____

EXERCISE 2   Insert semicolons and commas where necessary in the following sentences and circle them. Then in the spaces at the right, indicate how many semicolons and commas (total) are necessary.

1. Ms. Wagford has been promoted to manager she certainly deserves it.
2. The project seems easy therefore Anna Jim and I will complete it.
3. The team tried hard however they cannot meet their goals.
4. There is a budget constraint thus we will be making cutbacks.
5. The sale worked well we were able to reduce our inventory by 50 percent.
6. Our neighbor's daughter is doing well she is now a lawyer.
7. They were married June 7 1996 it was a beautiful ceremony.
8. Financial reports go to Bob statistical reports go to Annie.
9. Ms. Estokowski has the skills for the job furthermore she has the experience.
10. She investigated the case no evidence could be found.

1. _____
2. _____
3. _____
4. _____
5. _____
6. _____
7. _____
8. _____
9. _____
10. _____

EXERCISE 3   Insert colons and commas where necessary in the following sentences and circle them. In the spaces at the right, indicate how many colons and commas (total) are necessary.

1. The following faculty were selected to serve on the committee for
   curriculum development Drs. Cornwell Gotfryd Earle and Sherburn.
2. Here's a list of the items that we need for the project drawing paper
   a compass and a protractor.
3. Avoid these common redundancies in your writing *finish up over with*
   and *repeat again*.
4. Hint The document contains five misspelled words.
5. The Sherwoods were leaving on Flight 307 at 845 a.m.

1. _____

2. _____

3. _____

4. _____
5. _____

6. These are the steps call the client solve the problem document the call. 6. _____
7. Her goals are high complete college attend medical school and become a physician. 7. _____
8. Everyone has the same responsibility Keep the customer happy. 8. _____
9. These people have received an award Job Frances Jay and Debbie. 9. _____
10. Nominees for the office are as follows Sue David Anita Elijah and Hunter. 10. _____

EXERCISE 4 Insert commas, semicolons, and colons where necessary in the following sentences and circle them. In the spaces at the right, indicate how many of these punctuation marks are necessary.

1. I wanted to see the play he wanted to see the movie. 1. _____
2. I wanted to go to the mall however I promised Jan I would help her. 2. _____
3. The check hasn't arrived therefore the goods will not be shipped. 3. _____
4. Our new address will be effective July 1 please make a note of it. 4. _____
5. Both of you are qualified unfortunately only one of you can be chosen. 5. _____
6. This morning's meeting was at 830 this afternoon's meeting will be at 330. 6. _____
7. Marcy and Dan wanted to buy china however they could not agree on the pattern. 7. _____
8. Office hours will be 830 a.m. to 530 p.m. please tell everyone. 8. _____
9. Please order the following items for the office three staplers one dictionary and twelve pens. 9. _____
10. I appreciate your concern Millie I will let you know how the situation is resolved. 10. _____

WRITING ACTIVITY Write a sentence using the instructions that follow. Add a semicolon or a colon where needed. (Answers will vary.)

1. Combine two sentences with the conjunctive adverb, *however*.

_____

2. Combine two sentences using a semicolon.

_____

3. Use three nouns in a listing.

_____

4. Combine two sentences with a coordinating conjunction.

_____

5. Use three city and state combinations in a sentence.

_____

SHORT STORY Insert commas, semicolons, and colons where necessary in the following lines and circle them. Then in the space at the right, indicate how many commas, semicolons, and colons (total) are necessary. If the line needs no punctuation, write *OK*.

Fifty people were invited to attend the gathering however 1. _____
only forty people attended. A buffet meal was served that 2. _____
consisted of several selections beef chicken ham beans 3. _____
potatoes salad and dessert. Cathy was the hostess she 4. _____
had volunteered to replace Tom after he became ill. 5. _____
Everyone had fun and the evening ended too soon. 6. _____
Before everyone left Cathy gave out the following items 7. _____
party favors gag items and roses. Each guest thanked 8. _____
Cathy for the good company delicious food and 9. _____
entertaining conversation. 10. _____

DASHES, PARENTHESES, AND BRACKETS

USING DASHES, PARENTHESES, AND BRACKETS

THE DASH

The dash shares some of its use with the comma, the semicolon, and the colon. The dash, however, shows more emphasis:

The vice president—as well as the president—was adamant in his decision. The dashes emphasize *as well as the president*. Commas would not be so emphatic.

Three of our manufacturing plants—the ones in Tuscaloosa, Little Rock, and Stillwater—are being renovated. Commas would be confusing because the phrase *the ones in Tuscaloosa, Little Rock, and Stillwater* already contains two commas.

Use a dash before a word or phrase that has been repeated for greater emphasis.

Ted works hard—too hard—to make his business successful. The dashes provide the needed emphasis.

Dashes provide more emphasis than a semicolon or a colon can.

He wants to have the meeting at 9:00 a.m.—in fact, he thinks 9:30 might be too late! The dash provides more emphasis than a semicolon, although a semicolon would also be correct.

Our real estate agent told us the three most important factors in purchasing a home—location, location, location. A colon would be more formal but less emphatic.

Use a dash to set off a brief summary or before words such as *these, each,* and *all.*

Dishwashers, clothes dryers, and freezers—all make excellent gifts.

PARENTHESES

Use parentheses to give the reader extra information. Just as dashes are used to emphasize material, parentheses are used to de-emphasize material. Like dashes, parentheses enclose material that could be set off by commas.

You can place your order immediately by calling our toll-free number (800-555-3445). Here parentheses enclose a telephone number.

We want to thank you for your tax deductible gift of one thousand dollars ($1,000). Here parentheses are used to restate a dollar amount in figures.

The operator's manual provides complete instructions (see page 8). The parentheses enclose the independent clause *see page 8.*

The Springfield (Illinois) office houses our customer relations department. The parentheses here replace commas: *The Springfield, Illinois, office* would not be as clear.

The Oakville Company will merge with Springfield Metals (a Massachusetts firm). Parentheses enclose nonessential information.

Will you complete the following jobs for me: (1) call Ms. Whiting to set up an appointment, (2) e-mail Ms. O'Rourke with the name of the candidate, and (3) confirm the conference room for our meeting. Notice the colon before the listing. Use parentheses to enclose letters used for listing items within a sentence.

Use parentheses to enclose the abbreviation or acronym of an organization that immediately follows the full name of the organization.

The National Association for the Advancement of Colored People (NAACP) is having its annual convention in Atlanta, Georgia, this year.

CHECKUP 1 Use a caret ($_\wedge$) to indicate where to insert any missing punctuation marks in the following sentences. Then insert the punctuation mark above the caret.

1. You may reach me at my toll-free number $_\wedge$800-555-6400$_\wedge$.

2. The Raleigh North Carolina office serves as headquarters.

3. Two employees Troy and Faith are being promoted this week.

4. Two of the buildings the Skyrise and the Hytower were purchased by Financial Enterprises, Inc.

5. He loved his country so much so that he gave his life for it.

Other Punctuation Marks With Parentheses and Dashes Here are the *only* ways in which you can use other punctuation marks with dashes. Punctuation marks (such as question marks and exclamation marks) that belong only to the words within the dashes or within the parentheses should be placed *before* the ending dash or ending parenthesis.

The Portage office is too crowded—isn't it?—for additional staff.

The Portage office is too crowded—definitely too crowded!—for additional staff.

Now let's see how other punctuation marks may be used with parentheses.

The Portage office is too crowded (isn't it?) for additional staff.

The Portage office is too crowded (definitely too crowded!) for additional staff.

Unlike dashes, parentheses can be followed by other marks of punctuation.

You scored 40 points out of a total of 50 points (80 percent).
The period that ends the sentence *follows* the ending parenthesis.

Does anyone know why these forms are due twice a year (in April and October)? The question mark belongs to the sentence (not to the words enclosed in parentheses); thus the question mark is placed *after* the ending parenthesis.

It would be best if we met in the next month (by April 10 would be most convenient); by then we will have all the data we need. The semicolon belongs *after* the ending parenthesis.

When your six-month certificate of deposit comes due (October 17), consider renewing it for one year. Note the comma *after* the ending parenthesis.

BRACKETS

Use brackets to insert remarks, additions, or corrections (especially misspellings) made by another. Also use brackets as a substitute for parentheses within parentheses.

He said, "We have identified the winners [names were not given] of the New York lottery."

The headline read as follows: "ITS [sic] A SELLOUT!" Use brackets and the word *sic* to indicate that an error existed in the original material that is being quoted or referenced. In this example, *its* should be *it's*.

EXERCISES

EXERCISE 1 Use a caret (∧) to indicate where to insert dashes in the following sentences. Then insert the dashes above the carets.

1. Our managers Mr. Maly, Ms. Welz, and Mr. Kyle are in a meeting.

2. Two of our offices the one in Los Angeles and the one in San Francisco are closing.

3. The financial reports especially today's need to be completed by this evening.

4. In our marketing class we learned about promotional devices free samples, coupons, and discounts.

5. Do not delay it's too important submitting your proposal.

EXERCISE 2 Insert parentheses where necessary in the following sentences.

1. They inadvertently set the meeting date on a holiday Memorial Day.

2. Our department's budget is set for a maximum of ten thousand dollars $10,000.

3. Health Maintenance Organization HMO plans are becoming the dominant choice.

4. You can find information on this subject in your manuals see page 25.

5. The new provost a summa cum laude graduate, received her doctorate from Harvard.

EXERCISE 3 Insert brackets where necessary in the following sentences.

1. "It the new product is guaranteed for life," stated the inventor.

2. The operator said, "It the crane will not start."

3. The article stated "Odd's sic for the lottery improved.

4. All the workers (over 50 of them mostly veterans) attended the meeting.

5. Susan (Janices sic friend) responded to the call.

EXERCISE 4 Insert any missing punctuation marks (commas, dashes, parentheses, brackets, colons, and semi-colons) in the following sentences. Circle the commas. Use a caret to indicate where to insert the dashes; then insert the dashes above the carets. In the spaces at the right, indicate how many punctuation marks are necessary (a pair of parentheses or brackets counts as two marks).

1. Every year at least one alligator is seen in fresh waters ponds rivers or on land.   1. _____

2. When your contract ends this month on July 31 you may renew it if you wish.   2. _____

3. The report read "Alot sic of work was completed by a construction firm."   3. _____

4. The mother now living in another city is pleased with her choice.   4. _____

5. The school about 10 miles from my house has an excellent reputation.   5. _____

EXERCISE 5 Use a caret (∧) to indicate the punctuation error in each of the following sentences. Then in the space provided, indicate why each sentence is incorrect. If a sentence is correct, write *OK*. (Answers will vary.)

1. Janet is late—always late for our meetings.

   _____

2. You will be requested to make three oral presentations September, November, and December for this course.

   _____

3. Sharon had three requests: a she wanted to take her vacation in December, b she wanted an assistant, and c she wanted a laser printer.

   _____

   _____

4. That month's meeting December's was rescheduled.

   _____

   _____

WRITING ACTIVITY Write a sentence using each one of the phrases as shown. Insert punctuation where needed. (Answers will vary.)

1. (a) buy groceries (b) pick up prescription and (c) get gas.

   _____

   _____

2. Wait—

   _____

   _____

3. ($2,000)

   _____

   _____

4. (a newly created position).

   _____

   _____

5. [sic]

   _____

   _____

SHORT STORY Use a caret to indicate where to insert any missing punctuation marks (commas, dashes, parentheses, brackets, colons, and semicolons) in the following paragraph. Insert the needed punctuation marks above the carets. In the space at the right, write the total number of punctuation marks you supplied in each line (a pair of parentheses or brackets counts as two marks). If no punctuation is needed, write *OK*.

My friend Oscar he's been my friend for years helped   1. _____

me to write a letter. He told me to remember three   2. _____

things be polite be concise and be clear. He said, "Your   3. _____

image your personality is formed by the words   4. _____

you use. In fact the receiver of your letter will either   5. _____

think alot sic of you or not depending on how you write."   6. _____

I sat down to write my letter a short one to   7. _____

Ms. Townsend the Human Resource Director   8. _____

asking for summer employment however I had a hard   9. _____

time choosing the right words I wanted a positive   10. _____

image. Consequently my short letter took me hours to write.   11. _____

LESSON 47

QUOTATION MARKS, UNDERSCORES, AND APOSTROPHES

USING QUOTATION MARKS, UNDERSCORES, AND APOSTROPHES

QUOTATION MARKS

Use quotation marks (" ") to show that the words within the marks are someone's exact words. As you read the following examples, note where commas and periods are positioned.

Missy said, "Tomorrow will be a better day to hold our rummage sale." The quotation marks show Missy's exact words. Note the comma *before* the first quotation mark and the period *before* the end quotation mark.

"Tomorrow," Missy said to her neighbors, "will be a better day to hold our rummage sale." Missy's exact words are interrupted, so the quotation marks are "detoured" around the clause *Missy said to her neighbors*. The comma after *tomorrow* falls within the quotation mark.

Quotation marks are also used for words and phrases following such introductory words as *labeled*, *marked*, *signed*, and *stamped*.

Please stamp the material "overnight express."

Also use quotation marks to enclose titles that represent part of a complete literary work such as magazine articles, newspaper columns, chapters in books, essays, and songs.

Magazine article: The article "The World of Dinosaurs" was written by Claudia Grant.

Chapter in a book: Students were asked to read Chapter 7, "The Barriers to Good Listening."

Essay: Professor Zahn wrote an essay entitled "Year of the Ox."

Newspaper column: Stan Greeley writes the column, "Yes and No," for the newspaper.

Song: We sang "God Bless America" at the end of the program.

Question marks and exclamation points may go before or after the end quotation mark—it depends on whether the mark belongs with the speaker's exact words.

In her report Peg asked, "What is the difference between the two models?" Note that the question mark belongs with Peg's exact words, so it goes *inside* the quotation marks.

Why did Sam mark this "Confidential"? The question mark does not belong with Sam's exact words. It belongs with the entire sentence. The question mark goes *outside* the second quotation mark.

After working five hours on the problems, Debbie shouted, "I've got the solution!" The exclamation point belongs with Debbie's exact words, so it goes *inside* the second quotation mark.

Please don't forget to mark this box "Fragile"! The exclamation point goes with the entire sentence; thus it is placed *outside* the second quotation.

"Did You Say 'Quotation Marks'?" When a quotation appears within another quotation, use single quotation marks (' '), as shown in the following examples:

Pedro asked, "Why did Mario stamp this 'Top Secret'?" Note the position of the question mark; it does not belong with the words *top secret*; it belongs with the words being quoted.

The auctioneer said, "You folks need to bid so I can shout 'Going, Going, Gone!'" Here the exclamation point goes before the single quotation mark because it belongs with the words enclosed in the single quotations: *Going, Going, Gone!*

Periods and commas always go before the single quotation mark when they are at the end of a sentence.

Mike Foxtra said, "You need to place a sign on the lawn that says 'Danger—chemicals.'"

Doug said, "Yes, I'll place the sign 'Danger—chemicals' on the lawn."

CHECKUP 1   Insert punctuation marks where necessary in the following sentences. Circle your marks.

1. Our assignment was to read Chapter 5, "Special Techniques for Reports."
2. The article is titled In a Dream.
3. Cherry said We should go shopping before she left.
4. Don't forget to mark this paid.

UNDERSCORES

Use a continuous underscore or italics for titles of books, magazines, newspapers, operas, and movies or plays.

Opera: They went to see <u>The Marriage of Figaro</u> in New York City.

Underscores are also used for emphasis and for words used as words (usually preceded by phrases such as *the word, the term,* or *the expression*).

It is <u>imperative</u> that we all agree to stay.

The word <u>accommodate</u> is quite frequently misspelled.

APOSTROPHES

Use apostrophes to form *contractions* (a word or word group shortened because letters are omitted).

***There's* no reason for us to accept the wrong merchandise.** The letter *i* in *is* has been omitted in the phrase meaning *there is. There's* is a contraction.

***He'll* be happy to forward the invoice copies to you.** *He'll* is a contraction for *he will.* The letters *wi* in *will* have been omitted.

Here is a list of some frequently used contractions:

it's (it is, it has)	**who's (who is, who has)**	**doesn't (does not)**
we'll (we will)	**she'd (she had, she would)**	**I'm (I am)**
I'd (I had, I would)	**that's (that is, that has)**	**we've (we have)**
they're (they are)	**there's (there is, there has)**	**you're (you are)**

Many rules govern the use of the apostrophe to form the possessive of words. Note the apostrophe in this sentence to form the possessive of a singular noun.

***Jessica's* preparations for the presentation were quite a success.**

CHECKUP 2   Decide where the apostrophes are missing from the following sentences. Underline each word that needs an apostrophe. Then write the words correctly in the space at the right.

1. <u>Arent</u> you finished with that game yet?
2. Whos going to proofread the proposal for us?
3. Youll be asked to give your version of the accident.
4. If it werent for her father, Jayne wouldnt have the job.

1. <u>Aren't</u>
2. _____
3. _____
4. _____

Name _____ Date _____ Score _____

EXERCISES

EXERCISE 1 Insert punctuation marks, including end punctuation marks, where necessary in the following sentences. Circle the marks. In the spaces, indicate how many punctuation marks are necessary.

1. The winner declared I do believe the best person won
2. When the tree fell the man yelled Timber
3. In jubilation Robert cried out We found it
4. Computers said the director will be with us for a long time
5. Get the package marked Handle with Care

1. _____
2. _____
3. _____
4. _____
5. _____

EXERCISE 2 Insert apostrophes where necessary in the following sentences and circle them. In the spaces at the right, indicate how many apostrophes are necessary.

1. Theyre about to start play.
2. Im positive that youll be invited to Ricks party.
3. Havent you decided what youll be wearing yet?
4. Arent you excited about starting your new job?
5. Thats the reason were moving to Montana.

1. _____
2. _____
3. _____
4. _____
5. _____

EXERCISE 3 Insert underscores where necessary in the following sentences.

1. Three key words are accuracy, efficiency, and competency.
2. Will you be reading The Diary of Anne Frank in your class?
3. My favorite magazine is Reader's Digest.
4. Our local newspaper is The News & Observer.
5. Here's the March 5 issue of Times that you asked for.

EXERCISE 4 Insert punctuation marks, including end punctuation marks, where necessary in the following sentences. Circle the marks. In the spaces, indicate how many punctuation marks are necessary.

1. Will Mr and Mrs Royal be attending the ceremony
2. Don received his PhD from the University of Illinois in Urbana Illinois
3. Judy called the caterer the florist and the musicians
4. Heres the sample let me know what you think of it
5. Hal signed the contract and then he gave it to Mr Balwinder

1. _____
2. _____
3. _____
4. _____
5. _____

EXERCISE 5 Use each of the following punctuation marks correctly in a sentence. (Answers will vary.)

1. an apostrophe in a contraction, used at the beginning of a sentence

_____

2. an apostrophe to show the possessive of a noun

_____

3. an underscore for the title of a book

_____

4. an underscore for the title of a magazine

_____

5. an underscore for the title of a newspaper, used in a quote

_____

6. single and double quotation marks for a quotation within a quotation

_____

7. quotation as a chapter in a book

_____

8. an underscore for the title of a play

_____

9. an underscore to show emphasis

_____

10. an underscore for a word used as a word

_____

WRITING ACTIVITY Follow the directions given to write each sentence. Insert punctuation marks where necessary in each sentence. (Answers will vary.)

1. I love to play sports (used as a quote)

_____

2. The Blue Whale (as the title of a book)

_____

3. Ten reasons to smile (as the title of a magazine article)

_____

4. Nick doesn't (as a sentence)

_____

5. Go immediately (as a sentence placing emphasis on the word *immediately*)

_____

SHORT STORY Insert all the necessary punctuation in the following paragraph and circle each mark. In the space at the right, write down the total number of punctuation marks in each line.

Dan and Jon are best friends Dans house is two blocks   1. _____
from Jon's. One day Dan said Jon lets go to the   2. _____
arcade and play some games Sure Jon replied   3. _____
They went off to the arcade While walking to the   4. _____
arcade Jon told Dan about the article in the magazine   5. _____
Sports Illustrated Dan in response mentioned the   6. _____
article The Life of an Athlete which was in the same   7. _____
magazine Suddenly Jon blurted out Wow We even   8. _____
read the same things at the same time No wonder were   9. _____
best friends Dan laughed in agreement They finally   10. _____
arrived at the arcade however it was closed in   11. _____
observance of a holiday Figures Dan said The   12. _____
one day we have off from school and the arcade is   13. _____
closed Yeah replied Jon So do you want to   14. _____
go fishing   15. _____

UNIT 11

WORDS AND NUMBERS

UNIT 11 OVERVIEW

Understanding the eight parts of speech is certainly important to your becoming a good writer; however, other rules of the English language are equally essential to know in order to write clearly and fluently. In this unit, you will learn how to apply the rules of capitalization. By writing a word with a capital letter, you have another tool of communication; you are saying this word, this title, this name, and so on are important.

Numbers are extremely important. Think of all the numbers you use almost daily—age, date, money, address, time. In this unit you will learn the correct way to write these and other numbers.

The last part of this unit presents words that people oftentimes misuse, and by doing so, attach a different meaning to the message. These are words that you must know how to use so you can communicate the correct message in both speaking and in writing. Learn them well!

UNIT OBJECTIVES

When you complete Unit 11, you will be able to:

- demonstrate when to use capital letters in your writing.

- apply the major rules governing the use of numbers in writing.

- select the correct word to complete the meaning of a sentence.

CAPITALS

RULES OF CAPITALIZATION

FIRST THINGS FIRST!

Three "firsts" that must be capitalized are (1) the first word of every sentence, (2) the first-person pronoun *I*, and (3) the first word of the salutation in a letter and any noun or title in the salutation and the first word of a complimentary closing, such as *Sincerely yours*.

Also, always capitalize proper nouns, and always capitalize the title of *President of the United States*.

> **While touring the *West Coast*, we visited the *San Francisco State College* campus, the *Golden Gate Bridge*, and *Disneyland*.** *West Coast* designates a specific region. *San Francisco State College, Golden Gate Bridge*, and *Disneyland* name specific places.

Capitalize adjectives that are derived from proper nouns with the exception of a few (*french fries, india ink*, and *roman numerals*) that are now considered common.

> **We sang the national anthem as the *American* flag was raised.**

Capitalize trademarks and brand names. Do not capitalize the common noun following the name.

> **They purchased an *Aida* dishwasher and a *Tundro* snow blower.**

CHECKUP 1

Underline any letters that should be capitalized in the following sentences. Then in the spaces at the right, indicate how many letters should be capitalized.

1. we plan to go to myrtle beach for our vacation.
2. the salutation in your letter should read "dear mr. haley."
3. Sally, do you have any dr. pepper to drink?
4. do not aggravate mrs. frank with your bohemian dress.
5. They toured the south in a vintage rolls royce.

1. _3_____
2. _____
3. _____
4. _____
5. _____

FAMILY RELATIONSHIPS

Capitalize family titles such as *aunt, cousin, mother*, etc., when they stand alone:

> **Give *Mother* your coat.**   **Is *Grandpa* here?**   **Please ask *Uncle* to write to me.**

Capitalize family titles when they are followed by a personal name:

> **Is *Grandma Lucas* okay?**   **Watch *Uncle Matt* paint.**   **Call *Cousin Marty*.**

Do *not* capitalize a family title that is preceded by a possessive (*his, my, our*, etc.) that simply identifies a relative's position within the family:

> **I have never met my *cousin* Kasandra.**

Capitalize a family title that is preceded by a possessive if you always think of the title and name as *one unit*. If you can't imagine the name without the title that distinguishes it, the title does more than just identify a relative's position within the family—it signifies a perceived relationship:

> **My Cousin Kasandra visits us faithfully every week and tells us great stories.**
>
> **I love my Aunt Jane because she is always so kind to us.**
>
> **My Aunt Jane and my Cousin Kasandra are coming for Thanksgiving.**

ABBREVIATIONS

Some abbreviations are always capitalized.

FCC   CPA   IRS   YMCA   NASA   UCLA   IBM   AT&T   NYSE

SEASONS, POINTS OF THE COMPASS, DAYS, AND MONTHS

Capitalize the days of the week and months of the year, but not the seasons and points of the compass.

Monday   Sunday   April   July   spring   summer   north   south

CHECKUP 2   Underline any letters that should be capitalized in the following sentences. Then in the spaces at the right, indicate how many letters should be capitalized.

1. ask mother or dad if we can stay overnight at aunt Mary's house.   1. _5_
2. my new coworker moved to the united states from england.   2. _____
3. my son is a cpa in washington d.c.   3. _____
4. when in chicago, illinois, we belonged to the ymca.   4. _____
5. last monday, my uncle vince visited us as usual.   5. _____

IN TITLES

In titles of movies, books, articles, and so on, the first and last words are always capitalized. In addition, important words are also capitalized. Do not capitalize articles (*a, an, the*), conjunctions (*and, but, or, for*), and prepositions (*in, of, off, to, at*) with fewer than four letters unless they appear at the beginning or the end of the title.

> **The publisher approved *The Nuts and Bolts of Car Repairs*.** *The, and,* and *of* have fewer than four letters, but *The* is capitalized because it is the first word in the title.

IN PERSONAL TITLES

The titles *Mr., Miss, Mrs.,* and *Ms.* are always capitalized. When a business title is used in place of *Mr., Miss, Mrs.,* or *Ms.,* capitalize the title.

> **Regional Director Baylor is in England.** The business title *Regional Director* is used in place of another title such as *Mr.* or *Ms.*

ACADEMIC SUBJECTS AND DEGREES

Capitalize titles of specific academic courses but not names of subjects, except for proper nouns and their derivatives. Languages are always capitalized because they are derivatives of proper nouns.

> **Leling took a speech course, a Spanish course, and Math II.** *Speech* is the name of a subject, not a specific course; *Spanish* is the derivative of the proper noun Spain; and *Math II* is a specific course.

Capitalize the abbreviations of degrees when they are used alone or after an individual's name.

> **Kyla Ostertag, Ph.D., will be the speaker.   Kyla received her Ph.D. last June.**

CHECKUP 3   Underline any letters that should be capitalized in the following sentences. Then in the spaces at the right, indicate how many letters should be capitalized.

1. read stephen r. covey's book, the seven habits of highly effective people.   1. _10_
2. regional manager martin is at the raleigh, north carolina, store.   2. _____
3. the vice president of sales, mr. c. l. hammond, has retired.   3. _____
4. dr. nelson buyer, who graduated from harvard, is my mentor.   4. _____

EXERCISES

EXERCISE 1 In each of the following pairs of sentences, select the sentence in which capitals are used correctly. In the space at the right, write the letter of the sentence that is correct.

1. a. Mary Dawson, a student at UCLA, earned her Ph.D. degree this summer.   1. _____
   b. mary dawson, a student at ucla, has earned her ph.d. degree this summer.

2. a. My Sister Irene will be visiting us in august.   2. _____
   b. My sister Irene will be visiting us in August.

3. a. Jay Harris, our area manager, is retiring this fall.   3. _____
   b. Jay Harris, our Area Manager, is retiring this fall.

4. a. our trip to rome, italy, ended too quickly.   4. _____
   b. Our trip to Rome, Italy, ended too quickly.

5. a. Did you wish to visit your favorite uncle Andy this summer?   5. _____
   b. Did you wish to visit your favorite Uncle Andy this summer.

EXERCISE 2 Underline each letter that should be capitalized in the following sentences. Then in the spaces at the right, indicate how many letters should be capitalized.

1. people sat in their homes and watched news reports of unrest in asia, latin america, and the persian gulf.   1. _____

2. as a cpa, ms. rose fountain worked for president mitchell at industrial supplies, inc., in dayton, ohio.   2. _____

3. the new management trainee took management 200 and accounting I when he was at boston college.   3. _____

4. dr. steinbach, who received her d.d.s. degree from wayne state university, has been my dentist for several years.   4. _____

5. karen checked the ads in *the main street journal*.   5. _____

6. dr. harvey gold's latest article, "the importance of physical examinations," appeared in the july issue of *medical review*.   6. _____

7. do not ask dr. smith for the july issue.   7. _____

8. in april, sherry will submit her article, "five easy steps to good health."   8. _____

9. *of mice and men* was recently shown on t v and was sponsored by a t&t.   9. _____

10. he wrote the article "how to get on a t v game show" and sent it to c b s for their edit.   10. _____

EXERCISE 3 Underline any letters that should be capitalized in the following sentences.

1. he and his sister, jane, will be at the ymca convention.
2. on may 6, missy will graduate from virginia polytechnic institute.
3. grandpa and grandma will be visiting me this summer.
4. her courses include spanish, english 101, and business statistics.
5. on monday, august 15, we'll be going to yosemite national park.

EXERCISE 4   Rewrite each item listed below correctly in the space at the right. If an item is correct, write *OK*.

1. United States senate   1. _____
2. jefferson memorial   2. _____
3. an experienced cpa   3. _____
4. Sincerely Yours   4. _____
5. spring   5. _____
6. far east   6. _____
7. *The Taming Of The Boar* (book)   7. _____

WRITING ACTIVITY   Write seven sentences following the directions. (Answers will vary.)

1. Use a day of the week.

_____

2. Use a month of the year.

_____

3. Use the name of a public building.

_____

4. A family relation

_____

5. Use a season

_____

6. Use an academic degree

_____

7. Use the title of a book.

_____

SHORT STORY   Underline each letter that should be capitalized in the following paragraph. Then in the spaces at the right, indicate how many letters should be capitalized. If the line is correct, write *OK* in the blank.

When i was a student at the middle school level   1. _____
i used to think that some day my name would read   2. _____
erin murphy, m.d. But as a sophomore in school   3. _____
i could picture my name reading erin murphy, r.n.   4. _____
My aunt amelia had completed her nurse's training   5. _____
at the university of wisconsin, and i wanted to be like   6. _____
her. After taking accounting and finance courses in   7. _____
my senior year, i now decided that my name should read   8. _____
erin murphy, cpa. After graduation i spent the summer   9. _____
working at long's fashion store, and i loved it. Now i   10. _____
started thinking that fashion design or retailing should be   11. _____
my college major. Was i wrong in changing my mind   12. _____
again? My dad said he changed his mind often on what   13. _____
career to pursue; in fact, he was a junior at u c l a before   14. _____
he could make up his mind. Maybe i should talk with   15. _____
grandma about what to do; she always has the answer.   16. _____

NUMBERS

NUMBERS AS FIGURES OR WORDS?

In business letters, memos, and reports, numbers can be expressed as words or figures. In general, use words for the numbers one through ten and use figures for numbers above ten.

> **Please make *ten* copies.** (NOT: *10* copies) **We expect *50* replies.** (NOT: *fifty* replies)
> BUT: ***Fifty-four* people finished the test.**   Spell out a number that begins a sentence.

ABBREVIATIONS

Use figures for numbers used with abbreviations.

> **During our travels, we saw many road signs such as *SR 405, US 66, I-80,* and *Hwy 31*.**

ADDRESSES

In addresses, express house numbers in figures except for house number *one*. Spell out street names that are numbered one through ten.

> **Adam's address is *One Hilltop Drive*, and Dawn's address is *398 Tenth Street*.**

Use figures for street names that are above ten. When figures are used for both the house number and the street name and there is no intervening word, such as *East* or *West*, use the ordinal form (1st, 2d, 3d, 4th) for the street name to avoid confusion.

> **Derek is looking for *243 South 22 Street*, not *22 24th Street*.**

ADJACENT NUMBERS

When two numbers are adjacent and one is part of a compound modifier, use a figure for one number and spell out the other one.

> **Send the *20 ten-page* reports to the director.   Hall bought *ten 32-cent* stamps.**

Separate with a comma adjacent numbers that are expressed the same way.

> **On page 19, 11 clues are revealed.   On page five, two clues are revealed.**

DATES

Express dates *after* the month in cardinal numbers and dates *before* the month in ordinal figures or words.

> **We leave on June 6.   We leave on the 6th of June.   We leave on the sixth of June.**

AMOUNTS OF MONEY

Use figures for amounts of money. Express whole amounts without the decimal and zeros; express amounts under a dollar with a number and the word *cents*.

> **I spent *$25.75* on food and *$10* on ice.** (NOT: *ten dollars*)
> **She has *50 cents* left for a phone call.** (NOT: $ 0.50)

DECIMALS AND PERCENTAGES

Use figures to express decimals and percentages.

> **Tad's car averaged *22.5* miles a gallon on the *500-mile* trip.**
>
> **Clare earned a *95* percent on her history exam.** Spell out the word *percent*.

FRACTIONS

Spell out fractions when they stand alone (without a whole number). Use figures for fractions when they are part of a mixed number (a whole number and a fraction), or when the spelled-out form is long and awkward.

> **We gave *two-thirds* of the profit.** (NOT: ⅔)
>
> **Classes last *1½* hours.** (NOT: one and a half)
>
> **The fabric for the drapes is short by *3/32* of an inch.** (NOT: three thirty-seconds)

TIME

Use figures to express periods of time and with *a.m.* and *p.m.*

> **The Sullivans took out a *30-year* mortgage on their house.** (a period of *time*)
>
> **I eat breakfast at *6:30 a.m.*** (A colon separates hours from minutes.)
>
> **I eat at *8 a.m.*   I eat at *8:00*.** (For hours only, use *a.m.* or *p.m.* *or* a colon and zeros.)
>
> **Our shop is open from *9:30 a.m.* to *6 p.m.*** (NOT: 6:00 p.m.)

AGES

In general, express ages in written form.

> **Pauline will be *twenty-five*, and Norman will be *twenty-nine*.**

Express ages in figures when the age appears directly after a person's name, when age is used in a technical sense, and when age is expressed in years, months, and days.

> **Ms. Bryan, *62*, will retire soon.   The voting age is *18*.   Jane is *3* years and *2* months old.**

ANNIVERSARIES

Spell out ordinals to express anniversaries except when more than two words are required. (A hyphenated word like *twenty-first* counts as one word.)

> ***first* anniversary   *twenty-first* anniversary   *115th* anniversary**

WEIGHTS, DIMENSIONS, AND OTHER MEASUREMENTS

Use figures for weights, dimensions, and other measurements.

> **We stored *2 tons* of paper in bins that measured *16 yards by 50 feet*.**
>
> **The boards measured *12 feet by 3 feet*.** (or *12' by 3'* in tables or in technical material)

FIRST OR *1ST*?

Spell out ordinal number—*first, second, third*—that can be expressed in one or two words. Hyphenate compound ordinals (*twenty-first* to *ninety-ninth*).

Name   Date   Score

EXERCISES

| EXERCISE 1 | Underline any errors in number usage in the following sentences. Then write your corrections in the spaces at the right. |

1. You need to take I-forty to get to the beach.   1. _____
2. Please date the letter May 12th, 1998.   2. _____
3. She is inviting 10 people to the party.   3. _____
4. We own a tent that measures twelve feet by nine feet.   4. _____
5. The meeting will begin at nine-thirty a.m.   5. _____
6. Our group raised over three hundred dollars for charity.   6. _____
7. May I borrow sixty dollars from you?   7. _____
8. The company's address is 1 South Park Drive, Fayetteville, Arkansas.   8. _____
9. By next year, we should have over one thousand more clients.   9. _____
10. The enrollment deadline is August 31st.   10. _____
11. We need one hundred ten people to fill the room.   11. _____
12. Dick lives at 2327 10th Street; Myrna lives at 989 64 Street.   12. _____
13. 25 employees earned bonuses this month.   13. _____
14. The company is moving its headquarters from 201 South 43 Street to   14. _____
    112 Seventy-eighth Street.
15. This station charges only one dollar per gallon of gas.   15. _____

| EXERCISE 2 | Rewrite correctly each incorrect item listed below. If an item is correct, write *OK*. |

1. ten dollars   1. _____
2. fifteen percent   2. _____
3. two-ounce bottle   3. _____
4. July 21   4. _____
5. June 30th   5. _____
6. thirty-five cents   6. _____
7. one hundred twenty-fifth anniversary   7. _____
8. five tons   8. _____
9. fifteen dollars and fifty cents   9. _____
10. the legal age is twenty-one   10. _____
11. 7:00 p.m.   11. _____
12. payable in fifteen days   12. _____
13. twenty-one two hundredths of a second   13. _____
14. .025 inch   14. _____
15. twenty five and one half percent   15. _____

Rewrite the following sentences to correct errors in number usage.

1. 350 people plan to attend the convention in Dallas, Texas.

_____

2. I'll need fifteen dollars for the membership fee.

_____

3. The Diamonds plan to return from their trip on August 10th.

_____

4. Would you believe that Cecilia spent four hundred fifty dollars for a computer?

_____

5. They increased profits by fifteen percent.

_____

6. The toll fee is fifty cents.

_____

7. The rates will go up in the year two-thousand one.

_____

WRITING ACTIVITY   Write four sentences following the directions given below. (Answers will vary.)

1. Write your street address.

_____

2. Use two adjacent numbers.

_____

3. Use a date.

_____

4. Use an amount of money.

_____

SHORT STORY   Underline any errors in number usage in the following sentences. Then write your corrections in the spaces at the right. If a line is correct, write *OK*.

On July 24th, we will attend a party for our   1. _____

neighbor's 43d wedding anniversary.   2. _____

Mrs. Sullivan is 63, and Mr. Sullivan   3. _____

is 65. They plan to start the celebrating   4. _____

at three p.m. because that was the time they were   5. _____

married 43 years ago. 5 members of their family   6. _____

will travel seven hundred miles and more   7. _____

to join the party. We plan to make a money   8. _____

card that will hold twelve twenty dollar bills   9. _____

to present to the Sullivans; 7 other people   10. _____

are making a money tree with forty-three   11. _____

ten-dollar bills. They will have enough   12. _____

money to buy something nice to remember   13. _____

the 24 of July.   14. _____

WORD USAGE

CHOOSING THE RIGHT WORD

Many words have similar spellings or similar sounds but very different meanings. Learn how these words are used so that your writing is clear and concise!

Accept **means "to take."** Please *accept* my sincere thanks.
Except **means "to exclude."** All *except* you may go.

Ad **is short for** *advertisement*. See the *ad* in the classified section.
Add **means "to join."** *Add* the figures.

Advice **is a noun meaning a "suggestion, a recommendation."** What's your *advice*?
Advise **is a verb meaning "to recommend."** I was *advised* to stay.

Affect **is a verb meaning "to influence, to change."** How will the prices *affect* your income?
Effect **is a verb meaning "to bring about," or a noun meaning "result."** I *effected* a change. It had an *effect*.

All right **means "okay."** There is no such word as *alright*. I am *all right*.

Already **is an adverb meaning "previously."** They have *already* gone.
All ready **means that "all are prepared."** They are *all ready* to go.

Between **is used to discuss two.** Divide the supplies *between* you and me.
Among **is used to discuss three or more.** Share the information *among* the five applicants.

Amount **refers to items that cannot be counted.** A large *amount* of trash was thrown away.
Number **refers to items that can be counted.** A great *number* of citizens came to the meeting.

Anxious **means "worried or concerned."** I am *anxious* about my grades.
Eager **means "intensely desirous."** She was *eager* to see the movie.

Assure **is a verb meaning "to promise."** I *assure* you that I will finish the report by noon.
Ensure **is a verb meaning "to make certain."** To *ensure* delivery, check the address.
Insure **is a verb meaning "to protect."** Please *insure* your car before you drive.

Capital **is a sum of money, an uppercase letter, or a seat of government.** Lansing is the *capital* of Michigan.
Capitol **is the building where the government meets.** Students toured Lansing's *capitol*.

Choose **is a verb meaning "to select."** We were able to *choose* the printer.
Chose **is the past tense of the verb** *choose*. He *chose* the printer.

Cite **means "to quote."** I need to *cite* two authorities in my paper.
Sight **means "to see."** My *sight* at night is not very good.
Site **means "a location."** Is this the *site* of the new store?

Complement **means "to complete."** His tie *complemented* his outfit.
Compliment **means "to praise."** *Compliment* your students frequently.

Continual **means "in rapid succession."** The bell rings *continually*.
Continuous **means "without interruption."** The river flows *continuously*.

Council means "an advisory group." The *council* meets today.
Counsel, as a noun or verb, means "advise." Seek his *counsel*. *Counsel* the students carefully.

Desert is a noun meaning "barren region." On our way to California, we crossed the *desert*.
Dessert is a noun meaning "the last course of the meal." We had cake for *dessert*.

Farther means "at a greater distance." They traveled *farther* than you.
Further means "additional." Do you have any *further* information?

Fewer refers to items that can be counted and modifies a plural noun. I made *fewer* pies.
Less means "a reduced amount or degree" and modifies a singular noun. I made *less* money.

Hear means "to perceive by ear." Can you *hear* me?
Here means "this place." Bring the book *here*.

Imply is a verb meaning "to suggest." The speaker *implied* that he would return.
Infer is a verb meaning "to deduce." The listener *inferred* that the speaker would return.

Regardless. NOT: *Irregardless*. *Regardless* of what you say, I will go.

It's is a contraction for *it is* or *it has*. *It's* raining.   *It's* easy.
Its is a possessive pronoun and never takes an apostrophe. *Its* owner has left.

Loose means "free." The strings are *loose*.
Lose means "to mislay." Please don't *lose* your tickets.

Passed is the past tense of the verb pass. She *passed* her exam.
Past means "over with" or "time gone by." That's in the *past*.

Personal means "private." These are my *personal* papers.
Personnel refers to a company's employees. Notify all *personnel*.

Precede is a verb meaning "to go before." What *preceded* the incident?
Proceed is a verb meaning "to continue." *Proceed* with plans.

Principal means a person who has controlling authority, a thing of primary importance, or a sum of money. She is *principal* of the school. The *principal* reason is time. I invested the *principal*.
Principle is a general truth, a rule. Name the *principles* of good writing.

Stationary means "fixed." The chairs in this room are *stationary*.
Stationery refers to writing paper. I wrote the letter on my favorite *stationery*.

Then means "at that time." *Then* there were only five left.
Than is used to complete a comparison. Sue is older *than* Kathleen.

There is an adverb indicating direction. *There* it is.
Their is a possessive pronoun. *Their* book is on the desk.
They're is a contraction for *they are*. *They're* going to class.

To is a preposition. We went *to* the office.
Too is an adverb that intensifies or means "also." I ate *too* much. She drove *too*.
Two is a number. *Two* of us were applying for the job.

We're is a contraction for *we are*. *We're* in Ms. Smith's class.
Were is the past tense of the verb *are*. We *were* in the office.
Where implies a place. *Where* did you go?

Who's is a contraction for *who is* or *who has*. *Who's* there?
Whose is the possessive of who. *Whose* book is this?

EXERCISES

EXERCISE 1   Read the following sentences carefully. Select the word from each pair in parentheses that better conveys the meaning of the sentence. Underline the correct word.

1. Who can throw the ball (*further, farther*)?
2. If it is (*all right, alright*) with you, I'll finish this project first.
3. There are (*fewer, less*) people attending this year.
4. Please order a ream of office (*stationary, stationery*).
5. The (*amount, number*) of entries this year is rather high.
6. (*Its, It's*) engine needs repairing.
7. People are (*continually, continuously*) complaining.
8. Madison is the (*capital, capitol*) of Wisconsin.
9. Can you (*ad, add*) these figures for me?
10. Do you have any (*advise, advice*) regarding my situation?
11. This matter is (*personal, personnel*).
12. Write your letter on plain (*stationary, stationery*).
13. I would strongly (*advice, advise*) you to think before you speak.
14. The (*desert, dessert*) is a very hot area.
15. The ceremony was (*preceded, preceeded*) by a short musical interlude.
16. I (*to, too*) will be going to the concert.
17. (*There, Their*) are several issues we need to discuss.
18. The furniture (*complemented, complimented*) the decor in the office.
19. He found some (*lose, loose*) connections to the terminal.
20. (*We're, Were, Where*) have they put the office supplies?
21. I understand that (*it's, its*) difficult to do your job.
22. Are you trying to (*imply, infer*) that this is my fault?
23. Will you (*accept, except*) my reason for being absent?
24. Will you divide the proceeds (*between, among*) the two charities?
25. Have you been to the doctor to have your (*cite, sight, site*) checked recently?

EXERCISE 2   Underline the correct word from each pair of words in parentheses. Then write your answer in the space at the right.

1. I have a large (*amount, number*) of paperwork to do.   1. _____
2. There will be (*fewer, less*) of a crowd today.   2. _____
3. She gives (*advice, advise*) to people for a living.   3. _____
4. We will (*ad, add*) more space to the next room.   4. _____
5. Even (*though, through, thorough*) she was a new sales representative, she made her quota before the end of the year.   5. _____
6. I'm glad that you are (*all right, alright*).   6. _____
7. The (*capital, capitol*) building is right down the street.   7. _____
8. The water in the sink was running (*continually, continuously*).   8. _____
9. I will discuss the details with you (*further, farther*).   9. _____

10. The company owns (*its, it's*) own jet.   10. _____
11. She is now the (*principal, principle*) of the high school.   11. _____
12. I am taking a (*personal, personnel*) leave of absence.   12. _____
13. Do not (*lose, loose*) your tickets!   13. _____
14. I plan (*to, too*) address this matter during the meeting.   14. _____
15. He likes to (*compliment, complement*) the girls.   15. _____
16. She likes riding the (*stationary, stationery*) bikes in the gym.   16. _____
17. (*There, Their*) house is being remodeled.   17. _____
18. He (*passed, past*) the slow moving car.   18. _____
19. The trial will (*proceed, precede*) tomorrow.   19. _____
20. She made apple pie for (*desert, dessert*).   20. _____
21. Claudia had heard good things about the book, and she was
    (*anxious, eager*) to read it.   21. _____
22. I (*assure, ensure, insure*) you that I will be at the meeting on time.   22. _____
23. We (*we're, were, where*) at the mall when the storm started.   23. _____
24. I (*imply, infer*) from your statement that you would like a transfer.   24. _____
25. (*Accept, Except*) for John, the entire class attended the concert.   25. _____

WRITING ACTIVITY   Use the following words in a sentence. (Answers will vary.)

1. principal   _____
2. already   _____
3. assure   _____
4. chose   _____
5. farther   _____
6. advise   _____
7. compliment   _____
8. than   _____

SHORT STORY   Underline any word that is used incorrectly. Write the correct word in the blank at the right. If all words in the line are used correctly, write *OK*.

Our vet comes hear to our house today too   1. _____
check the health of our too dogs and four cats.   2. _____
In the passed we would go too his office, but   3. _____
after buying more pets, it was not easy two   4. _____
take them all in the car for there checkup.   5. _____
One of our dogs was lose yesterday, and   6. _____
we where very eager about finding her. Occasionally,   7. _____
she gets lose, but this time she ran further   8. _____
away then usual. We called and whistled too   9. _____
her to come home; however, she conveniently   10. _____
did not here her name. Irregardless of some   11. _____
shortcomings, she is a nice dog. The animals   12. _____
sense the vet is coming; they are all ready trying   13. _____
to find a place to hide out of his site. I don't   14. _____
blame them for not wanting to get they're shots,   15. _____
but I want to assure they're continued good health.   16. _____

UNIT 12

PARAGRAPHS

✓ Lesson 51. Creating Paragraphs

UNIT 12 OVERVIEW

The ability to write grammatically correct sentences is, of course, very important to all of us. However, much of our writing involves paragraphs in letters, memorandums, or reports. We need to know the writing techniques that will help us create a paragraph with one main idea supported by sentences that explain the idea. In this unit you will learn how to identify the main theme of a paragraph and how to achieve unity with the ideas that support the theme.

UNIT OBJECTIVES

When you complete Unit 12, you will be able to:

■ identify a topic sentence.

■ use transition words in a paragraph.

■ position words for emphasis in a paragraph.

■ write a paragraph that demonstrates unity of ideas.

LESSON
51 CREATING PARAGRAPHS

PARAGRAPH DEVELOPMENT

A paragraph is a portion of a written composition; it develops one main idea or topic. It can range in length from one sentence to many sentences. A one-sentence paragraph is dramatic; it focuses the reader's attention on a particular fact. However, most paragraphs contain several sentences. Remember: A shorter paragraph is more inviting to read.

> **You're right; pennies nowadays are worthless.** This one sentence can serve as an attention getter.

Usually we write a paragraph that contains several sentences.

> **Our textbook presents the eight parts of speech. These eight parts are: nouns, pronouns, adverbs, verbs, adjectives, prepositions, conjunctions, and interjections. Within the 12 units of the textbook, we have learned how to use the parts of speech to improve our ability to speak and to write correctly.**

TOPIC SENTENCE

Usually, a paragraph begins with a topic sentence. The topic sentence identifies the topic being discussed in the paragraph; it presents the central idea. The other sentences in the paragraph help explain this idea. Sometimes helping sentences are written with word clues. Some word clues are *first*, *next*, and *finally*.

> **Growing tomatoes in the garden takes several steps. *First*, one must dig a hole large enough to accommodate the plant. *Next*, add some top-quality fertilizer and sufficient water to wet the roots. *Finally*, cover the roots with dirt and tap around the plant to firm the soil.**

The topic sentence is *Growing tomatoes in the garden takes several steps*. It identifies the content of the paragraph. Notice how the words *first*, *next*, and *finally* link each sentence to the previous sentence making the paragraph easy to read and to understand.

CHECKUP 1 Write a topic sentence for each noun. (Answers will vary.)

1. whales   Whales are not fish; they are mammals.
2. tennis   _____
3. circus   _____
4. homework   _____
5. cars   _____

LINKING IDEAS IN THE PARAGRAPH

Sentences should "stick" together in a paragraph; each sentence is linked to the preceding sentence to give unity. Together all of these sentences provide details about the topic introduced in the *topic sentence*. Linking can be achieved in several ways:

Repeat a word that was used in the preceding sentence:

> **. . . and the decision was made to try. This decision . . .**

LESSON 51 ■ 225

Use a pronoun that represents a noun used in the preceding sentence:

... the decision was made. It will cost ... Because *it* means *decision*, the second sentence is linked to the first sentence.

Use *transitional* words such as *however, therefore, yet, nevertheless, consequently, also, in addition,* to connect one sentence to another smoothly:

... the decision was made. However, not all people agreed ...

CHECKUP 2 Write a supporting sentence for each of the topic sentences. Link your sentence to the topic sentence by repeating a word, using a pronoun, or using a transitional word or phrase. (Answers will vary.)

1. Summer school will start on Monday, June 13.
   It will last for 6 weeks.

2. We offer top-quality cellular phone cases made of durable soft mesh.

3. Host families are needed for students arriving from Scandinavian and European countries.

4. Have you thought about a career as a veterinary assistant care specialist?

5. People communicate in many ways.

EMPHATIC POSITIONS

The first and last words of a paragraph are in particularly emphatic positions. An idea that deserves emphasis can be placed in either position.

The *damage* inflicted by the windstorm was significant. *Damage* is the emphasized word in the topic sentence because sentences that follow will discuss the degree of the damage.

BEWARE! The word *I*, which is often used too much in a message, is especially noticeable if it appears as the first word. Try to minimize the use of *I* as you write.

I think it is important to realize that the damage inflicted by the windstorm was significant. Here *damage* is de-emphasized, but what the writer (I) thinks is emphasized.

CHECKUP 3 Underline the emphatic word in each set that would serve as the topic of a paragraph. Then write the word in the space at the right.

1. a. The <u>rain</u> delayed the game for three hours.
   b. The game did resume.

   1. <u>rain</u>

2. a. Chicago offers so much in culture and education.
   b. The Museum of Science is fascinating.

   2. _____

3. a. The editor of the newspaper spoke to the journalism class.
   b. He told the students to have an inquisitive mind.

   3. _____

4. a. Tornado season is here and we need to review emergency procedures.
   b. Go to a basement if you have one.

   4. _____

5. a. The graph does not adequately describe the situation.
   b. We need to show how sales have increased in Canada.

   5. _____

Name _____ Date _____ Score _____

EXERCISES

EXERCISE 1   There are three related ideas in each line. Write a topic sentence for each group of words. (Answers will vary.)

1. carrots, peas, lettuce   _____

2. cat, dog, turtle   _____

3. books, instructor, homework   _____

4. clauses, phrases, words   _____

5. ant, fly, ladybug   _____

6. bus, taxi, car pool   _____

7. flex time, child care, parking space   _____

8. stocks, bonds, earning   _____

9. rye, wheat, barley   _____

10. jazz, blues, rock   _____

EXERCISE 2   Look at each list of three words. If each set appeared in a paragraph, what do you think would be the topic of that paragraph? Write your answer in the blank at the right. (Answers may vary.)

1. raccoon, squirrel, deer
2. elephant, lion, tiger
3. house, apartment, igloo
4. spring, fall, winter
5. rain, snow, sleet
6. shoes, slippers, socks
7. poodle, collie, pug
8. adverb, verb, noun
9. Florida, swimming, boating
10. desk, file cabinets, computer
11. 401K, Keoghs, annuity
12. watch, clock, sundial
13. sports, full, compact
14. split-level, 2-story, ranch
15. hurricanes, tornado, monsoons

1. _____
2. _____
3. _____
4. _____
5. _____
6. _____
7. _____
8. _____
9. _____
10. _____
11. _____
12. _____
13. _____
14. _____
15. _____

Read through the sentences below. Select the one you think would make the best topic sentence. Label that sentence 1. Now create a paragraph by using all the remaining sentences to discuss the topic sentence. Sequence the sentences so that their order makes sense and they link together smoothly! Label the remaining sentences 2 through 11. Then write the sentences in order on the lines below. (Answers will vary.)

1. Logging has been accelerated.
2. This is because the extent of damage caused by weather is greater than in the past.
3. For example, floods are more damaging now because environmental factors that naturally reduce or prevent floods have been affected.
4. These wetlands absorb excess water in time of heavy precipitation, but with their absence, waters run and flood unabated.
5. A final example is where soil was once present to absorb the rains, asphalt now stands.
6. We seem to hear more reports of natural disasters these days.
7. Some human actions have contributed to the severity of the weather-related damage.
8. Rainfall that would have been slowed by forests now runs down bare hillsides.
9. Over half of the original wetlands have been lost due to draining or filling.
10. Rains pour off these nonabsorbent surfaces and enter into rivers and streams causing them to flood.
11. Another example is our wetlands.

_____

_____

_____

_____

_____

_____

_____

_____

_____

_____

_____

_____

_____

_____

_____

_____

_____

_____

_____

_____

UNIT 1

LESSON 1

CHECKUP 1

1. okay
2. like
3. what's up
4. dude

CHECKUP 2

	Word	Greek Root	Meaning
1.	asterisk	ast	star
2.	bicycle	cycl	circle, ring
3.	telegraph	graph	write
4.	biography	bio	life

CHECKUP 3

	Word	Latin Root	Meaning
1.	bankrupt	rupta	break
2.	location	loc	place
3.	suburb	urb	city
4.	audible	aud	hear

CHECKUP 4

1. brunch
2. modem
3. moped
4. splice

CHECKUP 5

1. auto
2. burger
3. exam
4. memo

CHECKUP 6

1. windshield
2. touchdown
3. sidewalk
4. doorknob

UNIT 2

LESSON 2

CHECKUP 1

1. NS
2. S
3. S
4. NS
5. NS

CHECKUP 2

1. Amy
2. friend
3. appearance
4. presentation
5. businesses

CHECKUP 3

1. program
2. (you)
3. manual
4. She
5. ability

CHECKUP 4

1. received
2. Read
3. wants
4. Buy
5 toured

LESSON 3

CHECKUP 1

1. promises
2. choir
3. car
4. author
5. glasses

CHECKUP 2

1. demolished
2. staying
3. played
4. worked
5. reading

CHECKUP 3

1. wagon, float
2. sheriff, prisoner
3. papers, pencils
4. brother, sister
5. men, women

CHECKUP 4

1. supervises
2. are
3. is
4. is
5. plan

CHECKUP 5

1. shook, rattled
2. plowed, disked
3. opened, distributed
4. combed, styled
5. studied, graduated

LESSON 4

CHECKUP 1

Answers will vary. See your instructor.

CHECKUP 2

Answers will vary. See your instructor.

CHECKUP 3

Answers will vary. See your instructor.

CHECKUP 4

Answers will vary. See your instructor.

CHECKUP 5

Answers will vary. See your instructor.

CHECKUP 6

Answers will vary. See your instructor.

CHECKUP 7

1. I
2. E
3. D
4. IM

UNIT 3

LESSON 5

CHECKUP 1

1. supplies, Ms. Rinehard
2. benefits, plan
3. Henry, tray, cafeteria
4. brush, dog

CHECKUP 2

1. captain
2. Alaska
3. briefcase
4. lush
5. democracy

CHECKUP 3

1. abbreviation, form, word, phrase
2. doctor, wife, results, test
3. carpenter, town, material
4. auditor, director, position

CHECKUP 4

1. night, sky, brightness
2. stars, astronomer
3. list, brightness, stars
4. stars, magnitude

CHECKUP 5

1. Oliver Medford;
   Boulder, Colorado
2. Ken Burns, Civil War
3. Green Bay Packers, Super Bowl
4. National Archives

CHECKUP 6

Answers will vary. See your instructor.

LESSON 6

CHECKUP 1

1. cartoon
2. tuba
3. curtain
4. tomato

CHECKUP 2

Answers will vary. See your instructor.

CHECKUP 3

1. spirit
2. liability
3. jealousy
4. system

CHECKUP 4

Answers will vary. See your instructor.

CHECKUP 5

1. sweatshirt, lighthouses, Great Lakes
2. oil wells
3. stopwatches, storeroom

CHECKUP 6

Answers will vary. See your instructor.

CHECKUP 7

Answers will vary. See your instructor.

LESSON 7

CHECKUP 1

1. P, P, S
2. S, P, S
3. S, P, P
4. P, P, S

CHECKUP 2

1. passes
2. pushes
3. taxes
4. marches

CHECKUP 3

1. fifties
2. policies
3. fineries
4. corollaries
5. holidays
6. attorneys
7. boys
8. bays

CHECKUP 4

1. twos
2. cellos
3. echoes
4. cameos
5. tariffs
6. proofs
7. beliefs
8. thieves

CHECKUP 5

1. rules of thumb
2. loaves
3. ponies
4. faxes

LESSON 8

CHECKUP 1

1. hero's   heroes   heroes'
2. witness's   witnesses witnesses'
3. ox's   oxen   oxen's
4. lady's   ladies   ladies'

CHECKUP 2

1. Tanya
2. Dick
3. Brown's
4. son-in-law's

UNIT 4

LESSON 9

CHECKUP 1

1. her
2. you, my, our
3. their, its
4. her

CHECKUP 2

1. her, her, Mother
2. his, student
3. his, Bob; their, presidents

CHECKUP 3

1. their
2. his (her)
3. their
4. her

CHECKUP 4

1. his *or* her
2. OK
3. its
4. he *or* she

LESSON 10

CHECKUP 1

1. He, she
2. I
3. You
4. They, they

CHECKUP 2

1. she
2. she
3. he
4. I

CHECKUP 3

1. them
2. them
3. him
4. her

CHECKUP 4

1. their
2. his
3. her
4. his

CHECKUP 5

1. my
2. your
3. our
4. His

LESSON 11

CHECKUP 1

1. I
2. I
3. he
4. me
5. I

CHECKUP 2

1. him
2. him
3. them
4. her
5. me
6. I

CHECKUP 3

1. We
2. we
3. us
4. us
5. us
6. us
7. us
8. us
9. us
10. We
11. We
12. us

LESSON 12

CHECKUP 1

1. Who
2. Who
3. who
4. whom

CHECKUP 2

1. that
2. that
3. which
4. that
5. which

CHECKUP 3

Answers will vary. See your instructor.

CHECKUP 4

1. that
2. who
3. which
4. none

LESSON 13

CHECKUP 1

1. himself
2. Whom
3. Which
4. whoever
5. yourself

CHECKUP 2

1. who
2. you
3. OK
4. OK
5. themselves

UNIT 5

LESSON 14

CHECKUP 1

1. expressed
2. Prepare
3. demonstrated
4. agreed

CHECKUP 2

1. statement
2. question
3. command
4. statement
5. request

CHECKUP 3

1. have-not
2. computer
3. proposal
4. have-not
5. home run

CHECKUP 4

1. receive
2. serve
3. displayed
4. handling
5. traveling

CHECKUP 5

Answers will vary. See your instructor.

LESSON 15

CHECKUP 1

1. declining, rapidly
2. seen, seldom
3. announced, finally
4. seen, not

CHECKUP 2

1. responded, past participle
2. bringing, present participle
3. prepared, past participle
4. arriving, present participle
5. running, present participle

CHECKUP 3

1. predicate adjective
2. predicate adjective
3. predicate pronoun
4. predicate noun
5. predicate noun

LESSON 16

CHECKUP 1

1. he sings
2. I teach
3. she runs
4. he draws
5. he manages
6. you plan

CHECKUP 2

1. you dance
2. they announce
3. we demonstrate
4. you fax
5. we compute
6. they compose

CHECKUP 3

1. I am appearing
2. he is walking
3. she is sending
4. they are examining

CHECKUP 4

1. she described
2. he replied
3. they acknowledged
4. she transferred

CHECKUP 5

1. he was rehearsing
2. it was fading
3. I was consuming
4. we were quoting

CHECKUP 6

1. he will arrest
2. she will call
3. they will release
4. I will teach

CHECKUP 7

1. he will be brushing
2. you will be speaking
3. we will be learning
4. they will be leading

LESSON 17

CHECKUP 1

1. arose, arisen
2. began, begun
3. bound, bound
4. clung, clung
5. flew, flown
6. drew, drawn
7. rang, rung
8. was, been
9. hid, hidden
10. took, taken
11. met, met
12. rode, ridden
13. heard, heard
14. fled, fled
15. dealt, dealt
16. blew, blown
17. ate, eaten

18. grew, grown
19. thought, thought
20. lent, lent

CHECKUP 2

1. began
2. took
3. blew
4. wrote
5. bought
6. met

CHECKUP 3

1. chosen
2. taught
3. forgotten
4. said
5. burst
6. sat

CHECKUP 4

1. dreamed *or* had dreamt
2. rode *or* had ridden
3. told *or* had told
4. took *or* had taken
5. rang *or* had rung
6. tore *or* had torn

LESSON 18

CHECKUP 1

1. is being
2. are being
3. is having
4. are having

CHECKUP 2

1. was being
2. were being
3. was having
4. was having

LESSON 19

CHECKUP 1

1. is doing
2. am doing
3. are doing
4. is going
5. are going
6. are going

CHECKUP 2

1. was doing
2. were doing
3. were doing
4. were doing
5. were doing
6. were going
7. was going
8. was going
9. was going
10. was going

CHECKUP 3

1. will be doing
2. will be doing
3. will be doing
4. will be doing
5. will be doing
6. will be going
7. will be going
8. will be going
9. will be going
10. will be going

LESSON 20

CHECKUP 1

1. they have created
2. he has supervised
3. you have created
4. she has walked
5. has arranged
6. have recommended
7. has prepared
8. has extended

CHECKUP 2

1. they had prepared
2. he had audited
3. he had managed
4. we had identified
5. had decided
6. had addressed
7. had notified
8. had performed

CHECKUP 3

1. you will have learned
2. he will have served
3. she will have operated
4. we will have reached
5. will have processed
6. will have walked
7. will have achieved
8. will have gone

CHECKUP 4

1. future perfect
2. past perfect
3. future perfect
4. past perfect
5. present perfect

LESSON 21

CHECKUP 1

1. walks
2. need
3. moves
4. has

CHECKUP 2

1. were
2. are
3. has
4. has
5. are

LESSON 22

CHECKUP 1

1. papers
2. carpet
3. have-not
4. pencils
5. have-not

CHECKUP 2

1. lie
2. lying
3. laid
4. lays
5. lays

LESSON 23

CHECKUP 1

1. sit
2. set
3. sat
4. setting

CHECKUP 2

1. rises
2. rising
3. raise
4. rose

LESSON 24

CHECKUP 1

1. leave
2. let
3. let
4. taught
5. learned

CHECKUP 2

1. bring
2. take
3. takes
4. bring
5. brings

CHECKUP 3

1. effect
2. effected
3. affect
4. affected
5. effects
6. effect

CHECKUP 4

1. borrow
2. lend
3. borrow
4. lend
5. borrow

UNIT 6

LESSON 25

CHECKUP 1

1. 2
2. 2
3. 1
4. 2

CHECKUP 2

1. the, lush, beautiful, the
2. The, famous, the, tired
3. a, steamy, August, a, ten-speed, a, the, downtown
4. A, an, the, young

CHECKUP 3

1. My, this
2. His, this, several
3. That, mine
4. This, his

LESSON 26

CHECKUP 1

1. Mexican
2. Japanese
3. Canadian
4. Chinese

CHECKUP 2

1. Yes
2. Yes
3. Yes
4. No
5. Yes

CHECKUP 3

1. No
2. Yes
3. Yes
4. Yes

LESSON 27

CHECKUP 1

1. flakier
2. coarsest
3. poorer
4. famous

CHECKUP 2

1. finer
2. best
3. unique
4. easiest

UNIT 7

LESSON 28

CHECKUP 1

1. waited
2. sign
3. played
4. proceeded

CHECKUP 2

1. when (*or* how often)
2. how much
3. when (*or* how often)
4. how much
5. when

CHECKUP 3

1. ADV, V
2. ADV, V
3. V, V
4. ADV, V
5. ADV, V
6. ADJ

LESSON 29

CHECKUP 1

1. harder
2. more (*or* less) closely
3. more (*or* less) supportive
4. more (*or* less) assertively

CHECKUP 2

1. worst
2. better
3. more
4. faster
5. clearly

LESSON 30

CHECKUP 1

1. I want only chocolate ice cream.
2. We almost lost the Oldani account.
3. Did you ever see such a sight!
4. I told only him the secret.
5. Only the parent was there for the child.

CHECKUP 2

1. I could hardly stop laughing.
2. Please finish your work, or you'll be late.
3. Please repeat what you said.
4. I have no money for you.
5. I haven't gotten any complaints.

CHECKUP 3

1. slow
2. angry
3. sweet
4. quickly
5. nervous

CHECKUP 4

1. sad
2. surely
3. bad
4. badly
5. sure

LESSON 31

CHECKUP 1

1. other
2. other
3. else
4. else
5. other

CHECKUP 2

1. well
2. really
3. OK
4. well
5. really

CHECKUP 3

Other answers may also be correct. See your instructor.

1. ; consequently,
2. ; therefore,
3. ; however,
4. ; then
5. ; otherwise,

UNIT 8

LESSON 32

CHECKUP 1

1. 2
2. 3
3. 4
4. 3
5. 2

CHECKUP 2

1. Monday, office
2. employees, picnic
3. you, me
4. hardware

CHECKUP 3

1. ADJ, ADJ, ADV
2. ADV, ADV
3. ADJ, ADJ
4. ADV
5. ADJ

CHECKUP 4

Answers will vary. See your instructor.

LESSON 33

CHECKUP 1

1. omit
2. omit
3. omit
4. omit

CHECKUP 2

1. between
2. at *or* about
3. me
4. among

CHECKUP 3

1. to
2. OK
3. to
4. from
5. from

LESSON 34

CHECKUP 1

1. and
2. and
3. or
4. but
5. and

CHECKUP 2

1. but
2. and
3. or *or* and
4. and *or* but
5. or

CHECKUP 3

1. or
2. but also
3. nor
4. but also
5. or
6. or
7. but also

LESSON 35

CHECKUP 1

Other answers may also be correct. See your instructor.

1. See either
2. implemented
3. She neither
4. neither discuss
5. competently

CHECKUP 2

1. run-on
2. comma splice
3. OK
4. comma splice

LESSON 36

CHECKUP 1

1. Hurrah!
2. Gee whiz!
3. Voila!
4. Three cheers!
5. Good! *or* Good,

CHECKUP 2

1. Yes, Yes! *or* Yes! Yes!
2. Ugh!
3. Wow!
4. Yippee!
5. Oh, *or* Oh!

CHECKUP 3

1. Well!
2. Rah-rah!
3. Oh, no!
4. Amen!
5. Help!
6. Hurrah!

CHECKUP 4

Answers will vary. See your instructor.

UNIT 9

LESSON 37

CHECKUP 1

1. to plan
2. to walk
3. to fix
4. to solve
5. to take

CHECKUP 2

1. Emphasizing
2. Motivated
3. Persuaded
4. Wanting
5. Given

CHECKUP 3
1. was
2. was
3. Donald
4. is
5. utilizes

LESSON 38

CHECKUP 1
1. NS
2. S
3. NS
4. after
5. before
6. before

CHECKUP 2
1. ADJ
2. N
3. ADJ
4. ADV

LESSON 39

CHECKUP 1
1. She has one daughter only.
2. The supervisor asked Geraldine twice to write the report.
3. Almost everyone elected blue for the team color.
4. Several of the callers asked for women's red dresses.

CHECKUP 2
1. Put your clothes that need to be washed in the laundry room.
2. Wearing a sweat suit, Carl ran five miles daily to stay fit.
3. The meeting that is about the budget will be tomorrow.
4. that
5. , which we will attend,
6. that

CHECKUP 3
1. Carrying a tray of food, Danny caught his toe on the wire.
2. We had a box of photographs that were lost in the move.
3. While swatting the wasp, I ran my car off the road.

LESSON 40

CHECKUP 1
1. verbs
2. subjects
3. adverbs
4. adjectives
5. objects

CHECKUP 2
1. to
2. in
3. a
4. to the

UNIT 10

LESSON 41

CHECKUP 1
1. period
2. question mark
3. period
4. exclamation point

LESSON 42

CHECKUP 1
1. but
2. and
3. or
4. OK
5. for

LESSON 43

CHECKUP 1
1. 2, nonessential
2. 2, nonessential
3. OK, essential
4. 2, nonessential
5. OK, essential

CHECKUP 2
1. essential
2. nonessential
3. nonessential
4. nonessential
5. nonessential

CHECKUP 3
1. 1
2. 1
3. OK
4. 1
5. 2

LESSON 44

CHECKUP 1
1. brother-in-law, Jason,
2. OK
3. walk,
4. doctors, she,
5. OK

CHECKUP 2
1. 2
2. 3
3. OK
4. 2
5. 1

LESSON 45

CHECKUP 1
1. 1
2. 2
3. 2
4. 1
5. 5

CHECKUP 2

1. 1
2. 3
3. 2
4. 1
5. 3

LESSON 46

CHECKUP 1

1. You may reach me at my toll-free number (800-555-6400).
2. The Raleigh (North Carolina) office serves as headquarters.
3. Two employees—Troy and Faith—are being promoted this week.
4. Two of the buildings—the Skyrise and the Hytower—were purchased by Financial Enterprises, Inc.
5. He loved his country—so much so that he gave his life for it.

LESSON 47

CHECKUP 1

1. Our assignment was to read Chapter 5, "Special Techniques for Reports."
2. The article is titled "In a Dream."
3. Cherry said, "We should go shopping," before she left.
4. Don't forget to mark this "paid."

CHECKUP 2

1. Aren't
2. Who's
3. You'll
4. weren't, wouldn't

UNIT 11

LESSON 48

CHECKUP 1

1. 3
2. 4
3. 3
4. 4
5. 3

CHECKUP 2

1. 5
2. 4
3. 7
4. 7
5. 4

CHECKUP 3

1. 10
2. 6
3. 5
4. 4

LESSON 49

No Checkups

LESSON 50

No Checkups

UNIT 12

CHECKUP 1

Answers will vary. See you instructor.

CHECKUP 2

Answers will vary. See you instructor.

CHECKUP 3

1. rain
2. Chicago
3. editor
4. tornado
5. graph

LIST OF COMMON PREPOSITIONS

about	beside	into	respecting
above	besides	like	since*
across	between	near	through
after*	beyond	of	throughout
against	but**	off ≠	til
along	by	on ≠	to
among	concerning	opposite	toward
around	down ≠	out ≠	under
as*	during	outside	underneath
at	except	over	until*
before*	for**	past	up ≠
behind	from	per	upon
below	in ≠	plus	with
beneath	inside	regarding	within
			without

   *   These prepositions are also used as subordinating conjunctions.

**   This preposition is also used as a coordinating conjunction.

  ≠   These prepositions are also used as adverbs.

WORD GROUPS USED AS PREPOSITIONS

These word groups are used as though the whole group were one preposition

apart from	back of	from outon	account of
according to	because of	in addition to	to the extent of
ahead of	by means of	in front of	with respect to
as far as	by way of	in place of	
as for	contrary to	in reference to	
as regards	devoid of	in regard to	
as to	from beyond	in spite of	
		instead of	

because is a subordinating conjunction when used by itself.

PRINCIPAL PARTS OF THE VERB TO BE:

Infinitive	Present	Past	Past Participle	Present Participle
to be	am, is, are	was, were	been	being

CONJUGATION OF THE VERB *TO BE*

PRESENT TENSE

Person	Number	
	Singular	Plural
1st	I **am**	We **are**
2nd	You **are**	You **are**
3rd	He, She, It **is**	They **are**

PRESENT PROGRESSIVE

Person	Number	
	Singular	Plural
1st	I **am being**	We **are being**
2nd	You **are being**	You **are being**
3rd	He, She, It **is being**	They **are being**

PAST TENSE

Person	Number	
	Singular	Plural
1st	I **was**	We **were**
2nd	You **were**	You **were**
3rd	He, She, It **was**	They **were**

PAST PROGRESSIVE

Person	Number	
	Singular	Plural
1st	I **was being**	We **were being**
2nd	You **were being**	You **were being**
3rd	He, She, It **was being**	They **were being**

PRESENT PERFECT TENSE

Person	Number	
	Singular	Plural
1st	I **have been**	We **have been**
2nd	You **have been**	You **have been**
3rd	He, She, It **has been**	They **have been**

PAST PERFECT TENSE

Person	Number	
	Singular	Plural
1st	I **had been**	We **had been**
2nd	You **had been**	You **had been**
3rd	He, She, It **had been**	They **had been**

FUTURE TENSE

Person	Number	
	Singular	Plural
1st	I **will be**	We **will be**
2nd	You **will be**	You **will be**
3rd	He, She, It **will be**	They **will be**

FUTURE PERFECT TENSE

Person	Number	
	Singular	Plural
1st	I **will have been**	We **will have been**
2nd	You **will have been**	You **will have been**
3rd	He, She, It **will have been**	They **will have been**

APPENDIX C

PRINCIPAL PARTS OF SOME COMMON REGULAR AND IRREGULAR VERBS

INFINITIVE	PRESENT	PAST	PAST PARTICIPLE	PRESENT PARTICIPLE
to arise	arise	arose	arisen	arising
to awake	awake	awoke, waked	awaked, woken	awaking
to be	am, is, are	was *or* were	been	being
to beat	beat	beat	beaten	beating
to begin	begin	began	begun	beginning
to bend	bend	bent	bent	bending
• to bid	bid	bid	bid	bidding
to bind	bind	bound	bound	binding
to bite	bite	bit	bitten	biting
to blow	blow	blew	blown	blowing
to break	break	broke	broken	breaking
to bring	bring	brought	brought	bringing
to build	build	built	built	building
• to burst	burst	burst	burst	bursting
to buy	buy	bought	bought	buying
to catch	catch	caught	caught	catching
to choose	choose	chose	chosen	choosing
• to climb	climb	climbed	climbed	climbing
to cling	cling	clung	clung	clinging
to come	come	came	come	coming
• to cost	cost	cost	cost	costing
to deal	deal	dealt	dealt	dealing
to dig	dig	dug	dug	digging
to dive	dive	dove	dove	diving
to drag	drag	dragged	dragged	dragging
to draw	draw	drew	drawn	drawing
to dream	dream	dreamed	dreamt	dreaming
to drink	drink	drank	drunk	drinking
to drive	drive	drove	driven	driving
to do	do	did	done	doing
to drown	drown	drowned	drowned	drowning
to eat	eat	ate	eaten	eating
to fall	fall	fell	fallen	falling
to fight	fight	fought	fought	fighting
to fit	fit	fitted, fit	fitted, fit	fitting

INFINITIVE	PRESENT	PAST	PAST PARTICIPLE	PRESENT PARTICIPLE
to flee	flee	fled	fled	fleeing
to fling	fling	flung	flung	flinging
to fly	fly	flew	flown	flying
to forecast	forecast	forecast	forecast	forecasting
to forget	forget	forgot	forgotten	forgetting
to freeze	freeze	froze	frozen	freezing
to get	get	got	got, gotten	getting
to give	give	gave	given	giving
to go	go	went	gone	going
to grind	grind	ground	ground	grinding
to grow	grow	grew	grown	growing
to hang (an object)	hang	hung	hung	hanging
to hang (death)	hang	hanged	hanged	hanging
to hear	hear	heard	heard	hearing
to hide	hide	hid	hidden	hiding
• to hit	hit	hit	hit	hitting
to hold	hold	held	held	holding
• to hurt	hurt	hurt	hurt	hurting
to know	know	knew	known	knowing
to lay	lay	laid	laid	laying
to lead	lead	led	led	leading
to leave	leave	left	left	leaving
to lend	lend	lent	lend	lending
to lie	lie	lay	lain	lying
to loan	loan	loaned	loaned	loaning
to lose	lose	lost	lost	losing
• to loose	loose	loosed	loosed	loosing
• to loosen	loosen	loosened	loosened	loosening
to mean	mean	meant	meant	meaning
to meet	meet	met	met	meeting
to pay	pay	paid	paid	paying
• to put	put	put	put	putting
• to quit	quit	quit	quit	quitting
• to raise	raise	raised	raised	raising
• to read	read	read	read	reading
to ride	ride	rode	ridden	riding
to ring	ring	rang	rung	ringing
to rise	rise	rose	risen	rising

APPENDIX C

INFINITIVE	PRESENT	PAST	PAST PARTICIPLE	PRESENT PARTICIPLE
to run	run	ran	run	running
to say	say	said	said	saying
to see	see	saw	seen	seeing
to seek	seek	sought	sought	seeking
to set	set	set	set	setting
to shake	shake	shook	shaken	shaking
to shine	shine	shone, shined	shone, shined	shining
to show	show	showed	shown or showed	showing
to shrink	shrink	shrank, shrunk	shrunk	shrinking
to sing	sing	sang	sung	singing
to sink	sink	sank	sunk	sinking
to sit	sit	sat	sat	sitting
to speak	speak	spoke	spoken	speaking
to spend	spend	spent	spent	spending
to spring	spring	sprang	sprung	springing
to stand	stand	stood	stood	standing
to steal	steal	stole	stolen	stealing
to sting	sting	stung	stung	stinging
to strike	strike	struck	struck, stricken	striking
to swear	swear	swore	sworn	swearing
to swim	swim	swam	swum	swimming
to swing	swing	swung	swung	swinging
to take	take	took	taken	taking
to teach	teach	taught	taught	teaching
to tear	tear	tore	torn	tearing
to tell	tell	told	told	telling
to think	think	thought	thought	thinking
to throw	throw	threw	thrown	throwing
to wake	wake	wake, woke	wake, woke, woken	waking
to wear	wear	wore	worn	wearing
to win	win	won	won	winning
to wring	wring	wrung	wrung	wringing
to write	write	wrote	written	writing

INDEX